Walking & Exploring
The
Battlefields of Britain

John Kinross

Walking & Exploring The Battlefields of Britain

DAVID & CHARLES
Newton Abbot   London

Page 1
Hanoverian siege artillery in action

Page 2
Fourteenth century knight in jousting armour (Marcher Lords)

For my father, J. B. S. Kinross CBE, who first took me to Sedgemoor in 1958

ACKNOWLEDGEMENTS

Thanks are due to many people, particularly Dr Newman of the Castle Museum, York; Dr Robert Dunning for help on Langport; Mr J. Sales of Bridport Museum; Miss B. Pittman; the staff of Killiekrankie and Bannockburn centres; Mr Miller of the Wallace Monument; H. Radcliffe of Newark Museum; the staff of Worcester Commandery, Devizes Museum, Edgehill and Naseby Battle Museums and Mr J. Dodgson of the English Civil War Society. Particular help on photographs from English Heritage and from Miss Murray-Flutter of the National Trust for Scotland. Finally thanks to my family for their patience and for allowing me to monopolise the kitchen table for four days over Christmas. The maps are drawn by Don Sargeant and an extra word of thanks to him for his patience.

J.S.K.
Bridgwater

British Library Cataloguing in Publication Data

Kinross, John, *1933.*
  Walking & exploring the battlefields of
  Britain.
  1. Great Britain, Battlefields – Visitors'
  guides.
  I. Title
  914.1'04858

  ISBN 0-7153-9180-1

Typeset by Typesetters (Birmingham) Ltd
Smethwick West Midlands
and printed in West Germany
by Mohndruck GmbH
for David and Charles Publishers plc
Brunel House   Newton Abbot   Devon

CONTENTS

LOCATIONS OF BATTLEFIELDS

1	Ethandum	878	16	Blore Heath	1459
2	Stamford Bridge	1066	17	Northampton	1460
3	Hastings	1066	18	Wakefield	1460
4	The Standard	1138	19	Mortimer's Cross	1461
5	Lewes	1264	20	St. Albans (II)	1461
6	Evesham	1265	21	Towton	1461
7	Stirling Bridge	1297	22	Hedgeley Moor	1464
8	Bannockburn	1314	23	Barnet	1471
9	Halidon Hill	1313	24	Tewkesbury	1471
10	Neville's Cross	1346	25	Bosworth	1485
11	Otterburn	1388	26	Stoke Field	1487
12	Pilleth	1402	27	Minster Lovell	
13	Homildon Hill	1402	28	Flodden	1513
14	Shrewsbury	1403	29	Pinkie	1547
15	St. Albans (I)	1455	30	Edgehill	1642
			31	Bradock Down	1643
			32	Stratton	1643
			33	Lansdown Hill	1643
			34	Roundway Down	1643
			35	Newbury (I)	1643
			36	Winceby	1643
			37	Newark	1644
			38	Cheriton	1644
			39	Basing House	
			40	Lathom House	
			41	Cropredy Bridge	1644
			42	Marston Moor	1644
			43	Lostwithiel	1644
			44	Newbury (II)	1644
			45	Auldearn	1645
			46	Naseby	1645
			47	Langport	1645
			48	Kilsyth	1645
			49	Philiphaugh	1645
			50	Dunbar	1650
			51	Worcester	1651
			52	Sedgemoor	1685
			53	Killiecrankie	1689
			54	Glen Coe	1692
			55	Preston	1715
			56	Sheriffmuir	1715
			57	Glen Shiel	1719
			58	Prestonpans	1745
			59	Clifton Moor	1745
			60	Falkirk	1746
			61	Culloden Moor	1746
			62	Fishguard	1797
			63	Slapton Sands	1944

miles

0   50   100

LONDON

THE COUNTRY CODE

When visiting the National Parks, take care to avoid damaging farm property by remembering this Code:

Guard against all risk of fire A cigarette thrown away or a pipe carelessly knocked out can start a raging inferno. Take care with camp or picnic fires and ensure that they are properly put out.

Fasten all gates Animals, if they stray, can do great damage to crops and to themselves too. Even if you find a gate left open, always shut and fasten it after you.

Keep dogs under proper control Animals are easily frightened – the chasing of a ewe or cow may mean the loss of valuable young.

Keep to the paths across farmland

Crops are damaged by trampling at any stage of growth. Remember that grass grown for hay is also a valuable crop.

Avoid damaging fences, hedges and walls If you force your way through a fence or hedge, you will weaken it. If stones from walls are rolled down slopes they may injure people, animals or farm property.

Leave no litter All litter is unsightly. Broken glass and tins and plastic bags are dangerous; they very easily harm livestock. So take your picnic remains and other litter home with you.

Safeguard water supplies Water is precious in the country. Never wash dishes or bathe in somebody's water supply or foul it in any other way.

Protect wild life, wild plants and trees Wild flowers give more pleasure to more people if left to grow. Plants should never be uprooted. Trees are valuable as well as beautiful and should be left alone.

Go carefully on country roads Country roads have special dangers. Blind corners, hump-backed bridges, slow-moving farm machinery, and led or driven animals are all hazards for the motorist.

Respect the life of the countryside The life of the country centres on its work. The countryman has to leave his belongings in the open; roads and paths run through his place of business, and the public are on trust. Be considerate.

CHAPTER 1
WHY EXPLORE BATTLEFIELDS?

Some people collect stamps or rare coins . . . I collect British battlefields. What is so special about them? Is there anything to be seen there anyway? These are some of the questions that may occur to the reader. The answer could be the famous mountaineering one of because they are there. However there is more than just exploring battlefields for historical research, and the following reasons, although varied, together provide an excellent picture of what motivates the enthusiastic battlefield explorer.

Firstly there are the connections with castles and roads that explain why battles were fought where they were. For example *Mortimer's Cross* on the Welsh border was fought where one army defended a bridge and ford crossing near their castle from another approaching from Wales.

The unlikely battle of *Wakefield* was fought where one army ventured unwisely out of a castle. *Bannockburn was fought because a castle needed to be relieved and Sheriffmuir*, nearby, was fought there because it was on the road between Perth and Stirling. *Hastings* was fought at Battle as it was on the road between Hastings and London. *St. Albans* and *Newbury* had two battles each, the first being on the London road to the North and the second on the road from Gloucester to London and also near Donnington Castle.

Secondly there are battles fought near rivers and bridges, where everything goes wrong because of the losing side being trapped by a river crossing. Thus many Welsh died at *Evesham*, drowned in the Severn; Royalists were trapped by the river at *Worcester*; Lord Lovell made a dramatic escape after *Stoke Field* by swimming his horse across the river. *Stirling Bridge* and *Stamford Bridge* were similar in that the losers were trapped halfway over the bridge.

Thirdly there are the battles that were in steep valleys with the winners usually on the high ground. Thus *Pilleth* and *Killiekrankie* have something in common, and *Glen Shiel* was a disaster for the Jacobites. On visiting the site, it is not surprising, as the Royal troops had the advantage of the high road and must have seen the ambush from a mile away. Had it been a few miles further on by the lake the outcome could have been different.

Firstly there is the battle which was touch and go throughout, and where the course of history was altered by the outcome. The prime example of this is *Bosworth*. Who can fail to be impressed by visiting *Bosworth* today? Leicestershire County Council museum service are to be congratulated in making it so interesting. There are flags on the fields, a diorama to explain what is happening and the white rose on the well placed by the Richard III Society, which tries to prove Richard's innocence of the murder of the two princes in the Tower.

Fourteenth century armoured warrior (Marcher Lords)

Archer in action defending a castle (Marcher Lords)

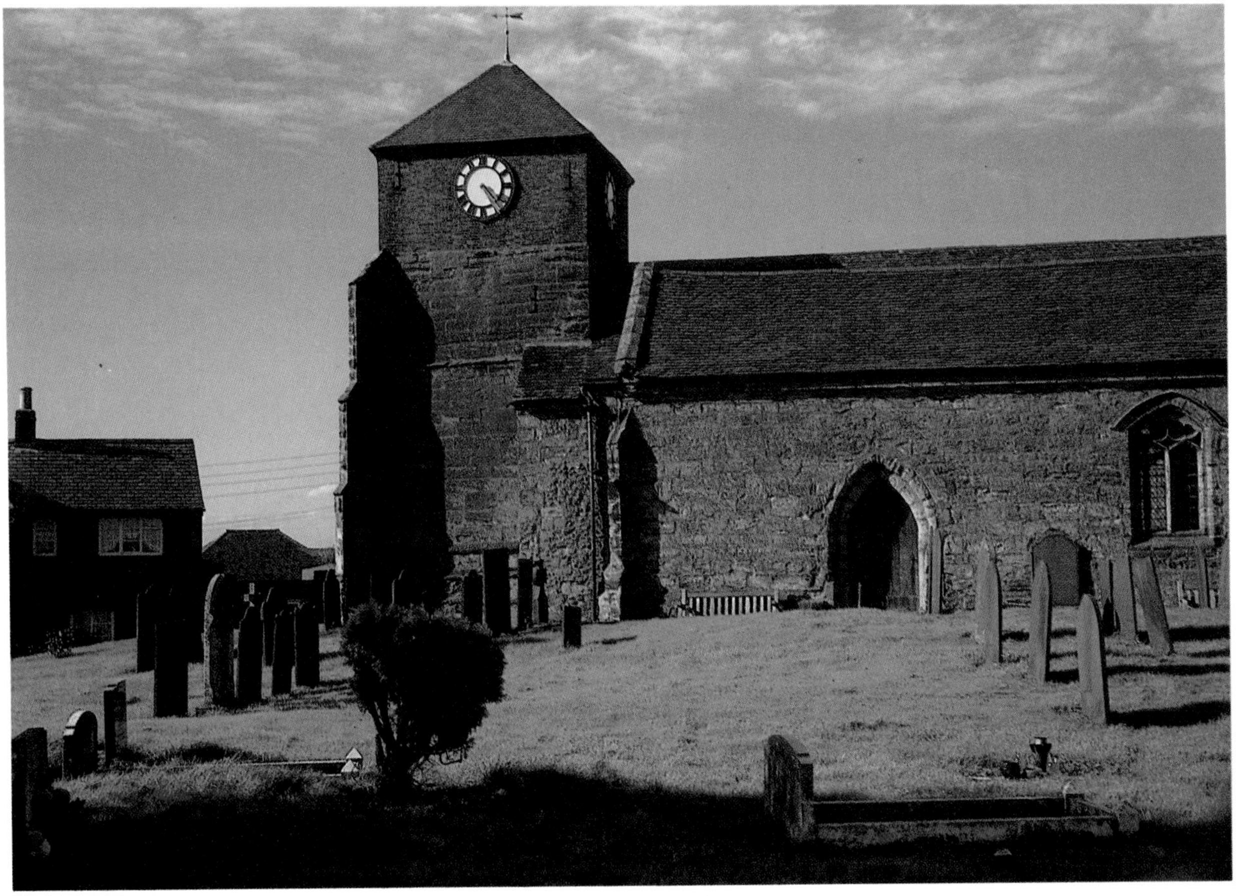

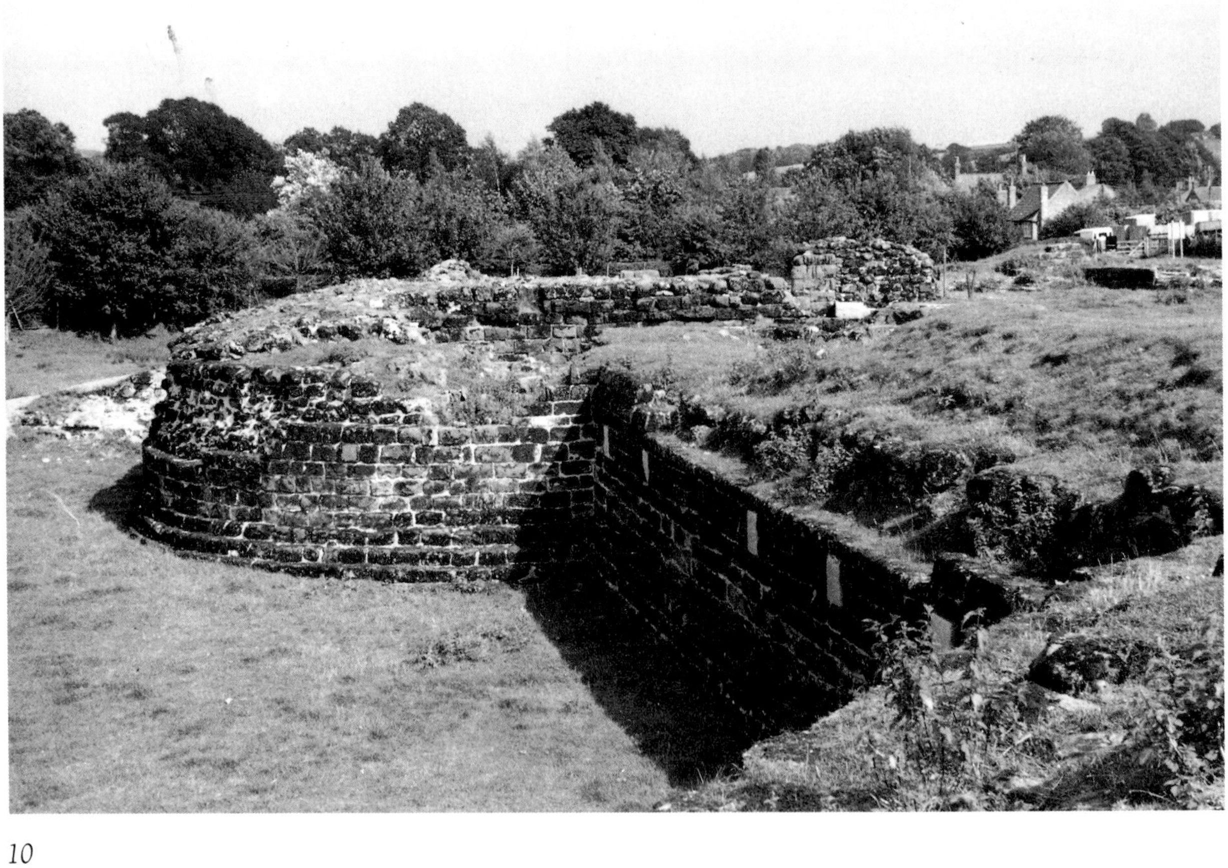

Shakespeare has much to answer for; his account of the battle in *Richard III* is generally considered inaccurate and so, too, is his military history in *Henry IV*. Sir Walter Scott is fairly accurate in his description of *Bannockburn* in *The Lord of the Isles* and the Battle of *Otterburn* would be nothing without the 'Ballad of Chevy Chase'. Lord Macaulay makes serious errors in his *History of England* and cannot even get Viscount Dundee's name correct. He calls him James Graham when his name was John Graham, and he generally blackens his name. Strangely Dundee's grave at Blair Atholl is hard to find, the stone being inside the wall of the ruined church.

Battle memorials are very interesting. That at *Towton* has recently been repaired by an Australian visitor. *Clifton Moor* has a simple one, recently erected inside the churchyard, to Bland's regiment. *Barnet* memorial looks like the crossroad pillar, *Mortimer's Cross* has a fine eighteenth century monument but it is not at the crossroads. *Naseby* has two monuments, *Marston Moor* has one recently repaired, *Winceby* has none at all though there is a large rock which will do, *Stamford Bridge* has one in English and Norwegian, *Newbury I* has one to Lord Falkland who was only a volunteer in the battle and held no command, *Newbury II* has no monument at all but is a fascinating battle. It was fought on two sides of the river at once and as far as walks go it is a varied, part river, part wood, part field walk during which such English sports as cricket and golf may be going on in an area that 344 years before would have seen a bloodthirsty struggle.

Culloden Moor (National Trust for Scotland)

(above left)
Sutton Cheney Church, Bosworth, where Richard prayed before the battle

(left)
Old Bolingbroke Castle, Lincolnshire. Remains of the fortress that was the birthplace of King Henry IV and features in the Battle of Winceby

Brass of Sir John and Lady Harsick
(Age of Chivalry Exhibition)

Then there are stories of ghosts. A lady talked on the radio recently of her strange forebodings at the Newark Castle scene of the murder of Montrose's followers. I myself had a ghostly experience when camping on the field of *Culloden* in April 1979. There are supposed to be ghosts at *Edgehill*; three suns were seen by the Yorkists before *Mortimer's Cross* and thereafter Prince Edward added the rising sun to the Yorkist white rose badge. Needless to say, his army was victorious at that battle.

Battlefields can be full of surprises. Abroad, the casual visitor to Waterloo would assume that the French had won the day as the Wellington monument is so hard to find. One gets the same sort of impression at *Bosworth* and few people have a good word to say for Henry VII. The hero is King Richard III though he was soundly beaten.

The most evocative of all British battlefields is probably *Sedgemoor*, a few fields away from my house. The rhine or ditch is no longer there but the moor is still easy to get lost on in low-lying mist. Even local people lose their way there and sheep and cows often have to be roped out of a ditch. There have been many accounts written about the battle and about Monmouth's men, but few have written a convincing account of the reason why so many thousands were prepared to die for a cause which must have seemed hopeless from the outset. There was no clan loyalty such as led to Bonnie Prince Charlie's followers fighting when their cause was lost, no financial reward, no dynamic leadership, no foreign mercenaries, no escape routes – only the terrific courage and the stubbornness of the Monmouth army itself kept it going on the road for three weeks in terrible weather until that final day.

History was made by our battles. What induced the Stanleys to attack King Richard at *Bosworth* and why did Northumberland look on and do nothing? Why, if the rhine was nearly dry at *Sedgemoor* did Monmouth's troops halt and go no further? How come Goring withdrew his artillery before *Langport*; did he expect to lose anyway? What induced King Charles to allow the very able and experienced General Skippon, whom he captured at *Lostwithiel*, to go free only to face him again with very different results at *Naseby*? These are some of the questions this book attempts to answer.

The illustrations are gathered from many sources. Some come from the Sealed Knot Society, who have re-fought many Civil War and other battles. In 1985 the re-enaction of Sedgemoor was so convincing that even the crowd were dressed up in seventeenth-century costumes and Monmouth's horse, returned to the local riding-school stable, now walks backwards as if in perpetual retreat.

Some people go to battlefields with metal detectors. This is only legal if they have permission in advance from the local landowner. The *Naseby* museum has a fine collection of such artefacts and others have been found at *Marston Moor*; especially buttons and bullets.

Strategy and tactics have to be studied when considering battles and they should not be confused. Strategy is the overall plan of a campaign, like a triple thrust on London. Tactics is the field commander's problem. One of the best users of tactics was Montrose. At *Auldearn* he was outnumbered; however by placing his standard on the hill on the right wing but putting himself on the left wing he was able to deceive his enemy into attacking one wing strongly leaving their flank open for a counter-attack. Bonnie Prince Charlie's general, Murray, was also

Culloden Moor. Battle sign (National Trust for Scotland)

Evesham battle monument

(pp 14–15)
Bosworth. King Richard's view

13

Robert de Bures. From All Saints, Acton, Suffolk (Age of Chivalry Exhibition)

a supreme tactician. He had no hope at *Culloden* however where the ground was chosen by Sullivan, who was not only no soldier but certainly no tactician.

The next two chapters will consider the different tactics and strategies used in the wars fought in the fields of our land. Most of the battles fall into the category of civil wars. Thus we start with Alfred's struggle against the Danes, then move on to King Harold and his struggle against the Vikings and the Normans. The invader then gives way to the civil war of Simon de Montfort and the very different battles of *Lewes* and *Evesham*. In Scotland we have the various struggles for independence and the border warfare that constantly divided England and Scotland, sometimes with Scots in both armies. It was not an English force that raided Cambuskenneth Abbey at *Bannockburn*, but a renegade Scots force under the Duke of Atholl.

In Wales we have the remarkable and very interesting battlefield at *Pilleth* and, at the other end of the country and in a very different age, the equally remarkable invasion at *Fishguard* that left a portion of Pembrokeshire in French hands for two days with, on paper at least, no effective army to prevent the enemy from running off in several directions and seizing a port for the French to ship in a large army from Ireland. It was a master stroke that neither Napoleon nor Hitler ever achieved – strategy devised by a forgotten French general and tactics devised by an unknown American Colonel with a taste for high living in his later years. Tate retired to live like an American tourist in a hotel in Paris with his lady friend.

Two main civil wars – the Wars of the Roses and the Civil War between King Charles I and Parliament – are considered in some detail. The first needs a good look at the family tree to understand who is who and the second needs a close look at the dates, for when the king was victorious in the west his army in the north was losing and when Montrose was successful in Scotland, his king was suffering in the south. *Naseby* was fought on 14 June 1645, *Alford* in Aberdeenshire (see page 27) was fought on 2 July 1645; the Royalists were defeated soundly at the first but won the second and followed it with another victory at *Kilsyth*. The Scottish battles had no effect on England except that Leslie set off to his surprise attack on Montrose at *Philiphaugh*.

There are the battles that do not really fit into any pigeon-hole. *Dunbar* and *Worcester* were Cromwellian victories in a second Civil War, it is true, but *Sedgemoor* cannot be called a Civil War battle or a Jacobite battle. It was anti-king, it is true, but Monmouth had been proclaimed king (outside the shoe shop in Taunton High Street it seems) so men were fighting for an anti-Catholic king rather than the Jacobite one whom Dundee, Mar and Bonnie Prince Charlie all fought for. It seems strange that the latter campaigned for his father whom so few had met and even fewer liked.

There may remain some readers who are still not convinced that this book is going to interest them. I hear them in the distance turning pages looking for a point of contact with the author. Perhaps they have teenage children who are studying history at school and want to know where to go to visit some of the battlefields? Good places to stay are York for those battles north and south of the city, Stirling for almost all the Scottish battles, Berwick-on-Tweed for those fought on the

Borders, and Gloucester for the Welsh border and surrounding area battles. All these towns have many other sights to visit which are mentioned after the walk descriptions, and are easy to get to by train or other means. Include Rugby as well for the Midlands battles and that leaves only a few like *Hastings*, *Lostwithiel*, *Fishguard* and *Glen Shiel* which are awkward to get to for those of us who don't live in the far-flung areas of Britain. But they are well worth a visit for the collector of battlefields, because that is what you will become when you have studied them in detail.

Two-handed sword from the collection at York Museum

Castles worth visiting because of their connection with battles are mentioned throughout the text, but of special interest are Edinburgh Castle, home of *Mons Meg*, the mighty cannon used at the time of *Flodden*, Carlisle Castle with its connections with the '45, Eilean Donan, the '19 Rising, Cawdor Castle for the Fishguard muskets, Taunton for its Sedgemoor relics, and the Tower of London for its Armoury.

CHAPTER 2
EARLY WARFARE

Where does one start with tracing battlefields? There is much contention about early sites and we must choose those that are accessible today.

The first battle in this book, *Ethandun*, was entirely fought on foot and the tactics of gaining the high ground and attacking out of the sun were similar to those used by Dundee at *Killiekrankie*. So many of our battles repeat each other in some aspect or other. The arms used by Alfred's men were very different however. They had shields, spears and swords; the *Anglo-Saxon Chronicle* speaks of a 'dense, shield-locked array' almost as if it was a rugby scrum. The Romans had influenced the method of warfare and their helmets were pointed and their shields locked together so that they could form a wall. This was the Saxon method of defence and they used slings and javelins for attack. At *Stamford Bridge* there was a similar method of attack, though Harold himself used a battle-axe and his men had shields with pointed centres. Banners, usually attached to spears, were used to rally the troops. There were Saxon javelin throwers at *Hastings*, where Harold's shield wall kept back the Normans for some time. William used his archers to shoot over the wall and his mounted knights to penetrate the Saxon defence. His men were better armed, with close-fitting mail armour and pointed helmet with an extended nose-piece. Their shields were round at the top and pointed at the bottom so that they could be formed into a pavise, a shield stuck into the ground behind which a man could squat to avoid missiles.

With the introduction of personal armour, the sword was not suitable for attacking your foe. Something heavier was required. The poleaxe was used at *The Standard* where the English army used its archers to such effect that the unarmoured men of Galloway were described as looking like 'hedgehogs with quills'. Maces were used at the Battle of *Lewes* where Prince Edward was free to roam the battlefield with his mounted knights, but like Prince Rupert at *Naseby*, in his absence his side was defeated. Strangely the horses themselves were still not protected and it was Robert the Bruce at *Bannockburn* who introduced a new type of tactic, that of rendering the horse a fair target for attack. His men dug pits covered in sticks and clods of earth to trip up the horses. His blacksmiths turned out small sharp calthrops, wicked triple-pointed spikes that caught in a horse's hoof and rendered the horse instantly lame. A calthrop is on view today at the Bannockburn centre.

The Scots under Wallace used the schiltron, a wedge of spearmen that moved forward like a giant porcupine and could also be used for defence, rather like the square at *Waterloo*, against cavalry. The heavy English knights were cut down in the wet boggy carse rather like the French knights at *Agincourt* a hundred years later. The tactics of allowing the knights to reach the boggy part of the field before ordering

The Percy Cross at Hedgeley Moor

the archers to release their arrows, breaking up the French charge with pointed stakes in the ground and then enticing the knights into a wood where they could be stabbed by the archers leaping on them from branches of trees, were enough to give Henry V a great reputation as a warrior.

Alas he spent so much time in France that his kingdom was allowed to deteriorate at home and his successor, Henry VI, a minor, was no soldier. The stage was set for the Wars of the Roses and as they form such an important chapter in the story of battles in England, we must examine the cause for them as well as the tactics and weapons used.

The end of the Hundred Years' War in Europe brought many soldiers home to England with, for most of them, no other trade to turn to than soldiering. They were unhappy at having such a weak king as Henry VI and watched with horror as possessions so hard fought for in France gradually disappeared from English control. By 1453 Gascony had gone and only Calais remained. Queen Margaret favoured the Duke of Somerset and appointed Richard, Duke of York, whom

Three archers at Towton (Marcher Lords)

she cleverly saw as a threat, to a post in Ireland. York had a clear claim to the throne through the Duke of Clarence (see family tree) and although at first he was loyal to Henry, he was upset by being excluded from Somerset's council on his return from Ireland. However in 1453 King Henry became temporarily insane and a regent had to be appointed. Somerset was out of favour due to the disasters in France and York was appointed regent and Governor of Calais. Miraculously Henry recovered in 1454 and dismissed York who retired to his castle at Wakefield. Somerset was released from the Tower and York at Wakefield made a useful ally in Richard Neville, Earl of Warwick, who had many fighting men at his command.

The stage was set for the first Battle of *St Albans*, where the Yorkists had a resounding victory. York now took over the king and the government, his ally Warwick becoming Governor of Calais. There was peace for some five years then the fighting started again. At this stage we should list the main battles and their results:

22 May 1455	*St Albans I*: Yorkist victory.
23 Sept. 1459	*Blore Heath*: Yorkist victory but followed by the Ludford affair, where superior forces trapped the Yorkists in Ludlow for two days, after which most of them ran away and their leaders took ship to France.
10 July 1460	*Northampton*: Yorkist victory (by Warwick).
30 Dec 1460	*Wakefield*: Yorkist defeat, Duke of York killed.
2 Feb 1461	*Mortimer's Cross*: York's son Edward defeats a Lancastrian force under Pembroke. Edward crowned king.
17 Feb 1461	*St Albans II*: Close-run battle but Warwick and Yorkists defeated.
29 March 1461	*Towton*: The largest battle of the Wars of the Roses; Yorkist victory.
26 July 1469	The Lancastrians suffered two minor defeats in the north at *Hedgeley Moor* and *Hexham*, but Warwick quarrelled with Edward and the Yorkists were defeated on 26 July at *Edgecote*. York was captured by Warwick but later released.
12 March 1470	*Empingham* or *Loosecoat Field*: A strange battle as the Lancastrians ran away. Yorkist victory.
14 April 1471	*Barnet*: Yorkist victory, Warwick killed.
14 May, 1471	*Tewkesbury*: Yorkist victory.
22 Aug 1485	*Bosworth Field*: Edward had died in 1483 and his brother Richard III had become king. Lancastrian victory which was more of a Tudor victory and followed by a further victory at Stoke Field.
16 June 1487	*Stoke Field*: Final battle of the Wars. The Earl of Lincoln, Viscount Lovell and Lambert Simnel's army were defeated by Henry VII.

The arms and armour used in the Wars of the Roses can be seen in the exhibition at Bosworth Field. There are models of soldiers in quilted gambesons and kettle helmets. Archers carried arrows in their belts and some carried crossbows with bolts in their wallets and a crank-handle in their belts. The mounted knights wore complete armour with bascinet, visor and greaves, spurs and gauntlets. There were some

Battle Trail sign at Tewkesbury

primitive artillery pieces as well as petardiers, who threw burning material down from castles or into an advancing enemy. Warwick's Burgundian troops had some primitive handguns, but they do not seem to have been very effective. Early battles were fought with bills, but the halberd was longer and more effective as it had a spike that could pull a man off a horse. Finally the pike was longer; some were 18ft (5m) and could protect a body of footmen from cavalry attack. The two-handed sword was used by some knights – one is in the York Castle museum; but it was very heavy and many preferred to use a short-handled battle axe.

The main strategy of the Yorkists seems to have been to capture the king and later, when Edward made himself king, to keep the throne when he ousted Henry in 1461. London was always of strategic importance but so too were the Lancastrian strongholds like Harlech, and Bamburgh and Alnwick in the north. The generals were of mixed efficiency: Warwick, who changed sides and prolonged the war after *Edgecote*, was killed at *Barnet* where his army got in a muddle in the fog

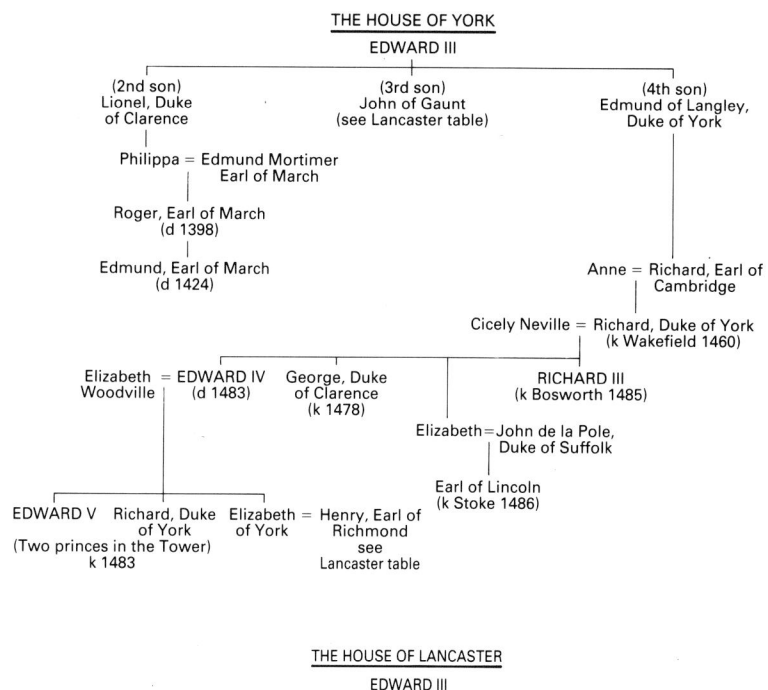

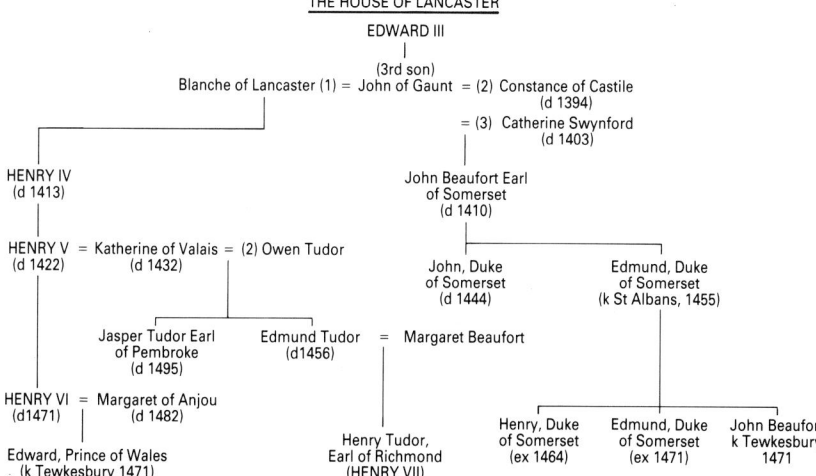

Knight's fighting at time of Neville's Cross (English Heritage)

and failed to recognise their own men. There were no outstanding leaders in the field like Montrose or Cromwell. Some men had their moments like Lord Salisbury at *Blore Heath*, by feigning a withdrawal, or King Edward's tactics at *Tewkesbury* when his small band of spearmen cut down Somerset's flanking move. Both sides made errors and many changed sides like Lord Grey at *Northampton* who allowed the enemy over the defences. In the final battle at *Bosworth* it was touch and go until the intervention of the Stanleys and the non-intervention of Northumberland, whose army walked off without fighting.

No further actions took place after Bosworth until the isolated Battle of *Stoke Field*, where the rebels had a largely mercenary army with semi-naked Irish fighting alongside experienced and well-armed Germans. Fortunately for King Henry VII, who was no soldier by inclination, the Earl of Oxford, veteran of *Barnet* and *Bosworth*, was on hand to lead his army to victory. After the battle the young Duke of Warwick was executed, thus finally extinguishing the house of York.

CHAPTER 3
THE CIVIL AND SCOTTISH WARS

The Tudors brought peace and prosperity to the country for a span of twenty-two years and it was not until 1509 and the advent of Henry VIII that there was further trouble. France had long been an ally of Scotland and when English troops invaded France in May 1513, Louis XII looked to James IV of Scotland to assist him and sent the Count d'Aussi to Scotland to instruct the Scots in the use of the 18ft (5m) pike and in artillery. James had seventeen large guns at *Flodden*, but apart from beating down the walls of Wark and Northam castles, they were not mobile enough for field work. The Earl of Surrey, son of Richard's gallant general, the Duke of Norfolk, was a very capable field commander. He may have been weak in horse, but he had some 25,000 men with his sons Thomas, Lord Admiral, and Edmund Howard as commanders, so he was not short of men.

Flodden was a resounding victory for Henry VIII and a disaster for Scotland. The English bill proved mightier than the Scottish pike and nearly 10,000 Scots were killed or captured. There was a further victory at *Pinkie* in 1547 where, for the first time, English ships fired on land-based troops. The tactics of *Bannockburn* had suddenly become out-of-date and the Scottish schiltrons were not the force they used to be.

Between 1547 and 1640 there was peace but with the reign of Charles I came the great Civil War and a complete change in warfare. Once again it was ideas from the Continent that influenced weapons and the conduct of war. King Gustavus of Sweden had many Scots like Alexander Leslie in his service. Leslie taught the Scots to fight in brigades with musketeers and pikemen. He also used small cannon. With leather guns made of iron bars bound in hide he could carry two barrels on one packhorse and his army thus became much more mobile.

The reasons for the Civil War are not easily summed up. The Scots' war led to the demand by Charles I for money from his parliament to raise an army. The impeachment of the five members and the persecution of dissenters speeded war on its way. Parliament refused to implement the Ship Money tax and demanded instant changes in the king's policy. Events moved swiftly towards war. The royal standard was raised at Nottingham on 25 August and soon the King had an army of 18,000 men, with his cousin Prince Rupert in command of the cavalry and Lord Forth in command of the rest of the army. Charles said to his troops:

Your consciences and your loyalty have brought you hither to fight for your religion, your King and the laws of the land. You shall meet

Seventeenth century basket-handled sword (York Castle Museum)

with no enemies but traitors, most of them Brownists, Anabaptists and Atheists; such who desire to destroy both Church and State, and who have already condemned you to ruin for being loyal to us.

Parliament declared the royalist army to be mostly delinquents and stated they would 'never lay down arms until his majesty should withdraw his protection from all persons who had been or might hereafter be voted delinquents'. Furthermore parliament wanted the delinquents to pay for the expenses of the equipping of Lord Essex's army. London remained firmly in parliamentary control but the country was either neutral or for parliament, like Hull and Portsmouth, or for the king like Chester and most of Wales.

The series of principal battles and their results are as follows:

23 Oct 1642	*Edgehill*: Drawn battle; way open for Rupert to advance on London, but at Turnham Green the London trained bands force him back.
19 Jan 1643	*Bradock Down*: Royalist victory in Cornwall.
16 May 1643	*Stratton*: Royalist victory on Cornwall–Devon border.
18 June 1643	*Chalgrove Field*: Royalist victory near Oxford.
5 July 1643	*Lansdown Hill*: Royalist victory by Hopton over Waller; Hopton wounded.
13 July 1643	*Roundway Down*: Royalist cavalry victory near Devizes.
20 Sept 1643	*Newbury I*: Drawn battle, but Essex, having relieved Gloucester, takes his army back to London.
11 Oct 1643	*Winceby*: Royalists defeated in Lincolnshire.
21 March 1644	*Newark*: Rupert defeats parliamentary besiegers.
29 March 1644	*Cheriton*: Waller defeats Hopton near Winchester.

Roundway Down. The steep incline is where the Parliamentary Horse came to grief

2 July 1644	*Marston Moor*: Fairfax defeats Rupert. The largest battle of the Civil War. Henceforth the North is in parliamentary control.
2 Sept 1644	*Lostwithiel*: Parliamentary army of Essex surrenders to the king in Cornwall.
28 Oct 1644	*Newbury II*. Charles relieves Donnington Castle in spite of a drawn battle.
14 June 1945	*Naseby*: King Charles defeated by Cromwell and Fairfax.
10 July 1645	*Langport*: Goring defeated by Fairfax. The West falls to parliament.

Edgehill Battle Museum at Farnborough Hall

While King Charles was losing battles and support in England, the Marquis of Montrose was having a series of remarkable royalist victories in Scotland. With a ragged, badly armed force of clansmen, mostly from the Outer Isles and Ireland, he defeated a Covenanting army at *Tippermuir* near Perth on 1 September 1644. Twelve days later the little army won another victory outside *Aberdeen*, which they captured. The next place to fall was Fyvie Castle (a National Trust for Scotland property open to the public for the first time in 1986), and after a terrible march across the Highlands in winter he defeated the Campbells at *Inverlochy* near Fort William on 2 February 1645. The Covenanters now sent Baillie and his Lowlanders to attack Montrose. With them was Sir John Hurry, once a royalist who had fought with Rupert at *Chalgrove Field*.

Montrose was driven out of Dundee and, moving quickly north into Gordon country, he took up a defensive position at the hamlet of

Auldearn. Hurry had lowland Campbells in his army and Auldearn has been described as a Macdonald-v-Campbell battle. For the first time Montrose used shock tactics. He was outnumbered and he placed his standard on a hill on the right wing, but hid his own force on the left wing. He had the cavalry of Aboyne to attack the centre; the four Covenant foot regiments were defeated and Hurry was forced to flee.

Alford on 2 July 1645 completed the defeat of Montrose's enemies in Aberdeenshire and he moved south and west to Stirling. Baillie, who still had most of his cavalry, had collected a new army, but it was committee controlled and so largely ineffective. At *Kilsyth* on 15 August 1645 Montrose had his last and possibly most thorough victory.

Unfortunately the old problem of desertion after victory happened after Kilsyth. En route for Glasgow, the Gordons left for Aberdeen and Leslie, with an army of experienced men who had fought at *Marston Moor*, came up from the south and caught the remnants of Montrose's little army at Philiphaugh (13 September 1645) on the banks of the Ettrick Water. He escaped with some thirty men to the Highlands but his army was put to the sword, many being rounded up into Newark Castle nearby and slaughtered.

Montrose himself escaped to Denmark and from there to Kirkwall in Orkney where he attempted to raise another army, but his Irish were no longer with him. With a few horsemen under Lisle, he defended himself against Colonel Strachan at Carbisdale but was routed and later

captured. The year of victories was over. Late in May 1650 Montrose was taken to the newly erected gallows on the Boroughmuir in Edinburgh and hanged by the neck. However in January 1661 there was a procession attended by fourteen earls to St Giles Cathedral where he was given a Christian burial and where there is now a monument to his memory.

Cromwell was not content with the final success of the Covenant in defeating Montrose and Leslie had to lead a Covenanting army that had accepted Prince Charles as their new sovereign as the prince was prepared to sign the Covenant and pretend he was an ardent Presbyterian. The Battle of *Dunbar* did not end Scottish resistance but it was a severe shock to their best general and Montrose's victor, Leslie. The following year the young Charles took an army to *Worcester*, where the original Civil War had begun with a skirmish at Powick Bridge. Once again Cromwell was victorious.

Some writers like to include *Sedgemoor* (6 July 1685) as part of the Civil War, but it falls into no specific category at all. If anything it was a royalist army putting down a Westcountry rebellion led by an able commander who had himself put down a rebellion in Scotland.

The final chapter of civil wars is part of the Hanoverian Succession, for the flight of James II in 1689 when William III landed at Torbay did not end support for the Jacobite cause. In Scotland it was only the beginning. The cause in Scotland was taken up by Viscount Dundee, who had fought under Monmouth at *Bothwell Bridge*. He was a very capable general but seems to have had trouble raising an army, rather like Montrose. After just one action the Scots had a tendency to pick up their plunder and go home. *Killiekrankie* was a victory for the Jacobites against Anglo-Dutch troops armed with cannon and muskets that had plug bayonets. There was little cavalry involvement and the death of Dundee was virtually the end of the rising. The 1715 was a better planned affair, although by the time the Old Pretender arrived the main action at *Sheriffmuir* was over and the English Jacobites had surrendered at *Preston*.

Archer at time of Bosworth (Marcher Lords)

(pp 30–1)
Three plotters (Dodgson)

Knight Templar at Lewes. He is armed with a mace (Marcher Lords)

Battles on the same ground are not very common in Britain. Newbury I and Newbury II were on two different sides of the town. Newbury II was two different battles as part of the parliamentary army went round the lanes to fight against the road block at Speen while the other half concentrated on Shaw House. *St Albans* was the scene of two battles during the Wars of the Roses, but two very different actions and fought on different ground.

In Scotland the only two actions that share the same ground are *Pinkie*, and Mary Queen of Scots' defeat at Carberry Hill, more a surrender than an action, but there is no mention of Carberry in accounts of *Pinkie*, though the armies must have occupied the tower.

CHAPTER 4
THE HANOVERIAN SUCCESSION 1715, '19, '45

Scottish ties with the Continent have always been strong, and with the exiled Stuart court abroad, they become even stronger. Plots abounded and leaders sailed to Scotland, but no invasion forces arrived. It was the support of the Highland clans that formed the Jacobite armies of 1715 and 1745. The small army of Scots and Spaniards that faced General Wightman at *Glen Shiel* was an exception, and most of the Spaniards returned home to Spain unharmed. The Mackenzies and Macleods that were out in the '15 refused to come out in the '45 when only twenty-two clans supported Prince Charles with ten against, in particular the Campbells, Grants, Munros, Sutherlands and Mackays. In some cases the chief stayed at home but sent his son or nephew. There were some French and Irish soldiers at *Culloden* but not enough to make much difference, and the few English supporters were left behind to surrender to Cumberland at Carlisle. Highlanders fought with a two-edged broadsword – the Hanoverians had a single-edged short sword more suited for the parade ground – leather and wood targe, dirk, and the chiefs carried pistols. Few had muskets and the Highlanders disliked artillery, so that proper use was not made of the guns captured from Cope at *Prestonpans* and Hawley at *Falkirk*. The Highlanders, Hawley stated in his Orders, 'come within a large Musket shot, or three score yards, the front Rank gives their fire, and immediately throw down their firelocks and come down in a cluster with their swords and targes making a Noise'. It startled new troops, as at *Prestonpans*, but Cumberland devised a new bayonet drill. After the three ranks had fired, they were to meet the charge with bayonets, each aiming at the Highlander to his right on the undefended side. *Culloden* was the outcome.

Cumberland's infantry had seen service abroad and were used to their new flintlocks, which were capable of a higher rate of fire than the old matchlock. In the English army was a young officer from Bath, James Wolfe. This was his first campaign and the world would hear more of him. The Scots, apart from Lord George Murray, had no officer of note and Murray himself did not always have enough sway over Charles and his favourites so that his ideas were not often listened to, with dire consequences. Finally the forgotten Colonel Belford and his artillery – brass 3-pounders that could fire up to 500yd (460m) and howitzers that could double that – did a wonderful job. His gunners

Battlefield of Sheriffmuir (top of hill) and Sterling University (centre) as seen from the Wallace Monument

*The 'Captain Scott' at anchor in Loch
Duich* (National Trust for Scotland).
Nearby is the battlefield of Glen Shiel

changed from solid to grapeshot at the appropriate times, and did most of Cumberland's work for him.

The Hanoverian Succession must be studied to realise the reasons for the Jacobite wars. The strange fact to note now is that James II, in spite of being driven into exile by his own daughter and her husband, lived until 1701 and that his son James, the Old Pretender, lived until he was seventy-eight, so that Bonnie Prince Charlie himself would not have become king until 1766 assuming he had won *Culloden* and there had been no further resistance. It is amazing that so many supported his cause when really they were supporting his father's and, unless they had been in Aberdeenshire in 1715, few had ever met the Old Pretender.

Jacobites had a very good claim to the throne. On the death of Henry, Cardinal of York, the claim was vested in the descendants of Henrietta and Victor Amadeus of Savoy who were rulers of Bavaria.

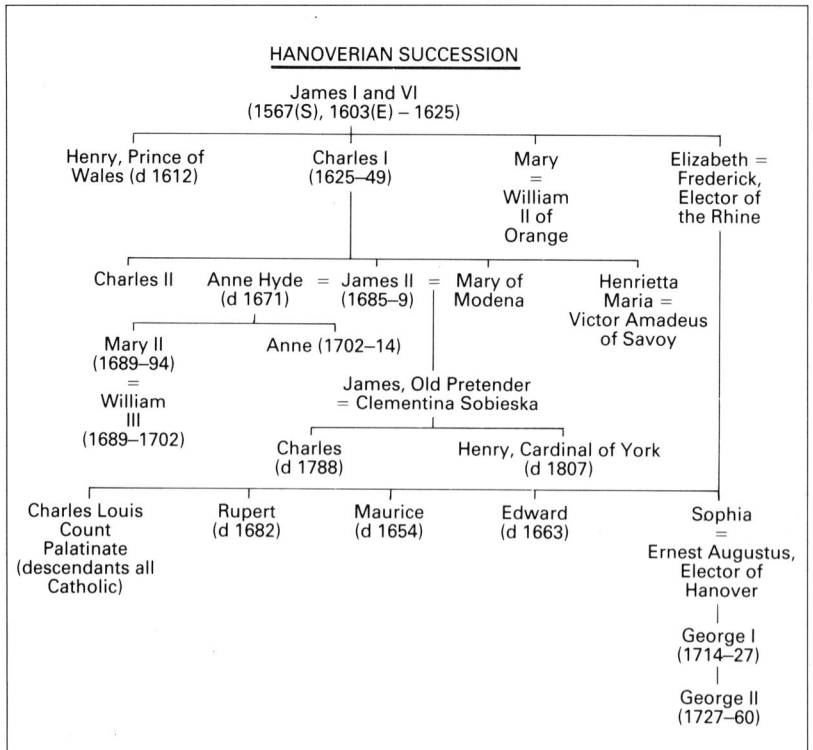

The problem of military leadership was not solely restricted to the Jacobites. The Hanoverian army relied largely on officers who purchased their commissions. Few had seen any action in the 1715 affair. General Wightman was a competent enough officer who did a good job at *Glen Shiel* against very poor opposition. In the '45 some had seen action on the Continent and in Prince Charles's army were men like Brigadier Stapleton who, with his Irish troops, had performed gallantly at *Fontenoy*. However Stapleton arrived too late to make any difference to the end result and Charles's French troops were not enough to help. The Duke of Cumberland took over when both Cope and Hawley had failed. The first was merely a gentleman soldier who was more at home in the gambling rooms of London. The latter – whose house at West Green, near Aldershot, is occasionally open to the public – was a different sort of person. Brutal and erratic, he came from a military family and was probably a friend of General Kirke (son

of the Sedgemoor Colonel Percy Kirke) whose tomb can be found in Westminster Abbey.

Lord George Murray was the discovery of the Jacobite command. He had the same instinct as Montrose in his handling of troops, but not the same respect from his fellow officers. The handling of the army before *Prestonpans*, by positioning them on the English side of Cope's men and charging before Cope could deploy his guns, was a brilliant move worthy of Dundee or the Earl of Surrey. The delaying action at *Clifton* was well handled and successful. The bitter cold battle at *Falkirk* was a strange affair and one wonders whether it was really due to Murray or to Stapleton filling in the gap on the left wing that won the day. Certainly Hawley, with his experienced fellow officers like Lord Ligonier, was not equal to the action when it started.

Cumberland took over a much more efficient army. He weeded out the riff-raff, and morale was excellent as the Aiken letters show. One of his young officers took note and used the experience of Culloden to good effect in Canada – James Wolfe, whose house in Bath is a few yards away from Bath Abbey. In the Abbey is a tomb to Lord Cawdor, the victor of *Fishguard* (1797).

British battles are all connected in an intimate network that spans the centuries. Let us hope that 1797 was the final action and that henceforward, though we do not forget them, the fallen rest in peace as in the two graves in Porlock, Somerset, churchyard. One is to a member of a bomber crew shot down in World War II and one to an RAF crew that crashed earlier in the war. I met a man putting a wreath on both graves last year. He was the ex-Luftwaffe pilot of the bomber.

(pp 38–9)
Warrior horse (Marcher Lords)

Battles and Walks

S   Short walk or no walk at all
M   Medium walk 15 minutes to 45 minutes
L   Long walk   1 hour or more

ETHANDUN
878

The Wiltshire Downs are an inspiration for walkers. Their broad scarp with the White Horse beckons you as the main railway line approaches Westbury station. What a splendid place for an army to attack from. The bald hills today may not have been quite so bald then or the Danes would have been waiting for them. Climb up to the top of the escarpment and look back at Alfred's view. He would have seen every step his enemy took and no better position could have been found from which to start an attack.

Ethandun or Edington was King Alfred's most dramatic victory against the Danes. There are two schools of thought about the site of the battle. The Somerset 'school' considers it was fought at Edington on the Polden Hills, only a short walk from Athelney where King Alfred spent the winter of 877–78 and now marked by a plaque erected in April 1987. The other 'school' places the battle at Edington in Wiltshire.

After his winter on the island in the swamp, Alfred according to the *Anglo-Saxon Chronicle* arranged a gathering of his trusty thegns at Ecgbryghts stane, a stone near Brixton Deverill, Wiltshire, near the modern Alfred Tower. He had men from Wiltshire, Hampshire and Somerset and they carried spears, strong-bladed swords and shields. The latter were round with metal centres sometimes spiked so that they could be used for pushing.

The Danes were at Chippenham in their fortified camp. They soon heard of Alfred's army through spies and Guthrun set out to meet him. Why they went to Edington is not clear but they failed to capture the hill above it. Alfred's army lay concealed in the long grass and, when the sunlight shone in the faces of his enemy, he gave the order to attack. 'He fought against all the army',

White Horse Hill near Ethandun battlefield

states the *Chronicle*, 'in a dense, shield-locked array, long maintaining a stubborn fight, and at length by Divine Will obtained a victory.' The Danes were chased to their camp at Chippenham where, after a fourteen-day siege, they were forced to surrender through hunger.

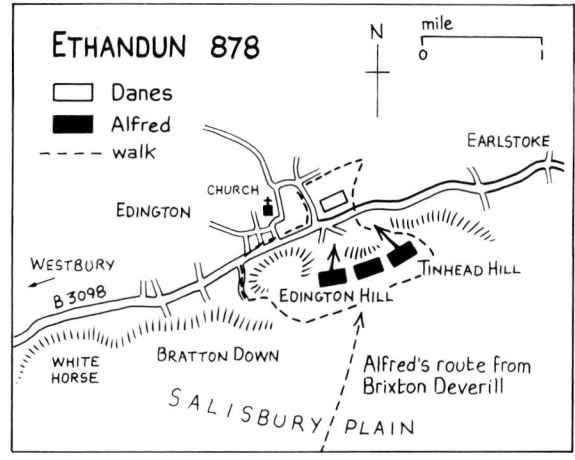

The interested student of King Alfred in the Westcountry should visit Athelney, just off the A361 Glastonbury to Taunton road, where there is a Victorian monument to the Abbey built there.

Nearby is Aller Church, where Guthrun was baptised, and in Wedmore Church there is a stained glass window representing Alfred as well as his prayer inscribed on the wall in Victorian times. The town of Winchester has a statue of him in the middle of the High Street.

THE WALK (L)

This starts at Edington Church (1351), reckoned by Pevsner to be one of the outstanding examples of Perpendicular style. It has a tomb to an unknown monk, which when I called was being inspected by the Church Commissioners with a view to being restored. Outside the way goes to the left along the church wall and across the Steeple Aston road towards some council houses. A small stile on the right leads into a large field. This and the field next door are where the Danes stood awaiting Alfred's attack. Go diagonally across the field to another stile, which leads onto the main Westbury to

TO SEE NEARBY

White Horse in the chalk at Bratton Down.

Devizes Museum, Long Street, Devizes, for fine examples of spears, shields, swords and helmets of the Viking period.

Battlefields Roundway Down, Devizes.

Edington Church. Starting and finishing place of the walk

Devizes road. Here the path continues opposite but it is difficult to find. There is a Post Office with two cottages to the left of it. One of them is called Sheba, so being Solomon-like in persistent exploration, I discovered a post with the word FOOTPATH written on it vertically so that long grass makes it hard to see. The path in fact is well worn and very narrow, but leads up to the downs. At the top of the hill the view back towards the church is magnificent. In the far distance is Chippenham some 12 miles (19km) away. The Danes had a long way to get home with Alfred's men at their heels. The path goes to the right through a gate and this is a good blackberry area in autumn. The famous White Horse cannot be seen as it is some 3 miles (5km) away on Bratton Down, but some say it was built to commemorate Alfred's victory.

The hill has numerous gullies in its slope which would make suitable places for hiding in the hawthorn and bramble bushes. There are sheep about and sheep paths through the chalk which after about 500yd (457m) lead down to a water trough. Here is a small tree that seems to be so covered in ivy it is difficult to know what kind of tree it is. Go through the metal gate to the right and you are now in Sandy Lane, which is welcome if only to provide cool shelter after the open down. The path winds down to Sandy Lane Cottage on the main road. It is so quiet that it is easy to forget the danger of fast traffic at the end. Flowers we noticed on the way down were bluebells, forget-me-nots, primroses, buttercups and violets. The downs are supposed to be a breeding ground for the small blue butterfly, but we did not see any. There was a cuckoo in the area and once we saw it, with its long tail stretched out behind, flying high up looking for a nest to 'poach'.

At the cottage turn right and carry on down the road to the fourth turning on the left where descend to the car park by the church. The walk has taken about an hour as we stopped at the top of the downs for a picnic and to admire the view. The Post Office sells ice-creams, postcards and everything one needs. There is a pub in nearby Erlestoke (a Danish sounding name), but it is a long hike down the road and not on the footpath.

STAMFORD BRIDGE
25 September 1066

Overshadowed by Hastings, the battle of Stamford Bridge is nevertheless of equal importance. Tostig, Earl of Northumberland and brother of King Harold, joined forces with King Hardrada of Norway in an attempt to get back his earldom. Harold had banished him for failing to control the north and given his land to Morcar. The latter had trouble controlling the north too and at Fulford, outside York, a Viking force under Hardrada defeated Morcar and Edwin (Harold's two brothers-in-law). Part of the Viking force consisted of Scottish levies who, like many Scots, took their booty and made for home. The weakened Viking army went to the east of York and camped at Stamford Bridge, defending it from attack from the west. On 24 September Harold was in Tadcaster and with 3,000 men was greeted by Morcar and Edwin in York, both of whom joined him on the short march to Stamford Bridge. Hardrada had left Olaf and a part of his army guarding his ships at Riccall so his force was only slightly larger than Harold's army. One Viking held up Harold's advance over the bridge until a local man stood in a swill tub and, from under the bridge, stabbed the Viking in the foot with a spear. Harold's archers rushed the bridge and commenced shooting from short range at the Viking army deployed on Battle Flats.

Hardrada was killed, Tostig was struck down by his own brother, and when Olaf arrived with reinforcements the battle was over. Harold allowed Olaf to withdraw with twenty ships, provided he did not trouble English shores again. The English army was exhausted and Harold had to leave almost immediately for the south having heard of William's landing. The Battle of Stamford Bridge was a harsh warm-up for Hastings and had it not happened the outcome of the latter might have been different.

THE BATTLEFIELD TODAY (S)

The present bridge is almost on the site of the old one if the Roman road continued across the river. There is a monument in English and Norwegian which says 'The Battle of Stamford Bridge was fought in this neighbourhood on September 25, 1066'.

> ### TO SEE NEARBY
>
> *York* Castle Museum, Viking Museum.
>
> *Stillingfleet Church* near Selby where ironwork on the door is supposed to represent a Viking ship.
>
> *Battlefields* Marston Moor and Towton.

Monument in both English and Norwegian at Stamford Bridge

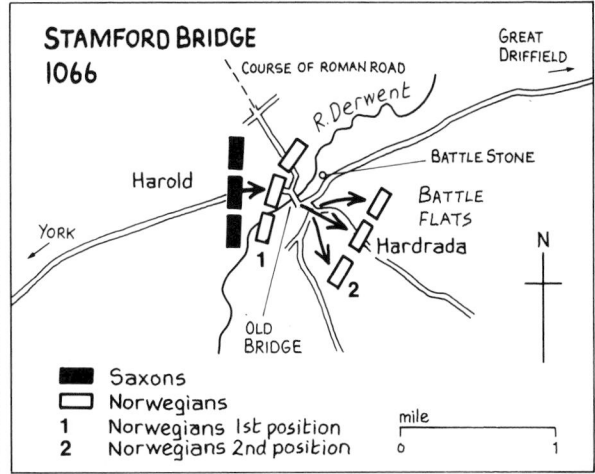

HASTINGS
14 October 1066

Ballista were of Roman or pre-Roman origin and consisted of large wheeled platforms with a see-saw like contrivance mounted on top. In one side there was a net that carried rocks, and the other had to be tied down with ropes so that when released the rocks shot up into the air. The modern word *ballistics* comes from the same derivation.

Harold's victory at Stamford Bridge was closely followed by the Norman invasion, when some 10,000 men landed unopposed at Pevensey. They had horses, boats that were suitable for living in while they were on shore, mailed armour and pointed shields and helmets. The Norman archers had small bows and short arrows, but had been trained to shoot up into the air so that their arrows landed in a rainshower on the enemy.

Harold's men made a rapid march south, stopping in London for reinforcements. His housecarls fought with axes and two-handed swords. Their long shields protected them when held, Roman style, in a wall. Some carried javelins. He had few archers and his ballista, or stone-throwing catapults, were of little use except in the siege of a flimsy castle or strongpoint.

Making for Hastings, Harold drew up his men in a long line at Battle Abbey, several miles short of the coast. William took Telham Hill and put his army in three divisions. Count Alan of Brittany took the left wing, Eustace of Boulogne with his French and Flemish soldiers took the right, and William himself took

Harold's Saxon army at Hastings
(Marcher Lords)

the centre. Archers were placed in front, then infantry and the Norman horse behind. Harold's shield wall did not break and the Bretons were pushed back. William ordered them forward once more and this time to deliberately retreat. Harold's right wing followed them, opening up the shield wall so that the Norman knights poured in. The famous arrow hit Harold, the housecarls finally retreated, turning on Eustace's men at a ravine called the Malfosse, where they cut them down. It was a costly victory and it was a further seven weeks before William was finally offered the crown.

THE BATTLEFIELD TODAY

The battle site has been given a number of interpretation panels and signs. In 1988 there is to be a video room showing what happened. Battle Abbey (English Heritage) was built by William as a thanksgiving for his victory, and the high altar is supposed to mark where Harold was killed. It is open at all times and there are walks in the grounds.

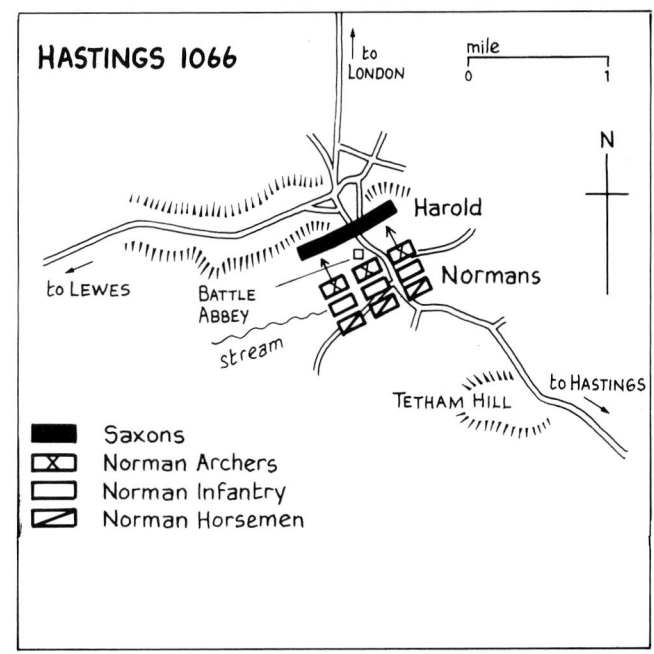

HASTINGS 1066

to LONDON

mile
0   1

N

Harold

Normans

to LEWES

BATTLE
ABBEY

stream

TETHAM HILL

to HASTINGS

- ■ Saxons
- ⊠ Norman Archers
- ▭ Norman Infantry
- ◪ Norman Horsemen

TO SEE NEARBY

Pevensey Castle, where the Normans landed.

Lewes (21 miles, 34km).

(pp 46–7)
Hastings re-enactment (English Heritage)

THE STANDARD
22 August 1138

The Scots under David I invaded England when Stephen came to the throne and, with the Earl of Gloucester in revolt in Bristol, Stephen was in no position to come to the aid of the people of York. However the archbishop, Thurstan, was a powerful force and he summoned the local forces to his banner – a huge mast on a cart, tipped by a silver pyx hung with the banners of St Peter of York, St John of Beverley and St Wilfrid of Ripon. His commanders included Walter Espec of Helmsley, Gilbert de Lacy and William le Gros, who later built Scarborough Castle.

Espec seems to have been in overall command of the English army and his knights fought on foot. The Scots were poorly armed. They had positioned themselves on Oaktree Hill and their wild charge was checked by the English archers; the men of Galloway in particular were described as looking like 'hedgehogs with quills'. Prince Henry of Scotland with his horsemen charged through the English lines, surrounding the baggage train; however Epec's

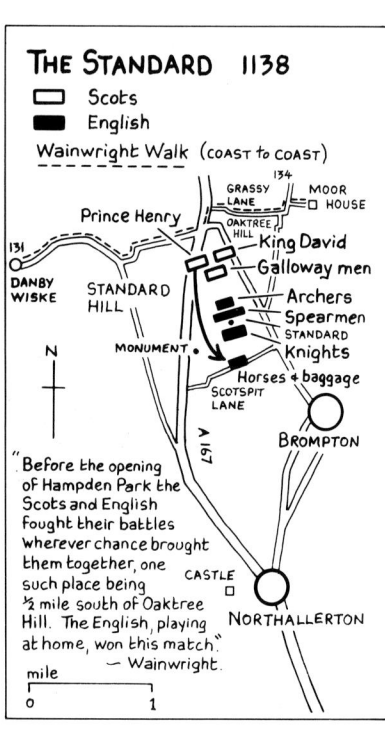

third line encircled the Scots and few survived. Henry and his father escaped to Carlisle. The Scots were killed in hundreds and their bodies buried in Scotspit Lane, which is still there connecting the main A167 from Northallerton to Darlington and Brompton Lane.

THE BATTLEFIELD TODAY (M)

There is a large stone monument on the right-hand side of the main road a few miles north of Northallerton, and on it can be seen the symbol of the archbishop's pyx or standard.

Strangely enough, although there is no obvious walk, the battlefield is included in Wainwright's *A Coast to Coast Walk* from St Bees head in Cumbria to Robin Hood's Bay in North Yorkshire. Wainwright did this walk in the 1970s and reckoned the dullest part was between Danby Wiske and Oaktree Hill where he had to keep to the road as the other routes were across fields well protected by barbed wire. He recommends walking up the A167 from Crowfoot Lane to Oaktree Hill, then on until taking a grassy lane on the right, 'a sylvan paradise by contrast', going north down Deighton Lane and then turning right to Moor House Farm. The route from point 132 to 134 on his map is about 16 miles (26km), and crosses the Scottish position; it is now one of the classic walks of England. Scotspit Lane is alas too overgrown for walkers.

TO SEE NEARBY

Battlefields Marston Moor, Stamford Bridge and Towton.

(left) *The battlestone at The Standard, Northallerton*

(below) *Standard Farm*

LEWES
14 May 1264

Knight at Lewes (Marcher Lords)

Helmet monument at Lewes. It has engravings of Simon de Montfort's life round the rim

The father of modern parliament, Simon de Montfort, Earl of Leicester, held his first meeting in Oxford in 1258 and followed this with a Barons' War against Henry III, who did not want a parliament, and ignored the Oxford resolutions. The king raised an army with Prince Edward as his leader of knights on horseback. Simon's men dressed in Crusader style with red crosses on a white shift. His army was blessed by the Bishop of Chichester and it occupied Offham heights north of Lewes, where de Warenne had declared for the king.

The Battle of Lewes in May 1264 was fought in stages. The impetuous Prince Edward led his knights out of the castle and attacked the Londoners on Simon's left wing, chasing them for miles. Meanwhile King Henry and his brother Richard, known as 'king of the Romans' because he had once claimed the Imperial Throne, took positions at the foot of the hill. The centre of Simon's army under Gloucester and his right wing under Seagrave with his sons Guy, Henry and Clare in the centre advanced down the hill to meet Henry's now depleted army. Richard was cut off from his men and captured in a windmill. Henry was forced to retreat to Lewes Priory, where Prince Edward, having attacked Simon's baggage train, later joined him having lost many of his knights on the way. Simon surrounded the priory and captured the king.

THE BONES OF LEWES

In 1846 a railway line was built through the site of the old priory at Lewes and the excavators discovered a mass of human bones in a well some 18ft (5m) below ground level. The workmen stopped work because the smell was too powerful for them to carry on and a special train of ten waggons appeared in which other men, presumably railway workers, put the bones, only to tip them out at Southerham corner where an embankment was being built. 'It is a source of deep regret', said the *Sussex Express* of 17 January, 'that human bones should have been employed for such a purpose'. A local surgeon, Gideon Mantell, wrote:

> In perfect accordance with the spirit of this railway age, this heap of skeletons of the patriots and royalists of the thirteenth century, which filled thirteen waggons [three more than the newspaper suggested] was taken away to form part of the embankment of the line in the adjacent brook.

Edward was sent under guard to Hereford, Richard to Kenilworth. The real fame of Lewes though was the setting up of the first Parliament of Knights from the shires with two representatives from the chartered boroughs.

THE WALKS (M and M)

Lewes is a town that is meant for pedestrians, everything of importance is clearly labelled and for the battlefield it is divided into a town walk and a country walk.

Town Walk: This starts from the castle ruins, in a dominant position at the centre of High Street. Visit the barbican with its museum of archaeology and the two towers on the motte which were added later. Then cross the street and go down St Martin's Lane into Garden Street and then into Priory Road. On the right is Anne of Cleves House, which is early sixteenth century and seems not to be really connected with the queen at all. It is now a museum and nearly opposite it is Cockshut Road with Southover Church on the corner. Go down here and through the railway tunnel. Turn sharp left and you are now in Lewes Priory, the first Cluniac priory in England and much demolished. Walls of the dormitory and reredorter remain, though one of them was nearly flattened by a falling tree in the great wind of October 1987. The monument to the battle is a large bronze helmet beside the children's playground. It was built by Enzo Plazzotta and unveiled by the Duke of Norfolk in 1964. Around the top, which shows inscriptions of the life of Simon, are the words:

> Law is like fire for it lights as truth, warms as charity, burns as zeal. With these virtues the King will rule well. Now Englishman read on about this battle fought at Lewes' Walls because of this you are alive and safe, rejoice then in God.

The walls can be seen nearby in Southover Road. Carry on back to High Street via Station Road.

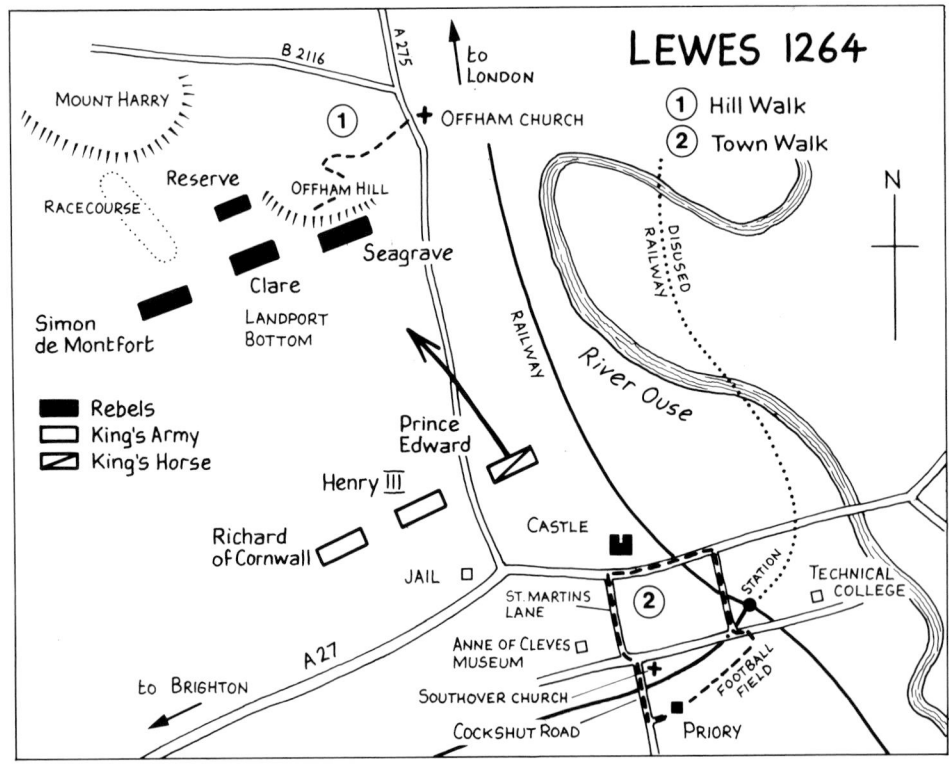

Simon de Montfort hunting. Seal
(Historical Association)

Country Walk: This starts from Offham on the London Road about 2 miles (3km) north of Lewes. Opposite the church take the footpath marked 'Blackcap 16A' with a vertical blue sign on a post. The path is muddy and chalky but leads round in a gentle curve to the top of Offham Hill with chalk pits on the left. Go through (or over) a stile then turn right to the small reservoir where there is a fine view of the town. As Colonel Burne points out, from here de Montfort could see the priory and Landport Bottom which was sufficiently flat for his horsemen. And it was on this hill that de Montfort's left wing of Londoners were chased off by Prince Edward's mounted knights. Return the same way; or for those with further energy there is a footpath to the top of Mount Harry where there is a small monument and which can also be climbed from the minor road between Offham and Hassocks.

THE PARLIAMENT OF KNIGHTS

King Henry III appealed to his barons in Oxford in 1255 to rescue him from his debts, mostly incurred by foreign wars. Simon de Montfort was the leader of the Council of Fifteen. Leaving their swords at the door, they pledged to 'Have the power of advising the King in good faith concerning the government of the kingdom'. It was decided that the King should hold three 'Parliaments' (the word is French in origin) a year at Michaelmas, Candlemas and in June. Simon took the arrangement as permanent and as he was Earl of Leicester, married to the King's sister and a man of firm resolve, it was not surprising that a mini or civil war was the result.

BANNERS

The British Army has its own regimental colours, some of which started as personal flags of their colonels.

Cavalry regiments carry a standard or a guidon, which is a split-ended flag on the end of a spear pole. Infantry regiments carry two colours, the sovereign's colour and the regimental colour. Nowadays colours are only used in ceremonial parades, but at *Evesham* they would have been rallying points, and latecomers to the battle would know where they should be by looking for their leaders' banners.

Visitors to *Bosworth* will see streamers or pennants on Ambien Hill, marking the site of Richard's position. The pennon was attached to a lance and is now used by lancer regiments, while the guidon, which can be gytton or geton, was often carried by an ensign or junior officer and is the standard now used by Dragoon regiments.

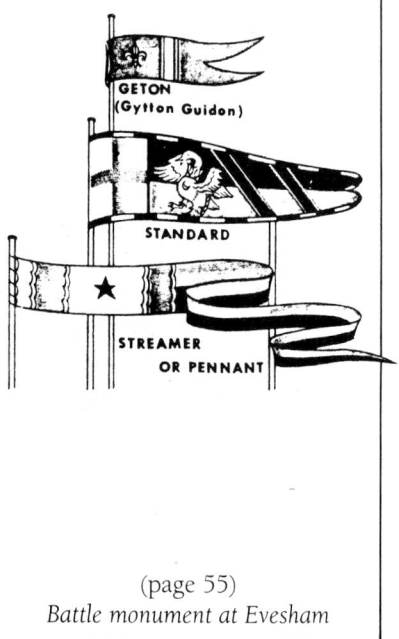

(page 55)
Battle monument at Evesham

EVESHAM
4 August 1265

Evesham was a trap. Prince Edward knew his enemy well. He caught him in the bend of the river so that Simon de Montfort, Earl of Leicester, and his sons had no other option than to fight with their backs to the town and the water. It is a peaceful, English scene today but in 1265 the river banks were covered with men trying to escape across the river at Offenham at a place called Dead Man's Bit. How many were drowned and how many killed by the enemy it is impossible to say.

Few prisoners were taken – Edward's vengeance was terrible. The earl's remains were buried by monks in Evesham Abbey and for many years it became a place of pilgrimage. His tomb was visited by the sick and deformed; all recovered as one of the monks has recorded. The entire village of Cordebregge near Reading was witness to a boy recovering his hearing after being deaf for three years. Guy de Phynele from Warwick recovered from paralysis after passing the string used for measuring the earl's relics round his forehead. There was an attempt to stop the pilgrims and eventually they ceased coming. Today a thanksgiving service is held to honour his memory on the Sunday nearest to 4 August.

The Battle of Evesham was therefore young Prince Edward's revenge after the disaster of Lewes. Simon de Montfort's guards had allowed Edward to escape and at Wigmore Castle (near Mortimer's Cross) he raised a large army to attack Simon, whose army was divided between Kenilworth where young Simon, his son, occupied town and castle, and Worcester. Edward attacked Kenilworth in the early hours of 1 August and captured many of Simon's men and banners, but failed to capture the castle. The main rebel army was now at Evesham awaiting young Simon. When they spotted his banners they naturally thought it was a relief force but it was Prince Edward and the Duke of Gloucester moving down from Green Hill, having first secured Bengeworth Bridge. Old Simon was now trapped and Evesham was his attempt to burst out.

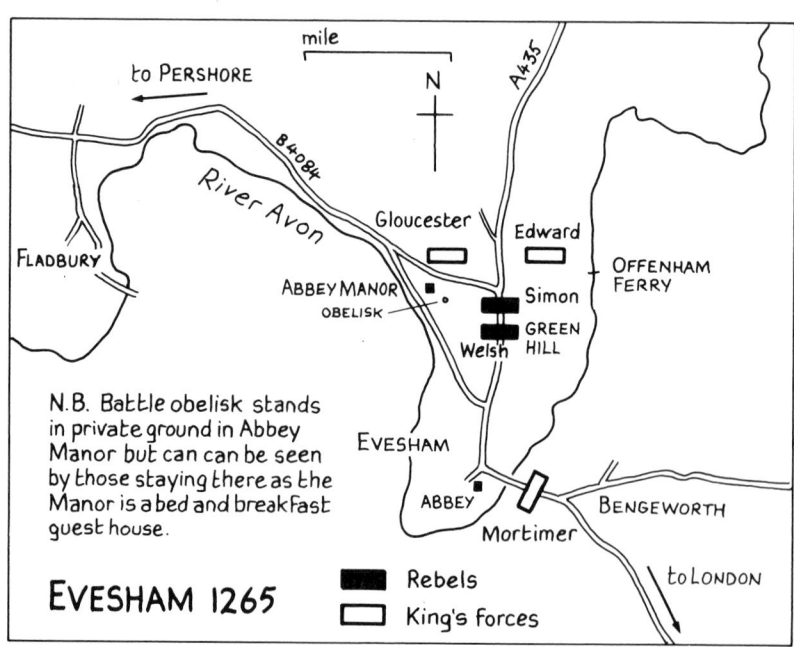

N.B. Battle obelisk stands in private ground in Abbey Manor but can be seen by those staying there as the Manor is a bed and breakfast guest house.

EVESHAM 1265

I AM HENRY OF WINCHESTER.
YOUR KING;
DO NOT KILL ME.

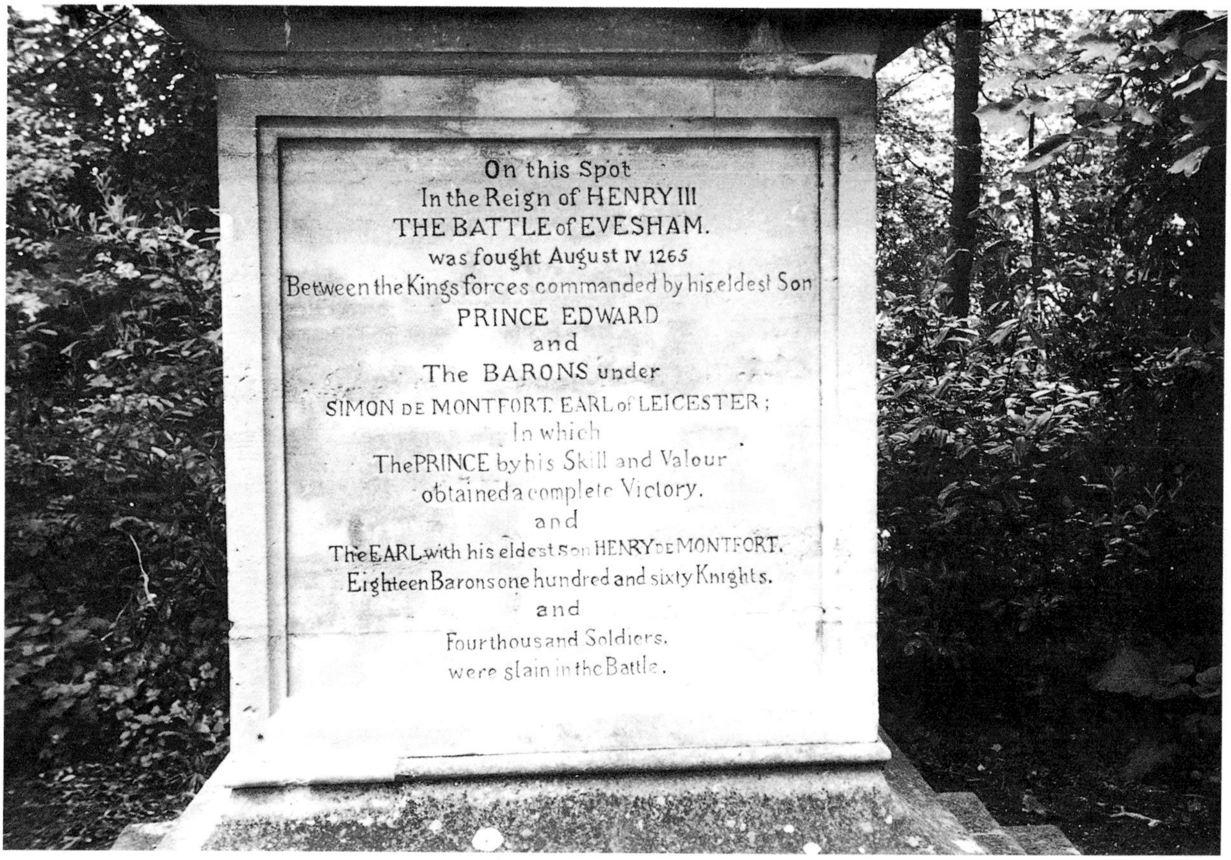

On this Spot
In the Reign of HENRY III
THE BATTLE of EVESHAM.
was fought August IV 1265
Between the Kings forces commanded by his eldest Son
PRINCE EDWARD
and
The BARONS under
SIMON DE MONTFORT EARL of LEICESTER;
In which
The PRINCE by his Skill and Valour
obtained a complete Victory.
and
The EARL with his eldest son HENRY DE MONTFORT.
Eighteen Barons one hundred and sixty Knights.
and
Four thousand Soldiers.
were slain in the Battle.

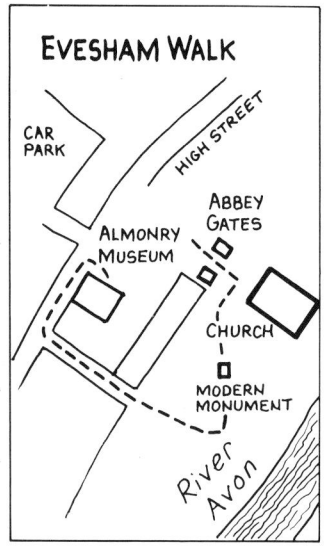

EVESHAM WALK

CAR PARK

HIGH STREET

ABBEY GATES

ALMONRY MUSEUM

CHURCH

MODERN MONUMENT

River Avon

The battle was fought in a thunderstorm and lasted over two hours but both Simon and his other son Henry were killed. The Welsh spearmen deserted. But there was no escape and Evesham was one of the most decisive victories in England. Kenilworth finally surrendered in December 1267 due to lack of supplies.

THE WALK (S)

Evesham is a short walk as the main battlefield is on private land. First take the abbey garden entrance and turn right to look at the de Montfort monument, a large block made from stone from the de Montfort castle ruins in France. It was opened by the Archbishop of Canterbury in 1965 and unveiled by the then Speaker of the House of Commons. A path past the

TO SEE NEARBY

Fladbury Church on the road to Pershore a few miles from Evesham has a north chancel window with the arms of Simon de Montfort and some of his fellow knights. The glass is supposed to have been brought here when Evesham Abbey was disolved by Henry VIII. In 1965 the window was restored. Also in this well looked–after church is a brass to Sir John and Lady Eleanor Throckmorton. He is in armour of the early Wars of the Roses period. On his belt there is a quick-release handle for getting into and out of his armour, and he is so thin it seems he wasn't allowed to eat anything in case his armour didn't fit him.

Kenilworth Castle Some 35 miles (56km) away, Kenilworth ruins are most impressive and belong to English Heritage. The moat is still mostly intact and the ruins are, like Raglan, worthy of being repaired. They are open to the public at all times.

monument turns right, back to the town. The field on the left is very often full of potato plants, a practical use to put to a field so near the centre of town.

The little Almonry Museum is at the end of this walk and worth seeing. Upstairs is the de Montfort Room with a montage of the battle.

For those staying the night in Evesham there is a chance to see the main battle monument. It is sited in the grounds of Abbey Manor, now a bed and breakfast guest house. Erected in the nineteenth century it has the inscription: 'The Earl and his eldest son Henry de Montfort, 18 barons, 160 knights and 4000 soldiers were slain in the battle'. An ice house and the Leicester Tower, a folly, are also in the Manor grounds. The field below where the battle took place is supposed to have a well, but this is just a damp spot today and not worth visiting.

Kenilworth Castle. In De Montfort hands but surprised by Edward before Evesham (C.C.)

STIRLING BRIDGE
11 September 1297

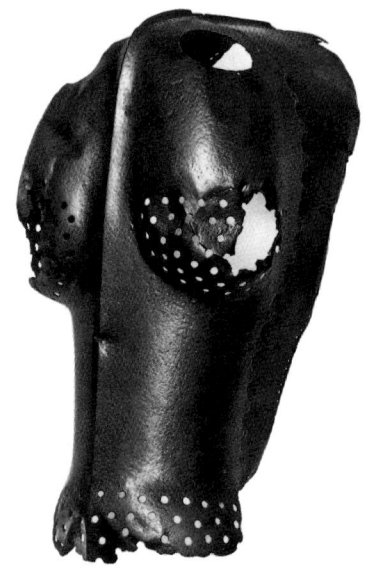

Fourteenth century knight in jousting armour (Marcher Lords)

The earliest breed of horse used in the Middle Ages was the *Shire*, or an early descendant of the modern Shire horse. It is over 17 hands high, weighs over a ton and can pull a load of five tons. The smaller *Clydesdale* was not introduced until the eighteenth century. The French horse, *Percheron*, a grey or black, was also a useful war horse.

Shaffron or horse-head armour (Age of Chivalry Exhibition)

The town of Stirling is clustered round its castle, which is similar in some respects to that at Edinburgh. There is no other similarity however. Here we are in the heart of Nationalist Scotland and the Wallace Monument is a shrine to Scotland's hero and to the independence of the country. Built in the Victorian age it is architecturally unattractive, but inside it serves its purpose admirably. Visit the Hall of Scottish Worthies: Sir Walter Scott, James Watt, Robert the Bruce, David Livingstone, Thomas Carlyle, William Murdoch (who discovered coal gas as a means of light), Robert Tannahill (an eighteenth-century Paisley weaver-poet), John Knox, Adam Smith (economist), George Buchanan (tutor to James VI and a poet), Hugh Miller (nineteenth-century writer), Thomas Chalmers (pulpit orator), Robert Burns, Sir David Brewster (inventor of the kaleidoscope and Chancellor of Edinburgh University at the time of the building of the monument) and, strangely, William Ewart Gladstone who was born in Liverpool but of Scottish descent. It is an incomplete collection, but it is important to realise that in 1861 these names were well remembered even if today some of them are a bit obscure.

It is impossible not to be stirred by the national pride inherent in the monument and by the view from its top of the surrounding hills and winding river where the 'Stuarts once in glory reigned' – the true heart of historical Scotland.

Part of that history was made in September 1297. On the death of Alexander III of Scotland in 1286, the Scottish throne became vacant with the nearest heir, the Maid of Norway, only three years old. King Edward I saw this as a golden opportunity to put his puppet king on the Scottish throne and keep the Border free from trouble. His choice fell on John Balliol, and the Scots naturally did not approve. They made an alliance with France, and a revolt under William Wallace and Andrew de Moray developed. An English army under Cressingham and the Earl of Surrey advanced on Stirling with about 1,000 armed knights and 50,000 foot. Wallace had 10,000 men hidden behind Abbey Craig. He waited until the English had partly crossed the old bridge (about ½ mile (8km) further upstream from the Old Brig that stands today) near Kildean Ford with their horses two abreast, before giving the

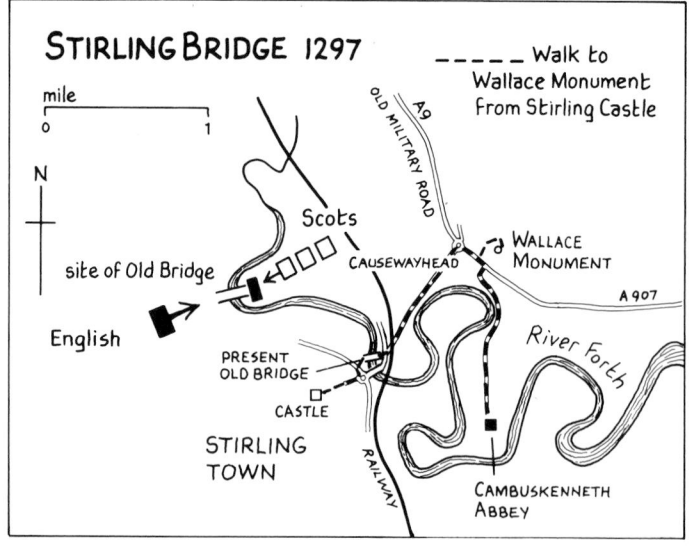

STIRLING BRIDGE 1297

— — — — — Walk to Wallace Monument From Stirling Castle

mile
0   1

N

Scots

site of Old Bridge

English

CAUSEWAYHEAD

WALLACE MONUMENT

A 907

OLD MILITARY ROAD

A9

River Forth

PRESENT OLD BRIDGE

CASTLE

STIRLING TOWN

RAILWAY

CAMBUSKENNETH ABBEY

signal to attack. Sir Marmaduke Twenge was one of the few knights to escape, for Wallace's carpenters removed the central section of the bridge so that the English were trapped and then they were set on by the Scottish spearmen. Some drowned in the river, others fled back to Berwick. The Scottish horse, few in number, crossed at a ford and harried the retreat. Cressingham was killed and Scotland had discovered a new hero.

Stirling Bridge and the Wallace Monument

THE WALK (M)
The bridge is no longer in existence, though at very low water the wooden stilts can still be seen. From the centre of Stirling proceed to Lawrencecroft Road and the little park by the Old Brig, built about 1600 and once gated. It had little houses for the gatekeepers built into the recess of the wall. Tolls were levied for its upkeep and today, though only a footbridge, it is in fine condition. Cross over it and take the road ahead to Abbey Craig and enter the park. The footpath to the Wallace Monument is steep and the 242 steps to the top should not be attempted unless you are fit. The view from the top is spectacular on a fine day. Not only can you see Bannockburn, but the sites of Sherriffmuir, the Stirling Bridge and the hill above Falkirk where eventually Wallace was defeated. The Victorian monument, built by John Rochead, was opened by a procession from the town, led by the provost, in 1861. Inside there is a slide-audio-visual show of the battle, Wallace's sword, some oil paintings and, as you climb the stairs, the room of Scottish Worthies with a commentary by Gordon Jackson is worth a halt (see also page 58). There are weapons in another room, placed high on the wall, and seemingly mostly nineteenth century in origin. The walk continues from the monument to the A407 and across it then down a straight lane to Cambuskenneth Abbey.

TO SEE NEARBY

Cambuskenneth Abbey On the far side of the Forth and approached from the road to Alloa, the abbey is open to the public. There is a triple-storey tower which can be climbed to enjoy the fine view from the top, and outlines of other buildings including cottages very close to the river bank. The much Victorianised tomb of James III and his wife is railed off. The king was killed at nearby *Sauchieburn* in 1488 after being defeated by his rebel lords. The other tombstones seem to belong to the Hunter family.

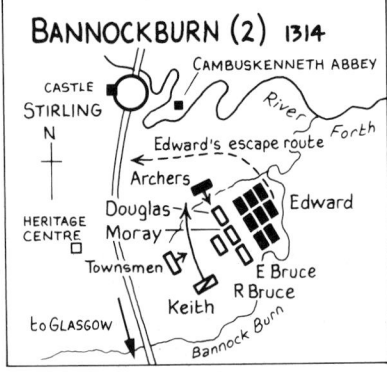

BANNOCKBURN
24 June 1314

The Bruce Monument (National Trust for Scotland)

TO SEE NEARBY

Battlefields Stirling is an ideal centre for battles. Stirling Bridge, Kilsyth, Sheriffmuir and Falkirk are nearby and are included in this book. The fields to the left of the Grangemouth road as you come into Stirling are supposed to be where the main battle of Bannockburn took place on the second day. There is no monument there and only in the last year or so have they ceased to be farmland.

After the death of King Edward I in 1307 the weak and ineffectual Edward II replaced him and the Scots under Robert Bruce were given fresh heart. There was an English garrison in Stirling Castle and Bruce obtained a honourable agreement that, unless relieved by Midsummer Day, Mowbray, the governor, would surrender the castle to the Scots. On 23 June some knights under the Earl of Clifford attempted to break through, but Moray's spearmen blocked the way and this preliminary skirmish was the prelude to the day-long battle at Bannockburn.

Bruce had a mere 8,000 against an English army of 22,000. It meant a good position was essential as the Scots were weak in horse. He scattered calthrops – one can be seen in the Heritage Centre museum; surprisingly small, it has four points so that always one is uppermost to maim a horse – and dug pits covered in brushwood and turf. His right was covered by scrub and forest and his left by St Ninian's kirk and the carse, rough land leading to the River Forth. There were bogs by the Bannock river, for it was more of a river than a burn in 1314, and Edward's approach from Falkirk took him into the carse for he crossed the Bannock Burn and positioned his army rather close together, but allowed Gloucester's knights to attack along the left flank while the Welsh archers were positioned out on the right wing to fire into Douglas's men. The attack by Keith's horse on the unprotected Welsh archers was one of the crisis points of the battle. The other was the sudden appearance on Gillies Hill of a large body of flag-waving reinforcements. Edward decided the day was lost, and with 500 knights he left the field. Mowbray refused him entry to the castle and he escaped to Dunbar where he left by rowing boat for Berwick-on-Tweed. One of the English knights, Sir Giles D'Argentan, refused to surrender and attacked the main Scottish schiltron or hedgehog of spearmen with the words 'I am not accustomed to fly, nor shall I do so now'. These were his last words.

The English had one success. They captured Cambuskenneth Abbey with its supplies and killed the commander, Sir John Aith, and his men. Bruce claimed that the high point of his victory was the charge of his right wing of Macdonalds under Angus Og. Henceforth Macdonalds would always claim the right wing in Scottish royal armies, a problem Lord George Murray and others had to solve.

THE BATTLEFIELD TODAY (S)

Heritage Centre   The National Trust for Scotland runs the excellent Heritage Centre which has a bookshop, toilets and (next door) a restaurant as well as an adequate car park. There is a diorama of the battle with simple coloured illustrations by the same artist (Jim Proudfoot) as those in the 1984 guidebook. Outside there is the rotunda and city cairn and flagpole with, a cricket pitch away, the fine statue (1964) of Robert the Bruce by an Englishman, Mr C. J. Pilkington-Jackson. Those who prefer smaller statues can see a model of this one in the Clan Robertson Museum (see Killiekrankie page 169). There is a fine expanse of green grass for stretching the legs, but the real walking in the area is up the Wallace Monument (page 59).

TO SEE NEARBY

Stirling Castle   Also a good walk to get to and interesting as the home of the Argyle and Sutherland Highlanders' Museum as well as the famous carved Stirling Heads in the royal apartments.

The Clydesdale Bank of Scotland £1 note showing the Bruce and on reverse the Scots attack. Note the variety of helmets and the lack of a shaffron on the horse (Clydesdale Bank)

HALIDON HILL
19 July 1333

TO SEE NEARBY

Berwick town walls and castle ruins.

Museum and Art Gallery in The Barracks

Museum of the Kings Own Scottish Borderers
also in the Vanbrugh Barracks (c1717)

Flodden

King Edward III placed Edward Balliol on the Scottish throne as his puppet king but, in spite of his being crowned at Scone, Moray and Douglas decided they didn't want him so they replaced him with Robert the Steward and turned to France for help. The town of Berwick agreed to surrender to the English army by 11 July, unless relieved. Alexander Seaton, Governor of Berwick, was then replaced by Sir William Keith, an ally of King Edward, and the Scottish army when they reached Berwick found the English in three divisions placed on Halidon Hill. The area is very boggy, as anyone who has visited it will discover, and the English army used this fact to their advantage. The archers in the centre with Bohun on the right wing and Balliol on the left waited for the Scots to advance before cutting them down with a devastating fire. A hand-picked troop of horse under Lord Ross in the Scottish second row attacked Balliol and Ross was killed. Douglas was captured and the Scots retreated. The pursuit lasted all the way to Ayton some 5 miles (8km) to the north and the English lost only their Newcastle division, which had come late, and one knight.

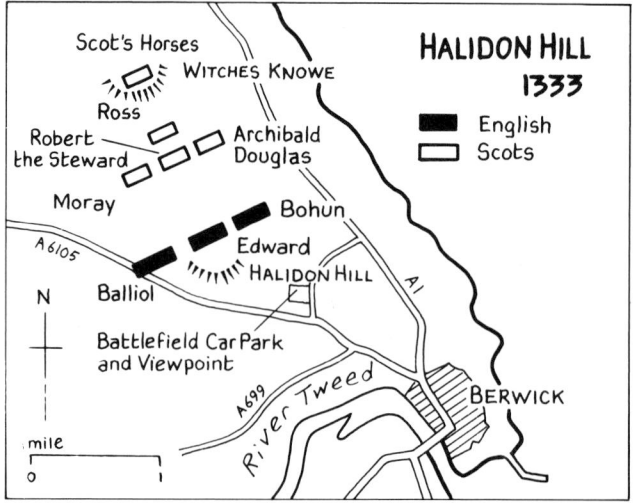

THE BATTLEFIELD TODAY (S)

This, with its car park, is easily found. Take the A6105 from Berwick towards Duns, turn immediately right and the car park is on the left. There is a viewpoint and a County Council battle map. For those wanting a walk, a very muddy track runs up towards the farm on top of Halidon Hill (537ft, 164m). Beware of the mud as only those well equipped with high boots can get through.

Sometimes the view from Halidon Hill can be breathtaking and a good pair of field glasses is of more use than a camera. The diagram in the car park indicates the main summits of the Cheviots, and on the other side the sea when we saw it late on a September evening was green rather than blue.

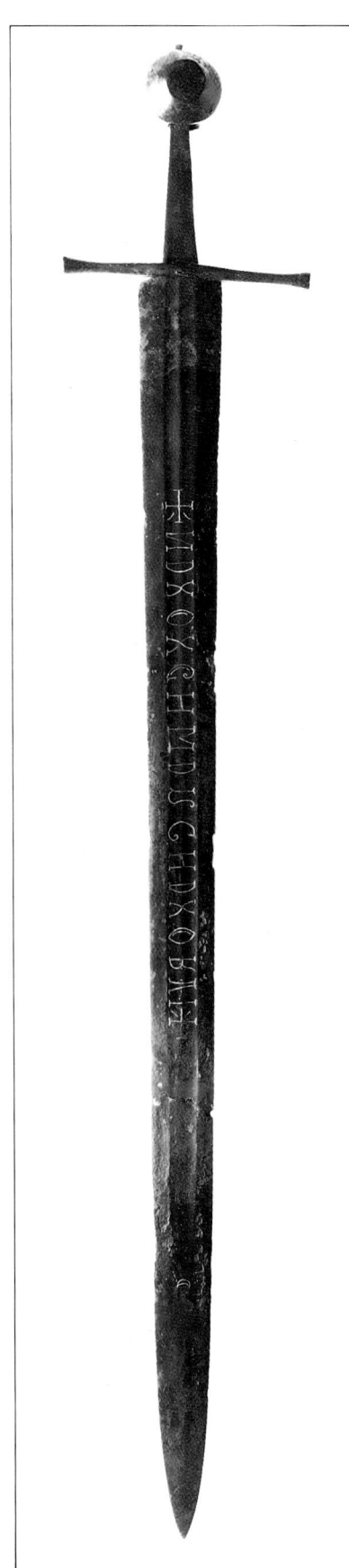

NEVILLE'S CROSS
17 October 1346

My first sight of the battlefield at Neville's Cross was from the steam train to Scotland, which slowed down just before Durham station. At the time I was a schoolboy going to visit relations, and the magnificent view of the castle and cathedral of this northern capital perched on the hill above the winding river was not to be forgotten. This was the view that the Scottish army had when they lay outside Durham.

Strangely the fighting bishops of Durham are not a thing of the past. When visiting the cathedral to see the Neville tombs, I tried to cross the road outside the building and was nearly mown down by a fast car. It stopped to see what I was doing and out jumped a young cleric, strangely angry at finding I was a mere tourist. He would have made a suitable warrior six hundred years ago.

The event leading up to Neville's Cross was the victory at Crécy earlier in 1346. This was a triumph for Edward III's army in France and the French king called on his Scottish allies to invade England and give France a breathing space. King Edward had planned for the Bishop of Durham, the Archbishop of York, Lord Percy and other barons to defend the Scottish border in the event of an attack. King David II of Scotland, with Robert the Steward and Douglas, entered the Esk valley but was delayed at Liddel Castle; however in October 1346 he camped at Bear Park outside Durham with 20,000 men. Lord Neville, commanding the English army, caught the Scots off guard at Sunderland bridge and drove them back. He deployed his army with Rokeby on the left and Percy on the right roughly along the line of the present-day railway line. In front were the archers, behind them the billmen, then the horse.

The Scots had the height advantage but, like so many battles from Homildon Hill to Edgehill, they had to descend the hill to get to grips with their enemy. Many were cut down in a narrow ravine before they descended the hill. In the centre Neville was pushed back and Percy on the right, by weight of numbers. Lord Lucy commanding the rearguard came up and, like Norfolk's men at Towton, tipped the balance. The Scots gave way and David II was captured crossing the Browney river. Rokeby and Percy advanced and the battle was over. King Edward, now the victor of Poitiers, was in a good position to make terms with France and Scotland. He could have taught Charles I a few lessons about what to do with his prisoners captured at Lostwithiel (page 135).

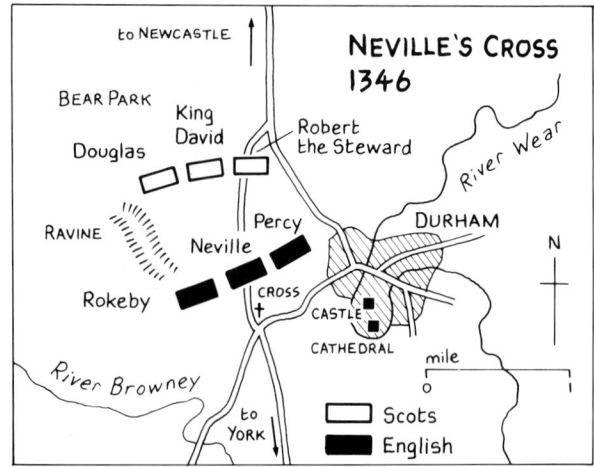

to NEWCASTLE

NEVILLE'S CROSS
1346

BEAR PARK

King David

Robert the Steward

River Wear

Douglas

RAVINE

Percy

DURHAM

Neville

N

Rokeby

CROSS

CASTLE

CATHEDRAL

mile

River Browney

to YORK

☐ Scots
■ English

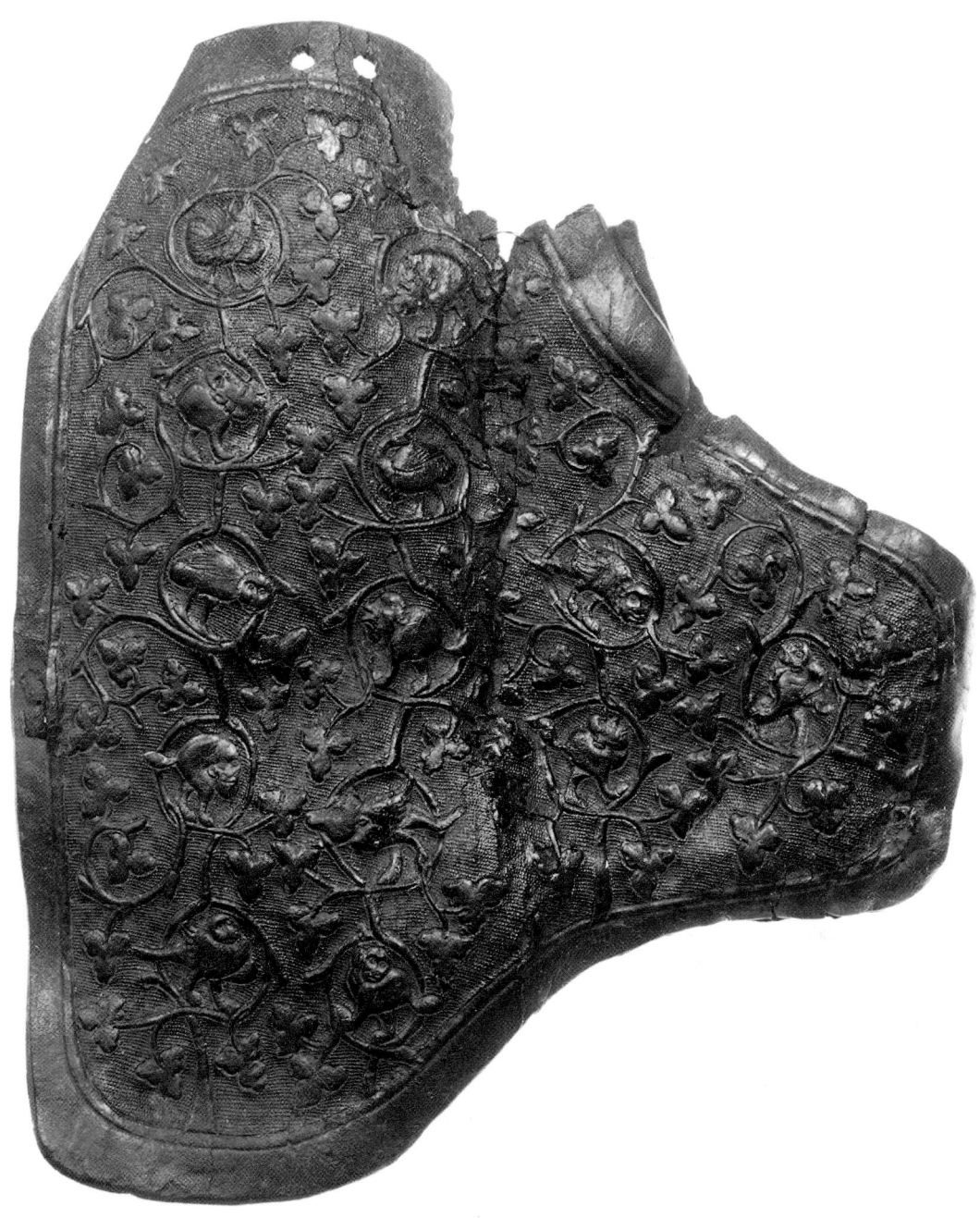

THE BATTLEFIELD TODAY (S)

The best view of Durham is from the railway line and Bear Park is still not completely covered in houses. The original cross is found on the main road at Neville's Cross (junction of A690 and A167) just outside Durham. It is on the right-hand side of the road coming from the south opposite a garage and stands high up above the pavement. Only the stump remains and there is no plaque to indicate its importance. Durham Cathedral and Castle should not be missed and on their horseshoe bend of the River Wear provide a pleasant walk; the city itself is well worth a visit though it can be a nightmare for motorists.

Fourteenth century leather arm defence. Note holes for lacing strap and also the design of grotesque creatures typical of the period (Age of Chivalry Exhibition)

(left) *Knight's sword c.1250. The inscription is in Latin and may refer to a prayer* (Age of Chivalry Exhibition)

OTTERBURN
19 August 1388

Otterburn was almost a private battle, Percy-v-Douglas. It is easy to imagine the two men having a private but chivalrous quarrel, which no one else would understand; rather like the American general who landed at Yeovil in 1946. It was a misty sunny day and his driver, an English sergeant, took him down the road to Montacute. The house, not then open to the public, was owned by a man keen on presenting dramatic reconstructions of Shakespeare in the open air. He was using his house as a backdrop and in the field at the rear were two knights on horseback, archers in chain mail and billmen lined up for a mock battle. The general, who was being taken to a Marshall Plan finance meeting, was astonished.

'Gee Sergeant, I knew your army was old-fashioned, but this really takes the biscuit.'

'Don't worry General, that's only the Home Guard practising.'

Steeped in legend, the battle of Otterburn which celebrates its 600th anniversary this year is one of the classics in medieval chivalry. Lord Douglas

attacked Durham on a raid, capturing Henry Percy's – Constable of Berwick Castle – pennon outside Newcastle. The Scots, laden down with booty, made their way home and halted at Otterburn, camping at Greenchesters, a wood north of the village where they defended their position with a barrier of trees. Henry Percy, known as Hotspur, was not slow in following the Scots; he reached Otterburn on 19 August, in the evening, and took up a position in the castle tower, now part of the Castle Hotel. He sent Sir Thomas Umfraville and a party of mounted knights in a wide sweep round the right flank to attack the Scots' camp. This they did most effectively, but Douglas had already left, so they decided to return in the dark by the route they had come.

Perhaps both armies were about 7,000 strong, but Hotspur had left men in the tower and also lacked Umfraville's knights. Dividing his force into two, Douglas moved up to the village and somewhere near where the cross stands engaged Hotspur. The archers on the English side were useless as it was too dark to fire arrows when you could hardly tell friend from foe. Early on, Douglas was killed but his men carried on the fight and both Hotspur and Ralph Percy, his brother, were captured. The Earl of Moray took command of the victorious Scots and only the onset of the Bishop of Durham with a new army prevented any further action. The 'Ballad of Chevy Chase' describes in many verses the terrible slaughter and three of them are quoted here.

This battle began in Cheviot
An hour before the noon,
And when even-song bell was rung
The battle was not half-done.

They took 'on' on either hand
By the light of the moon;
Many had no strength for to stand
In Cheviot the hills above.

Of fifteen hundred archers of
England
Went away but fifty-three;
Of twenty hundred spear-men of
Scotland
But even five and fifty.

THE WALKS (L and S)

Starting appropriately from the Percy Arms, there is a pleasant one-hour walk (L) on mostly flat land. Take the A696 in the direction of Jedburgh past the little church. There is a good path to the right of this road and after a short ½ mile (.8km) you come to a copse and the Percy Cross, erected in 1777, and a plaque stating that the larch trees surrounding the cross were planted by the National Trust to commemorate the Queen's Jubilee in 1977. A footpath opposite the cross, a short distance up the road by a school building, leads to a river footbridge and Garret Shiels farm, where you can pick up the line of the Roman road, Dere Street, make for Dunns Houses and then back to Otterburn via the main road, the mill and the B6320 to the Percy Arms.

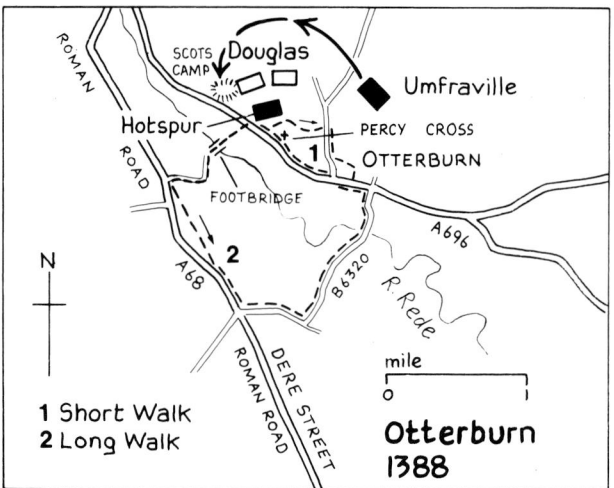

An alternative, and less uncomfortable walk (S) is to take the line of the old hedge up the field to the back of the Cross, then there is half a stile over the wall to another field, where follow the wall round to the right until it joins up with the army camp road. Here take the way back to the village but turn left to the back of the little church and churchyard where a sloping path leads down to the main road close to the Post Office. I asked the farmer about walking across his field, as there is no footpath marked on the map, and provided permission is obtained first (Townhead Farm) and there are no animals that might be disturbed or you don't have dogs, it doesn't seem to be a problem. The risk about wandering around this part of Northumberland is that the army uses live ammunition on the ranges and while walking near Rothbury one year my 5-year-old picked up a handful of live .303 rounds which seemed to have been dropped in a neat pile by the path. The army have a red flag flying when firing takes place and there is no possible chance of not seeing it or of not hearing the bangs.

Otterburn is a pleasant spot and an ideal walk for a fine day, but it could do, especially in anniversary year, with a proper Tewkesbury-style waymarked walk where there is no barbed wire and no red flags.

PILLETH
22 June 1402

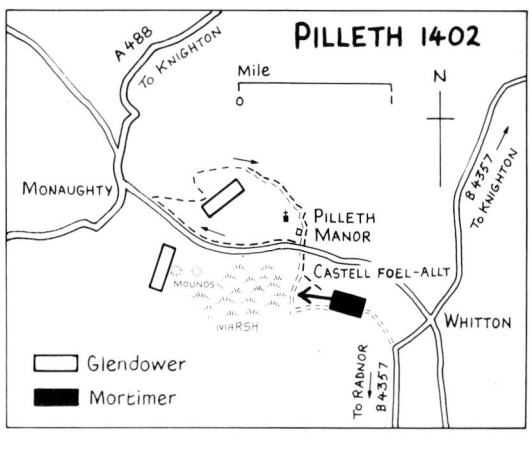

Owen Glendower was one of Richard II's allies and when Henry Bolingbroke seized the throne and Richard was shut up in Pontefract Castle where he died, there were some, including Owen, who claimed he was still alive and living in exile in Scotland. The revolt that broke out in Wales was not easy to stop and Henry gave the job to Edmund Mortimer, whose castle at Wigmore figures in the Battle of Mortimer's Cross. Edmund, who was related to Richard, was no lover of Owen, whose men had recently captured New Radnor Castle and beheaded the garrison.

Mortimer's army, mostly garrison men, made for Pilleth where the castle of Castell Foel-Allt, now a motte and bailey in the middle of a field, was a possible halting place. But it was a dangerous valley for just in front of the castle is a marsh. Mortimer's men walked straight into an ambush. They had no doubt been spotted by Glendower and his lieutenant, Rhys Gethin, as soon as they entered the valley. Glendower and his troops waited until Mortimer reached the foot of Bryn Glas hill, where the church stands today, before they surrounded his army and cut it to pieces. It was a case of well armed, nimble men against heavily armed less mobile troops. Also some of Mortimer's men were more Welsh than English, so may well have deserted.

Mortimer himself was spared and became one of Owen's men, even marrying his daughter. A few years later he was killed at the siege of Harlech Castle. Glendower sacked Cardiff after Pilleth but his dream of a free Wales with its own capital at Machynlleth never materialised and, although he was undefeated, he retired to Monnington Stradel near Bacton and was protected by Sir John Scudamore. His colleague, Rhys Gethin, was defeated by Prince Hal at Grosmont Castle in 1410, when the revolt finally ended.

THE WALK (L)
The road from Whitton comes to Pilleth Manor and in the field opposite is Castell Foel-Allt, with trees growing in the centre of the motte, one of which has a platform for observing horses as the field is used for eventing. The walk continues up the road and then turns right down a track to Pilleth Church, which stands on the bank of Bryn Glas. In 1870 some ploughmen dug up bones on the slope here and the owner, Mr Price, planted trees on the spot, so that they form a small plantation today. The footpath carries on through the Manor (a bed and breakfast house) back to the road.

Battlefield of Pilleth. On the left is the clump of trees where bones were found

Homildon Hill. The author on the summit in 1987

HOMILDON HILL
14 September 1402

TO SEE NEARBY

Battlefields Flodden, with Etal, Ford and Norham castles; Hedgeley Moor, south of Wooler; Otterburn; Halidon Hill.

There are many walks in the Cheviots from Wooler and the Ramblers' Association publish a useful little book with hand-drawn maps of the paths.

Misericord of falling knight from Lincoln Cathedral (Age of Chivalry Exhibition)

After Halidon Hill (Berwick-on-Tweed) there was peace on the Scottish borders, but in 1402 Sir Patrick Hepburn with a party of Scottish horses raided Northumberland and on their return were caught by Lord Percy and the Earl of March with the Berwick garrison and defeated at Nisbet Moor. Hepburn, who was a very popular leader, was killed.

The Scots were determined on revenge and chose their moment well. When Henry IV took an army to Wales to deal with Owen Glendower's revolt, Douglas with Murdoch Stewart, son of the Duke of Albany, took an army of 10,000 into England to revenge the defeat of Nisbet Moor. Percy was half expecting such a move and quietly collected an army at Dunstanburgh Castle. They moved to Wooler to block the Scots' return journey to Coldstream. Douglas seized the high ground north of Wooler and positioned his army on the top of Homildon Hill, but Percy's archers saw the sun glinting on the Scots' armour and, though on a hunting trip, they reported to Percy. He sent them up Harehope Hill, where they fired into the Scots army, sure of no return fire

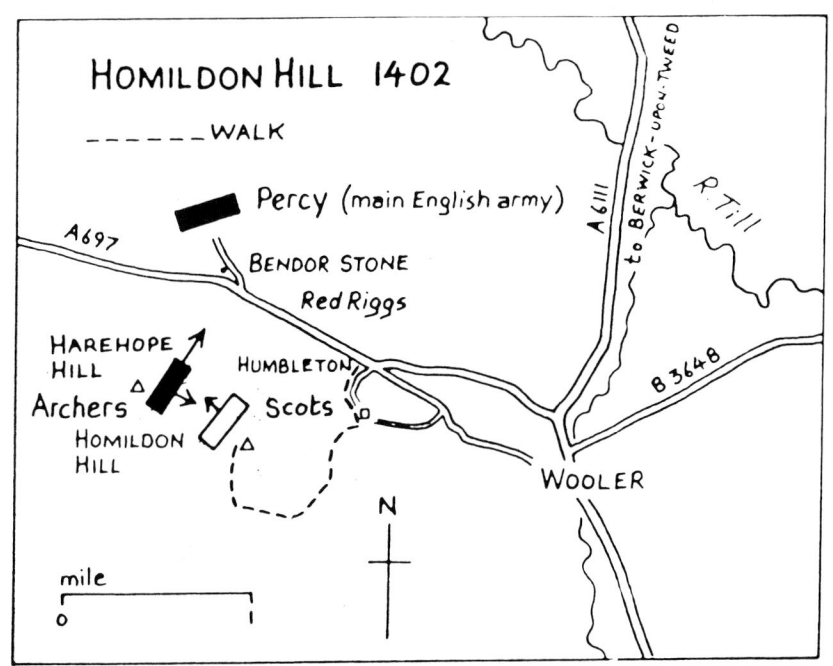

HOMILDON HILL 1402

------ WALK

Percy (main English army)

A697

BENDOR STONE

Red Riggs

A6111

to BERWICK-UPON-TWEED

R. Till

HAREHOPE HILL

HUMBLETON

B3648

Archers

Scots

HOMILDON HILL

WOOLER

N

mile

0   1

BOWS

The English bowmen first came into their own in the wars of King Edward I. Early bows made of elm, but later yew from Spain or Italy was preferred. The famous fifteenth century arrows were flecked with grey goose wing feathers, and a fletcher was a highly paid craftsman. The arrow was the length of a man's arm and as this was the same measurement as a bolt of cloth in width, it became known as the *Clothyard*.

Archers could discharge twelve arrows a minute and the arrow was accurate up to 220 yards. Scots bowmen used much shorter bows and on the Continent the cross-bow was more common, perhaps because it was easier to carry and was often used in a siege by the defenders. When captured, bowmen often had their two fingers of their draw hand removed.

as they were out of bowshot of the Scots, whose archers used smaller bows. Hotspur and March put their horsemen in a field known as Red Riggs, now marked by the Bendor Stone, which unfortunately is not visible from the top of Homildon, as it is too close to the foot of the hill. Sir John Swinton and Adam Gordon, two of the Scots' knights, took their horse down the hill and charged the English ranks. They were a mere hundred, and March and Hotspur cut them to pieces. Douglas did not follow up until it was too late. The English archers repositioned themselves and Douglas was wounded in the eye and captured, along with Stewart and the Earl of Angus. The Scots were chased to the Tweed and many were shot crossing the river.

THE WALK

This is easily found by taking the A697 from Wooler, the Bendor Stone is on the right after about ½ mile (.8km). Opposite this is Homildon Hill.

Take the steep hill up to Humbleton village and turn right at the telephone box. Go past the farm with ducks and the road comes to an end. The footpath to the top of Homildon (called Humbleton on some maps) starts from the new gate about 50yd (45m) further on. It is a steep climb and on a fine day the view is excellent over Wooler and towards Chillingham. Harehope Hill can be seen nearly with a gully between.

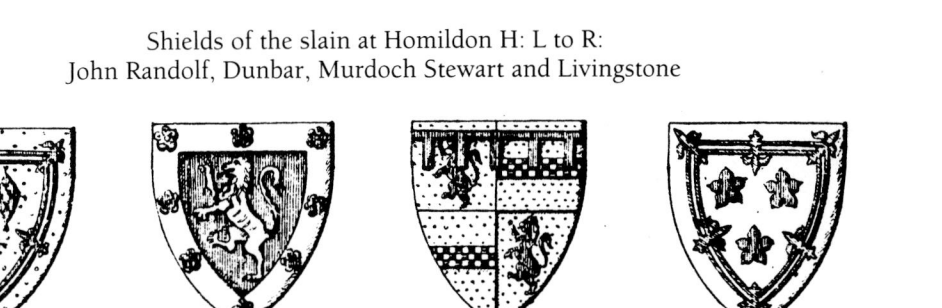

Shields of the slain at Homildon H: L to R:
John Randolf, Dunbar, Murdoch Stewart and Livingstone

Shield of Sir Walter Blount

Shields on the hammerbeams on either side of the church.

From the East End
Henry IV
Earl of Dunbar
Sir Hugh Stanley
Sir John Cockayne
Sir Nicholas Gausel
Sir Hugh Mortimer
Sir Hugh Shirley
Sir Robert Malveysin
Sir Madoc Kynaston
Sir Richard Sandford
Sir Francis Bromley
Sir Edward de Rowson
Henry, Prince of Wales
Earl of Stafford
Sir John Clifton
Sir Walter Blount
Sir Robert Gausel
Sir John Massey
Sir Thomas Wendesley
Sir Reginald Mottershead
Sir Jenkin Hamer
Sir Richard Hussey
Sir Russell John
Sir Mac of Salop

The hatchments commemorate members of the Corbet family.

Shield of Sir Richard Hussey

Shrewsbury
21 July 1403

The deposition of King Richard II by Henry Bolingbroke left many arrogant rebel barons who had been prepared to support the weak Richard but were not happy with the more powerful Bolingbroke. Northumberland and his son Hotspur, who had defeated the Scots at Homildon Hill, were not prepared to hand over their prisoners to Henry without some financial recompense. In fact Hotspur and Douglas became firm friends and planned to join Owen Glendower and defeat Henry. Young Prince Hal, later Henry V, was in Shrewsbury with a small army watching Owen Glendower. Here Percy and Douglas came in July 1403, occupying the shallow ridge between Albright Hussey and the main road north from Shrewsbury. The Abbot of Haughmond Abbey attempted to interpose between the two armies in vain. Prince Hal, reinforced by the king, had an army of about 12,000 and he moved out from Shrewsbury walls to occupy the area now called Battlefield, facing Hotspur. Because a king was so conspicuous a person on the battlefield, several volunteers dressed up as kings and Henry himself wore plain armour like any other knight.

Hotspur's Cheshire bowmen stopped the royal advance and Prince Hal was wounded in the face. Henry was forced back by Hotspur, and Prince Hal saved the day by leading his men round by Albright Hussey lane and catching Hotspur in the rear. The latter was killed by an arrow and Douglas, who killed at least two 'Henrys' as well as the standard bearer, Sir Walter Blount, was also killed. The king won the day but it was a very costly victory and he founded a church on the site together with a monastery, now no longer visible. The church is still used from time to time and has a display of coats of arms of those who fought in the battle (see below). The gargoyles are meant to represent the rebels.

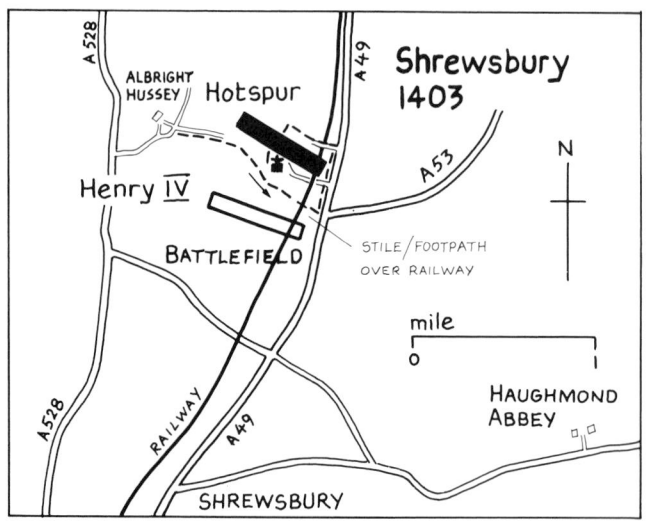

THE BATTLEFIELD TODAY
Nothing but a Victorianised church and farmland covers the battlefield. It is an evocative place though and all the familiar names of English history were present. Here was Sir Hugh Stanley, ancestor of the Earls of Derby; Sir John Clifton, whose ancestors were killed off in the Wars of the Roses; Sir Robert

Malveysin, whose name comes from *malvoisin*, an artificial mound thrown up outside a castle for siege-engines; Stafford, Blount, Hamer and Hussey. All their shields can be seen in the church and it is easy to imagine them fighting with their retainers against Hotspur and his recently acquired friend, Douglas.

THE WALK (L)

This is a pleasant 2 mile (3km) round walk, but it needs a fine day. Take the footpath from Albright Hussey (a restaurant now, but still a fine early Tudor house). Turn right into the ploughed field just before the wood and enter the wood where the path leads through into a field to the right of the church. Cross this field and over the railway line by the two high cross-stiles. Turn left and then onto the main road to Battlefield Farm. The lane crosses over the railway (a good place for a photograph) and then through the farmyard down to the cottage by the church. (The lady here lent me the two keys needed to see the church.) Follow the path past the church to link up with the route back to Albright Hussey.

Battlefield Church, Shrewsbury
(Redundant Churches Commission)

ST ALBANS I
22 May, 1455

The Duke of Somerset was one of the legendary family of Beaufort and the family were legitimised by Richard II by letters patent of 1407. Henry IV added a proviso that they were debarred from succeeding to the throne. They were loyal Lancastrians.

John, Captain of Calais and Deputy Constable of England died in 1410. Henry, who was Bishop of Lincoln at 21, became a cardinal. Thomas the third Beaufort was an admiral and general and became Duke of Exeter. John's two sons were John junior, who was the father of Margaret Beaufort (mother of King Henry VII). Edmund, Duke of Somerset, was killed at St Albans, leaving two sons, Henry and Edmund to carry on the line.

The Beauforts were descendants of John of Gaunt and his third wife, Catherine Swynford. The fact that they had a rightful claim to the throne, inspite of Henry IV's proviso, may have helped Henry Richmond when he finally became King at Bosworth.

When King Henry VI became insane in 1453, the Duke of York was declared Chief Councillor. His rival, the Duke of Somerset, promptly tried to exclude him from the government. However York had many supporters – the Earls of Warwick, Salisbury, Worcester, Pembroke and Norfolk with their retinues. When in 1455 King Henry regained his senses, Somerset was freed from the Tower where York had placed him and the latter with his Neville supporters, Warwick and Salisbury, hastened to the north to raise an army. Henry with support from Buckingham, Clifford, Northumberland and Somerset left London and, at St Albans, Buckingham decided they should barricade the town to prevent York from passing through on Watling Street to London. Using the old town ditch and bank, the Lancastrians defended it but without much enthusiasm. York's emissary wanted Somerset to be tried for treason, but Henry could not accept this and York advanced along Victoria Street and Sopwell Lane. At the same time Warwick, with his own men, forced the ditch near where the modern London Road now stands, and broke out into St Peter's Street. Taking the defences in the rear, Warwick cut down Clifford, Somerset and Northumberland as well as the son of the Duke of Buckingham. King Henry was captured, but treated with great respect and taken back to London, where there was a temporary peace for four years. At the second battle of St Albans (1461) the Lancastrians were victorious.

THE WALK (M)

The town of St Albans is easily reached by public transport from London. The main street, St Peter's Street, and Holywell Hill are still the same as in 1455, but Victoria Street was then Shropshire Lane and London Road didn't exist.

Starting at the Tourist Information Bureau my walk was in pouring rain. I found opposite the Bureau the Leeds Building Society has a plaque stating where Somerset was killed, for this corner was the old Castle Inn. Carry on up

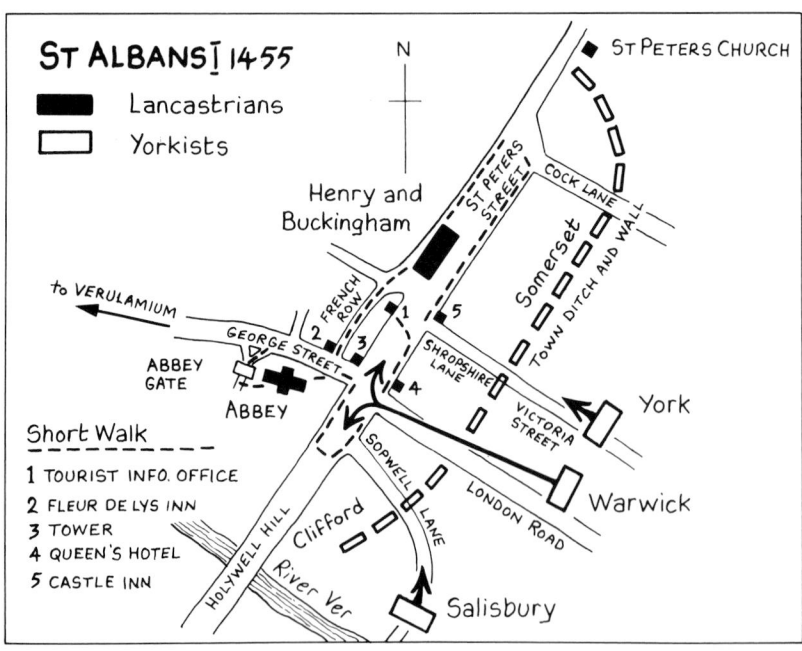

ST ALBANS I 1455

■ Lancastrians
□ Yorkists

Short Walk - - -

1 TOURIST INFO. OFFICE
2 FLEUR DE LYS INN
3 TOWER
4 QUEEN'S HOTEL
5 CASTLE INN

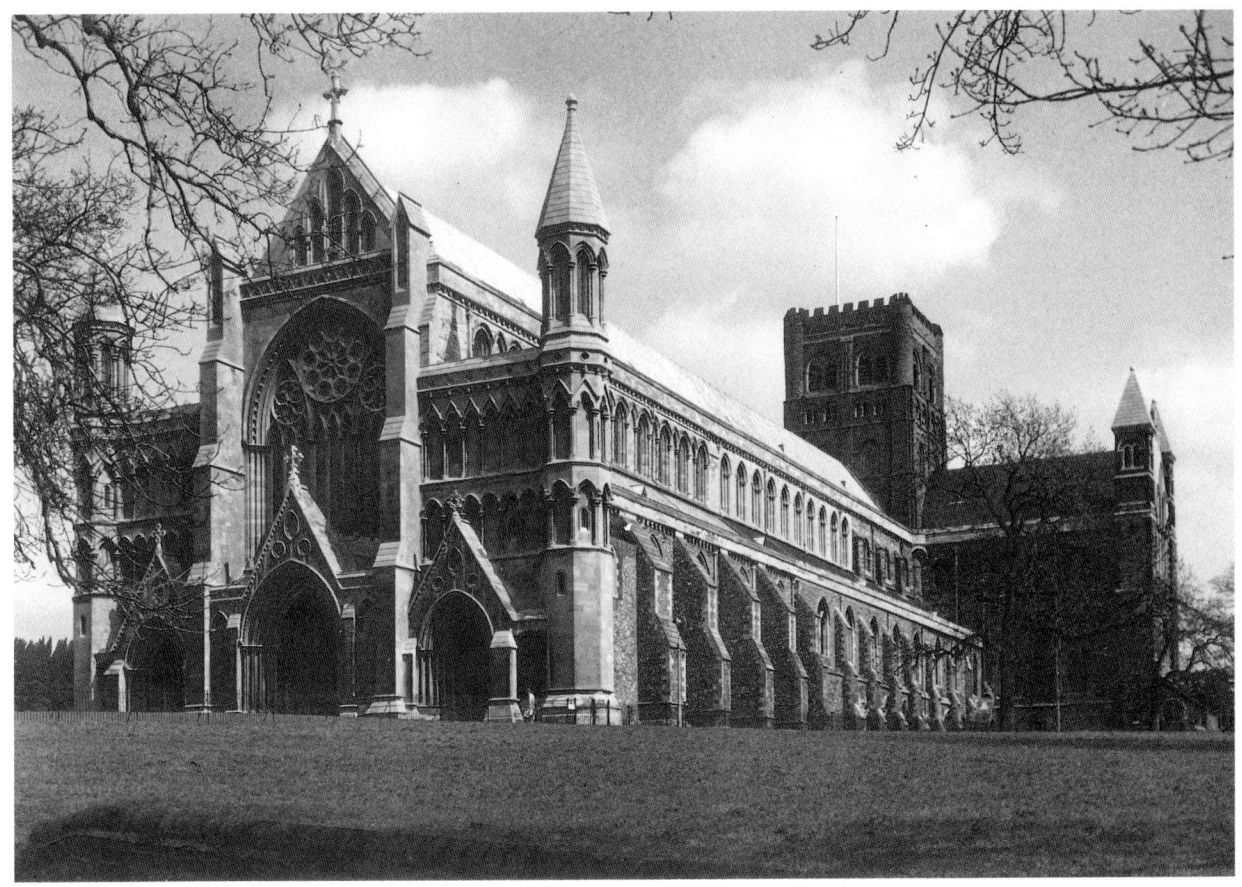

St Peter's Street to Cock Lane, where some of the Yorkists attacked, and over to the other side of the road where Henry and Buckingham stood, some accounts say unarmed. Then carry on down the narrow lane, French Row, to the Fleur de Lys inn where King John was briefly imprisoned after capture at Poitiers in 1356. Opposite is the old Clock Tower, a rare surviving curfew tower that can be climbed in summer for photography. Turn right into George Street with its attractive timber buildings and take the lane through the abbey gate and into the abbey, or cathedral as it now is. The inside is remarkably dark, but look for the tomb of Humphrey, Duke of Gloucester, brother of Henry V and a great warrior in the battles with Joan of Arc. Queen Margaret and her son sought sanctuary here during the battle in the streets of St Albans and she seems to have escaped unharmed.

The intrepid tourist can carry on to Roman Verulamium by going down Romeland, Fishpond Street and left into Michael Street; but we returned through an arcade to George Street and then down Holywell Hill to Sopwell Lane, near where Clifford was killed and Shakespeare gave Young Clifford his long revengeful speech. The Queen's Hotel, then called the Chequers, is supposed to be where Warwick attacked – and here we ended our wet walk.

For those with more time and fine weather, there is a St Albans Town Trail. Leaflets about it can be obtained from the Information Centre, 37 Chequer Street. Allow about ½ hour for my walk, but at least 1½ hours for the Town Trail.

St Albans Abbey (Woodmansterne)

TO SEE NEARBY

Battlefield   Barnet (1471).

BLORE HEATH
23 September, 1459

(left) *Fifteenth century armour* (Marcher Lords)

The passage of time from the first Battle of St Albans (1455) to 1459 was a period of uneasy truce between the Red and White Roses. In September 1459 Queen Margaret was at Eccleshall Castle openly distributing badges depicting the swan, emblem of her son the Prince of Wales, to her supporters. Lord Audley, with a party of Lancastrian troops, was at Market Drayton and Lord Salisbury, with an army of about 3,000 Yorkists, was en route from Middleham Castle, Yorkshire, to Ludlow. The queen ordered Lord Audley to intercept Salisbury (the father of the Earl of Warwick) at Market Drayton, but the Yorkist spies discovered this so Salisbury halted his army on Blore Heath, now farmland, outside the town.

The battle on 23 September was on the steep banks of the Hemp Mill Brook. Salisbury withdrew his centre and Audley thought he was in retreat but the Yorkist archers, unexpectedly reinforced by some deserting Lancastrian archers, took their toll. Audley's knights, on foot, were cut down as was Lord Audley himself and the surviving Lancastrians retreated to Eccleshall, some 9 miles (14km) away. Queen Margaret, who is supposed to have witnessed the battle, retreated to Mucklestone where the blacksmith, William Skelhorn, reversed her horse's shoes so that she could not easily be followed.

Although it was a Yorkist victory, Salisbury's army disintegrated at Ludford near Ludlow. The Earl of Warwick had brought over the Calais garrison under Lord Talbot; during the night Talbot took his very experienced troops over to the Lancastrian camp and both Salisbury, Warwick and the other Yorkist leaders fled before a battle took place. As an example of a smaller force defeating a larger one, the Blore Heath battle is worth studying, and the ground is not spoilt so far by buildings so that the Yorkist positions can be easily imagined.

THE BATTLEFIELD TODAY (S)

To see the Audley Cross (see map), enter the field opposite Audley Farm which is a mile or so out of Market Drayton on the Newcastle-under-Lyme road. Where the field dips to the stream the cross, or what is left of it, can be seen enclosed in a battered railing. The village of Mucklestone is a few miles further on to the right and the anvil stands inside the churchyard opposite the cottage that was built on the site of the forge. For walkers there is a path from Blore village to the main A53 that crosses the Hemp Mill Brook.

> **TO SEE NEARBY**
>
> *Eccleshall Castle Shrewsbury* (see page 74).

> As an example of a smaller force defeating a larger one the *Blore Heath* battle is worth studying. The ground has been left unspoilt and the Yorkist positions can be easily imagined. The Lancastrians under Lord Audley were in no position to deploy and when their leader was killed they fled. The wily Salisbury kept his weaker force hidden until the crucial moment. A similar event occurred with Montrose at *Auldearn* (see page 143).

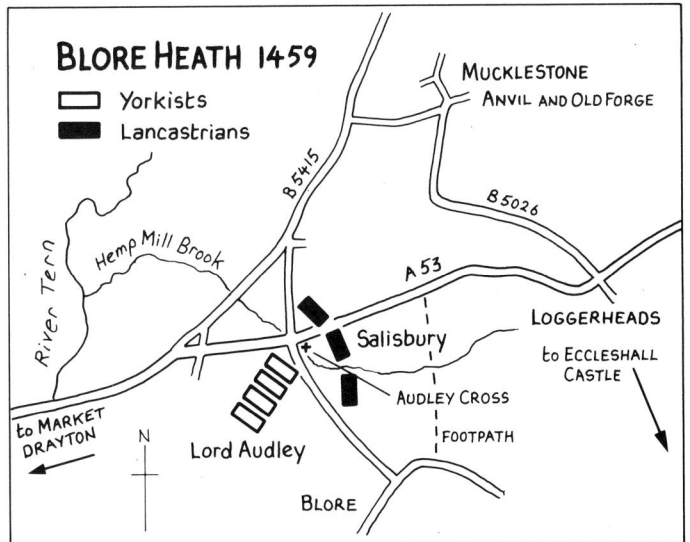

NORTHAMPTON
10 July 1460

The Battle of Northampton was rather like St Albans II in reverse, for instead of the Yorkists on the defensive, this time it was the Lancastrians who took up a defensive position on the River Nene, having marched south from Coventry. The Duke of Buckingham appears to have suggested to the king that they should take the position to guard the road to London, now in Yorkist hands, and so that their guns could prevent the enemy from capturing the town from that side. Although his front was well protected by sharp stakes and a bank, his rear was the unfordable Nene.

Edward, Earl of March (later Edward IV), left London with Warwick and Lord Fauconberg commanding the centre and rear of his three divisions. Having camped on Hunsbury Hill outside Northampton, he attacked at first light on 10 July. Warwick had made a pact with Lord Grey of Ruthin, on Buckingham's right wing. He ordered his men not to attack men wearing Lord Grey's badge of the black ragged staff. Instead Grey helped Warwick's men over the defences so that Buckingham was soon surrounded. His archers did what they could but Buckingham himself, Shrewsbury, Egremont, Beaumont and 700 others were killed before they could escape over the Nene. The queen escaped with a few others and made for Chester but luckless King Henry was led in triumph to London by Edward of March whose father came back from Ireland and was made Lord Protector.

THE BATTLEFIELD TODAY (S)

Delapré Abbey, where the bodies were buried after the battle, stands close to the battle site. It houses the County Record Office and is mostly a sixteenth- and nineteenth-century building today. The area is much overlaid with houses and roads, but the Eleanor Cross is still visible beside the A508, one of three to survive. Hunsbury Iron Age Camp is also still intact. Northampton's great Norman castle was destroyed long ago and the site is now a railway station. Lord Grey, who became Lord Treasurer of England, was buried in style in Westminster Abbey.

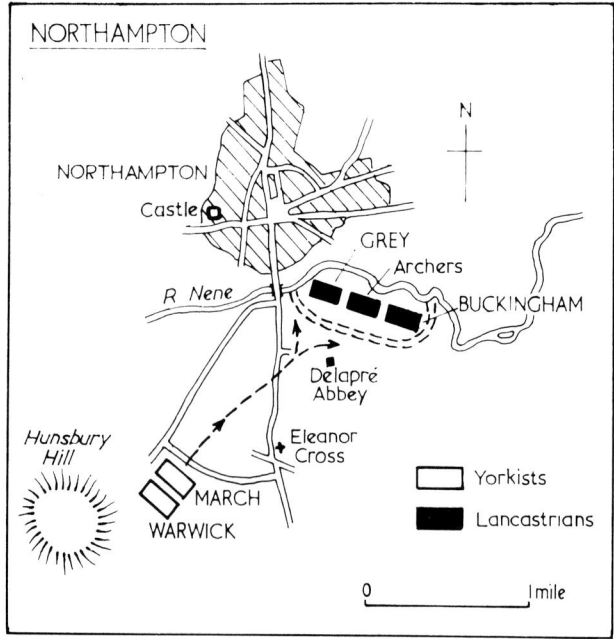

WAKEFIELD
31 December 1460

On 10 October 1460 the Duke of York declared in an Act of Settlement that he was heir to the throne and that his son Edmund, Earl of Rutland, was his heir. Henry's son, Edward, was excluded and the Lancastrians were very annoyed. Queen Margaret gathered her troops together in York and moved to Pontefract where she had an army of about 15,000 men under Lords Clifford, Wiltshire and Roos. The Earl of York with Lord Salisbury was outnumbered, but he occupied Sandal Castle outside Wakefield which was impregnable and commanded a fine view in all directions. After a Christmas truce, Lord Clifford's force appeared before the castle, and the very impetuous York, perhaps short of supplies, led out his troops to do battle. He had not seen Lord Roos's horse in a nearby wood and Wiltshire's men were also out of sight. Roos wheeled round to prevent York's return to the castle and Wiltshire actually entered it. The battle was soon over and it is alleged 2,800 Yorkists were killed including York himself and his son, who was cut down near Wakefield Bridge. The heads of the Yorkist leaders were hung on Micklegate Bar in York 'so York might overlook York' and Lord Clifford had his revenge for the killing of his father in St Albans I.

THE BATTLEFIELD TODAY (S)

Sandal Castle is easily found just off the A61 south of Wakefield. It was excavated in the 1960s and is excellently looked after though there is not much to be seen. There are some recently planted trees and, when I visited it in summer 1987, not a scrap of litter was visible. The little chapel on Wakefield Bridge is mostly Victorian, but N. Scatcherd in *The Chapel of King Edward III* (1862) says it was originally built in 1357 so that it is unlikely to have been constructed as a resting place for the murdered prince. There is a pleasant ten-minute walk round the castle and into the ruins, which are much the same as they appeared in the eighteenth century print by Nathaniel Buck.

Buck's print of Sandal Castle ruins

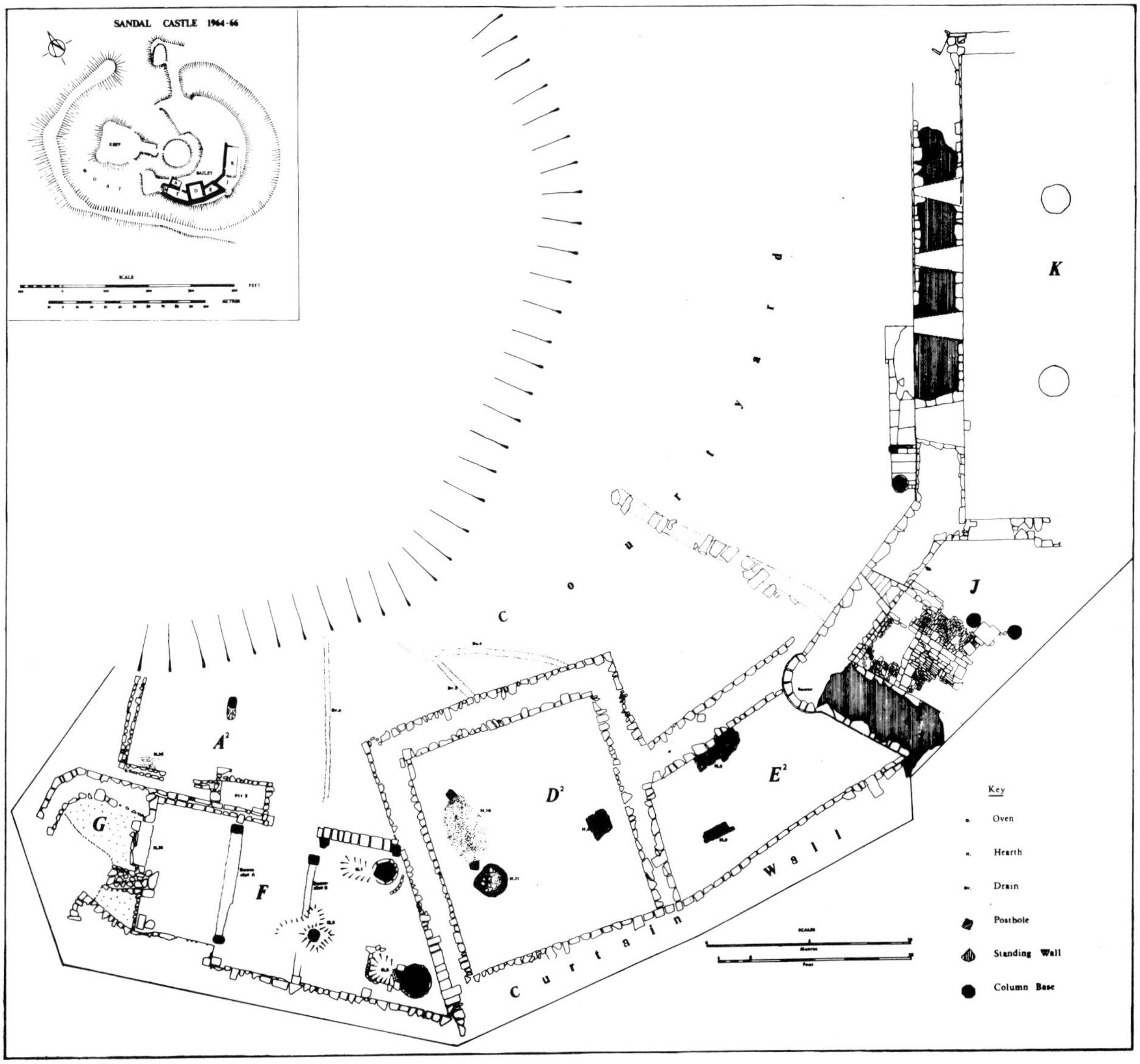

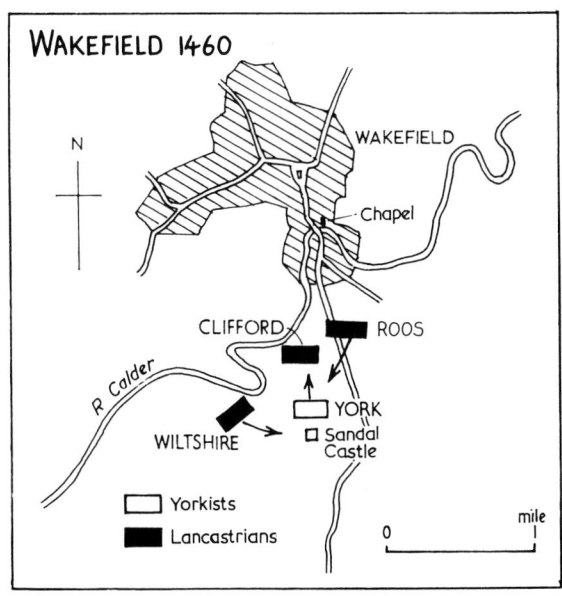

Plan of Sandal Castle during its restoration (Wakefield Historical Society)

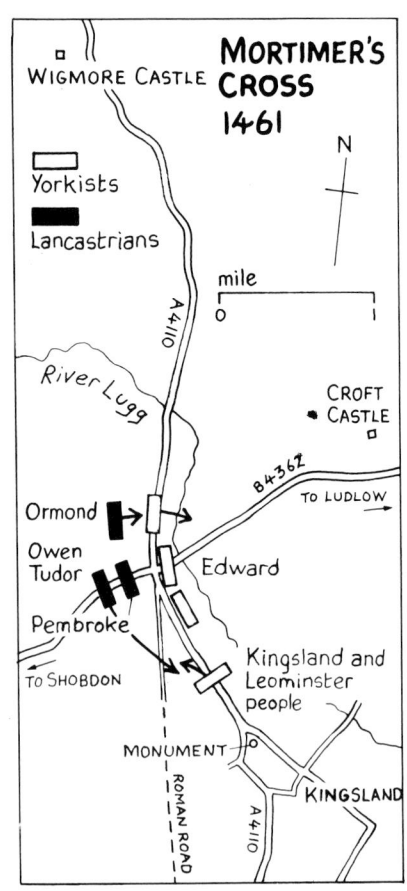

MORTIMER'S CROSS
2 February 1461

The death of the Duke of York and one of his sons at Wakefield did not mean the end of the Yorkist hopes. In fact young Edward, Earl of March, was gathering a fresh army in Gloucester when he heard that Jasper Tudor, a party of French and Irish troops under the Earls of Wiltshire and Ormond, and Owen Tudor were making for the Midlands. With his army he moved out of Wigmore Castle to defend the river crossing at Mortimer's Cross. He decided on the advice of Sir Richard Croft, who lived at Croft Castle nearby, to rely on his archers and position himself on the crossroads with the river behind him. It seems an odd decision as there is high ground soon after the River Lugg on the Ludlow road. However he successfully stopped Jasper Tudor's untried army from linking up with the successful Wakefield one.

The battle was in fact three small battles, as Ormond attacked Edward's right wing and pushed it over the river; Edward himself won the central battle against Jasper and Owen Tudor tried to move towards Kingsland but was stopped and surrounded by the men of Leominster and Kingsland who captured him somewhere near the present monument on the A4110 and B4360 junction. Ormond and Jasper Tudor escaped but Owen Tudor was executed in Hereford the following day.

THE BATTLEFIELD TODAY (S)
Mortimer's Cross is a small hamlet with an inn and a garage. There is a mill which is occasionally open to the public but no footpath. The Monument Inn with the 1799 pedestal in front of it is at a fork in the road 3 miles (5km) away towards Kingsland. There is supposed to be buried treasure in the area and recently some Australians dug up the old bar of the inn in search of it. They were unsuccessful but it was one way of working up a thirst!

The Mortimer's Cross monument

TO SEE NEARBY

Wigmore Castle and *Church* There is a pleasant walk up a lane to Wigmore Church and about 200yd (180m) beyond to the very ruined and overgrown castle, home of Anne Mortimer, Edward of March's grandmother.

Croft Castle This is a National Trust property on the road to Ludlow. It has some fine beech trees, and the tomb of Sir Richard Croft, who also fought at Towton and Stoke, is in the church.

ST ALBANS II
16 February 1461

The second battle of St Albans was a very different affair from the first. The Lancastrian victory at Wakefield meant that the Yorkists had quickly to regroup to stop Queen Margaret entering London. Warwick took command and positioned his army at St Albans with his archers in the town and his knights blocking the roads to the north at Harpenden and Sandridge. The king was placed inside the abbey and Warwick relied on his Burgundian troops with their flaming arrows, handguns firing darts, pavises and calthrops. But he did not move his army quickly enough when Margaret attacked on 16 February from the Dunstable direction. The queen took him by surprise by entering from George Street, thus his defences were useless and his guns more dangerous to the firers than the enemy. However he withdrew his men to a defensive position at Barnard's Heath, but his men from Kent under Lovelace deserted to Queen Margaret and the Lancastrians were triumphant. Warwick was forced back from his second position at Barnard's Heath to a third and final position at Nomansland Common. During the night he withdrew his army to Chipping Norton where he linked up with Edward's successful troops returning from their victory at Mortimer's Cross.

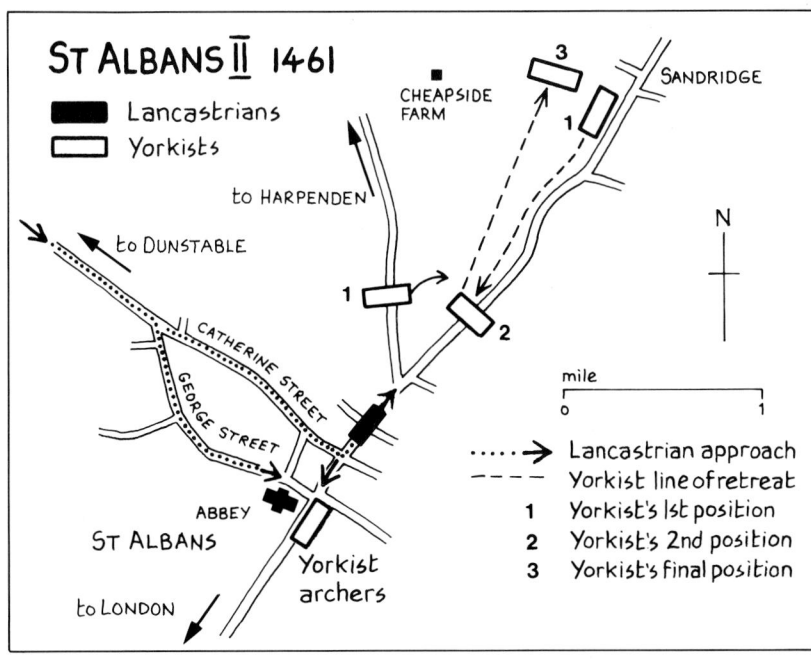

St Albans II was a muddled affair and great credit to the Lancastrian commanders, Somerset and Trollope; but they were helped by spies giving details of Warwick's defences and particularly the desertion of Lovelace.

THE BATTLEFIELD TODAY (S)
Barnard's Heath is now a suburb of St Albans but at Sandridge a playground near the Cricketer's Inn is where the Yorkists turned and retreated. The final position near the Old Albanians rugby ground is still an open field.

English bowmen from the Luttrell Psalter c1340

TOWTON
29 March 1461

The Towton battle monument – recently repaired by an Australian tourist

Just as Marston Moor was the largest battle of the Civil War so the action at Towton, just a few miles away, was the largest and mightiest struggle of the Wars of the Roses.

The two victories of the Lancastrians at Wakefield and St Albans II were followed by Prince Edward's resounding victory for the Yorkists at Mortimer's Cross. Edward reached London after that action and reorganised his army. Angered by the failure of Warwick at St Albans and the execution of Lord Bonville and Sir Thomas Kiriel who had been looking after the king, the Yorkists were keen to defeat Margaret's Lancastrians once and for all. With Warwick's uncle, Lord Fauconberg, in command of the London troops, Edward set out for Pontefract. He was opposed by a massive army of nearly 30,000 Lancastrians under Northumberland, Somerset and Exeter. The king and queen remained in York. Edward, who was in command of almost 25,000 men – the Duke of Norfolk's contingent had yet to arrive – sent a force under Lord Fitzwalter to cross the Aire at Ferrybridge (near the present power station). This was cut to pieces by Lord Clifford's Lancastrian horse. Unperturbed, Edward sent Lord Fauconberg and his men from Kent to cross the river further up, which he did and caught the Lancastrians at Dintingdale where a lucky arrow killed Lord Clifford.

It was now 29 March, Palm Sunday, and by all accounts snowing so that the wind and snow blew into the Lancastrian army. Edward ranged his troops above Saxton village and commanded his archers to fire and withdraw so that the Lancastrians, firing into the wind, fired short and the arrows in the ground could be reused by his own archers as well as providing a difficult calthrop-like surface for horsemen. But Somerset had placed an ambush party in Castle Hill wood on Edward's left flank and gradually the sheer weight of the Lancastrians pushed Edward back. Three hours of fighting passed before the Duke of Norfolk's banners were seen and the Yorkists took heart. Norfolk's men (the Duke was ill) took the right wing and gradually encircled the Lancastrian left. Suddenly the Lancastrians gave way and men were cut down in their hundreds trying to cross the River Cock.

Lord Dacre was killed as he rested by a tree. He is buried with his horse outside Saxton Church. William Paston wrote to his brother John:

> First our Sovereign Lord hath won the field and upon the Monday next after Palm Sunday he was received into York with great solemnity and processions. On the King's part is slain Lord Fitzwalter [at Ferrybridge] and Lord Scrope sore heart, John Stafford and Horne of Kent be dead. On the contrary [Lancastrian] part is dead Lord Clifford, Lord Beville, Lord Welles, Lord Willoughby, Lord Henry Stafford and by supposition the Earl of Northumberland, Andrew Trollope and many others, gentle and common to the number of 20,000.

Paston may have exaggerated the numbers killed, but it was an overwhelming success. York seized the throne (note Paston calls him a King) and entered London again in triumph.

THE BATTLEFIELD TODAY (S)

Saxton Church can be seen by collecting the key from the corner cottage opposite. In the churchyard the tomb of Lord Dacre can be recognised by its criss-cross pattern. The battle cross is small and isolated and can be found on top of the hill on the B1217. The track that leads past it comes to an abrupt

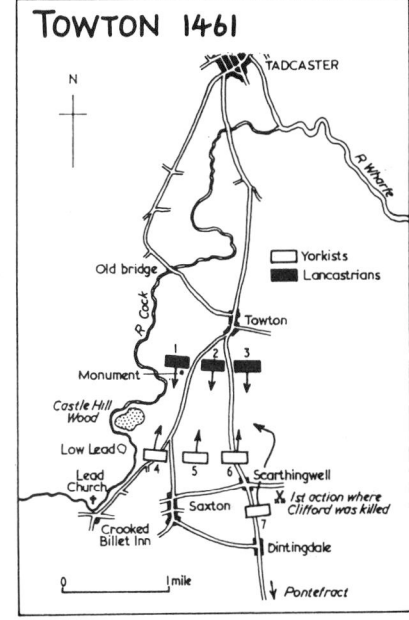

TOWTON 1461

1 Northumberland
2 Somerset
3 Exeter
4 Edward
5 Falconberg
6 Warwick
7 Norfolk's men
(Norfolk himself was
absent)

end at a locked gate and a sudden drop to the Cock Beck. There are some grave mounds further down the hill on the right-hand side, and Castle Hill wood where Somerset placed an ambush party can still be seen. Bloody Meadow, where the thickest fighting took place, is halfway between the wood and the cross (the latter kindly repaired by an Australian tourist). Some of the dead were buried at Towton, for Brooke writes that when he visited Towton Hall in 1857 the owner told him that a large quantity of human bones were found when the hall's cellars were enlarged. When we visited the battle site in late September, the locals were picking sloe berries on the few trees on the side of the road to Towton. This is very densely farmed country and apart from a footpath between Cattle Hill Farm and the wood, and Saxton and Saxton Grange, there seems to be distinct discouragement to ramblers.

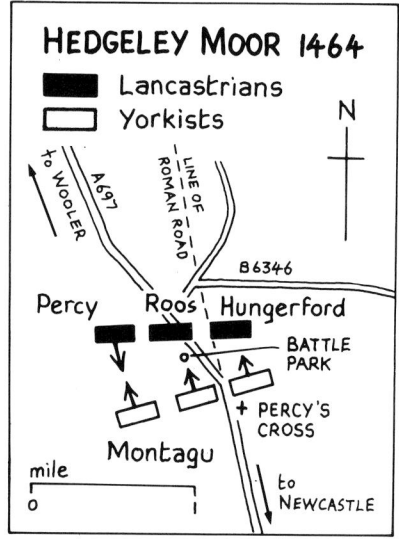

HEDGELEY MOOR
25 April 1464

A described railway line, a small copse and a large carved stone cross standing in a private garden – not much you might think to stop for. However you would be wrong because the little Battle Park has stones marking Percy's Leap – the leap of a dying man. The present owner of the cottage and garden that contains the cross was most helpful. He was a tall young man with a Northumberland accent. Perhaps his ancestors had fought with Percy on that day and at the very spot where he lives today. It reminded me of a friend who worked in a new electronics firm built inside an old maternity home. When his mother brought him some sandwiches on his first day, she recognised the wallpaper. James was working in the very room in which he had been born.

After Towton the Lancastrians had take time to re-emerge as a force and it was not until 1464 that they seized Norham Castle and Skipton Castle. Recruits were slow in coming in and York put his army into the capable hands of Warwick's young brother Lord Montagu. With 2,000 men, mostly from Newcastle, Montagu headed for Norham, but changed direction when he heard that a Lancastrian force was camped outside Wooler. Roos and Hungerford left the field early on but Percy, with his retainers, stayed to fight only to see the Lancastrian army disintegrate. He urged his horse to make a huge leap at what he thought was the weakest part of Montagu's line and was wounded. The animal staggered on for a few yards finally releasing its mortally wounded rider on the other side of the road, just a path then. Percy died with the battle over, where the cross stands today, both friend and foe listening to his famous dying words 'I have saved the bird in my bosom', meaning he had died for a lawful monarch. His army was mostly trapped in the marshy land, but Lords Roos, Hungerford and Somerset escaped to fight again at Hexham on 15 May. Somerset's army was still outnumbered but on that day he positioned his troops near Newbiggin on Hexham Levels with their backs to the Linnel river. Montagu struck quickly as he had at Hedgeley Moor and drove the Lancastrians into the water. Somerset was wounded and captured and Lords Roos and Hungerford were also captured. All three were later executed. The castles of Norham, Alnwick, Dunstanburgh and Bamburgh surrendered and the North was freed of Lancastrians.

THE BATTLEFIELD TODAY (S)

This battlefield is easily missed, but has been given a plaque recently by Northumberland County Council. The small park or walled enclosure with two boulders marking Percy's Leap is beside the A697. Percy's Cross, in the garden of one of a pair of cottages, is on the other side of the road about 500yd (460m) further south, surrounded by a railed fence. There is a metal gate leading to it and the garden owner does not mind photographers and tourists. The cross is a shaft of stone with indentations at the top, displaying the Percy coat of arms with that of Lucy. It is a much grander affair than that at Otterburn, but it needs a more commanding position. There is an old railway line nearby which one can walk down to Low Hedgeley and the Beamish River. It is not an easy walk as all the bridges have gone, so one has to come down to wet ground in between and leave the track. Perhaps someone will make it into an official footpath one day.

BARNET
14 April 1471

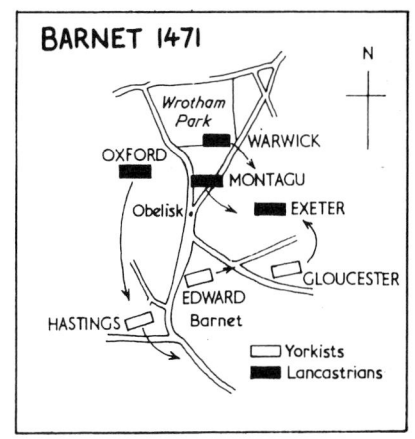

The Lancastrian power was by no means over after Towton. True, Edward seized the throne as King Edward IV, but he made himself unpopular with his marriage to Elizabeth Woodville and the Woodvilles plotted with Queen Margaret to put Henry back on the throne. The Battle of Edgecote in 1469 was a small affair where Edward's Welsh army under Pembroke was defeated by Robin of Redesdale. Warwick captured Edward and placed him in Middleham Castle. He tried unsuccessfully to run the country himself but was forced to release Edward as the country was in turmoil. In March 1470 Sir Robert Welles, a Lancastrian, was defeated by Edward at Empingham in Rutland – a battle called 'Loosecoat Field' because so many of the Lancastrians ran away without their coats. Warwick and Clarence were found to be behind Welles's attempt as papers were captured on the battlefield. Both fled abroad and, getting French support, they came back to England and this time Edward and his brother Richard of Gloucester were forced to flee to Charles of Burgundy from King's Lynn. Henry was placed on the throne again by Warwick, but Edward with a mere 2,000 men landed six months later at Ravenspur and set out for Coventry, being joined by Sir William Stanley, Sir James Harrington and others on the way. Clarence met him in Coventry and, instead of a battle, for Warwick and his brother Montagu were nearby at Warwick Castle.

Warwick had taken up a position near the Hadley High Stone on the St Albans to London road. He had Oxford on his right wing, Montagu in the centre and Exeter on his left. He himself was in reserve. His army was about 15,000 strong and Edward, in the darkness, took up his positions with Richard of Gloucester in his first command on his right wing and Lord Hastings on the left. He was outnumbered 3 to 1, but he had luck on his side. The Earl of Oxford's men had a badge with a radiant star not unlike Edward's badge of the sun with rays he had adopted after Mortimer's Cross. His men out-flanked Lord Hastings and chased his wing off the field (map 1). Gloucester outflanked Exeter's wing but the latter was reinforced by Warwick so that the battle here was fairly stagnant. The day was foggy and in the bad visibility the returning men from Oxford's wing approached Lord Montagu's men (map 2) from the south. They were mistaken as Edward's troops because of their badge and with cries of treason many fled in dismay. In the melée Montagu was killed. Edward launched himself and his reserve against Warwick, who withdrew to a wood where he had left his horse. (There is an area known as Dead Man's Bottom between the hospital and the High Stone where this probably occurred.) Here the lightly armed men from Edward's contingent cut down Warwick and of the Lancastrian leaders only Exeter, badly wounded, and Oxford escaped. Queen Margaret landed at Weymouth to hear the news of Barnet, too late to do anything about the result.

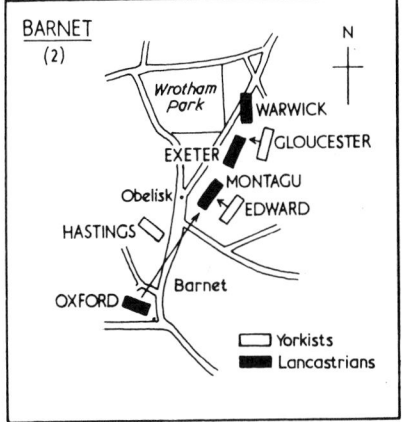

Clarence was the peace-loving and faithful brother to Edward. When Warwick and Montagu remained at Warwick Castle, Clarence joined Edward at Coventry and the two entered London in triumph. Yorkist prisoners were released from the tower and two days later Edward, leaving Clarence in London, turned to meet Warwick in battle at Barnet.

THE BATTLEFIELD TODAY (S)

The area is very heavily built over but the High Stone can be found by taking the A1000 out of Barnet towards Hadley Green. The golf course, where Oxford started his attack, is a good place (the third tee) to view the battlefield, but permission should be obtained from the golfers first and there is a danger of being hit by modern missiles. The obelisk was erected in 1740 by Sir Joseph Sambrooke and is one of the oldest surviving battle monuments.

(pp 90–1)
Archers at sunset (Marcher Lords)

TEWKESBURY
14 May 1471

Tewkesbury must be visited on a hot day. Queen Margaret's army arrived in the heat, throats parched and feet worn out with the walk from Weymouth. The Gupshill Inn must have made a fortune that day if it was open. The abbey vineyards were no doubt ransacked for food and berries; beer and water from the river would not be enough for men to fight on.

Walking round the Trail – and Tewkesbury has the best trail of any battlefield in this book – I began to wish I had started backwards so as to get to Gupshill Inn at opening time instead of an hour later. Once again it is not difficult to sympathise with the Duke of Somerset, no mean commander, who picked up his mace and bashed his supposedly treacherous ally Wenlock on the head. It must be much more satisfying to vent your wrath on someone you know than an enemy whom you don't.

THE BATTLE

One of the most decisive battles of the Wars of the Roses, Tewkesbury was Queen Margaret's final gamble. Her army had landed at Weymouth at the same time as the news came of the Lancastrian defeat at Barnet. She was advised that there were supporters for her cause in Wales and Lord Pembroke set off to rally them, the queen and young Prince Edward following. The Duke

Gupshill Manor, Tewkesbury. Sight of Queen Margaret's camp before the battle though she retreated towards the Abbey before taking up a defensive position. It is a fifteenth century manor house converted into an inn in 1955

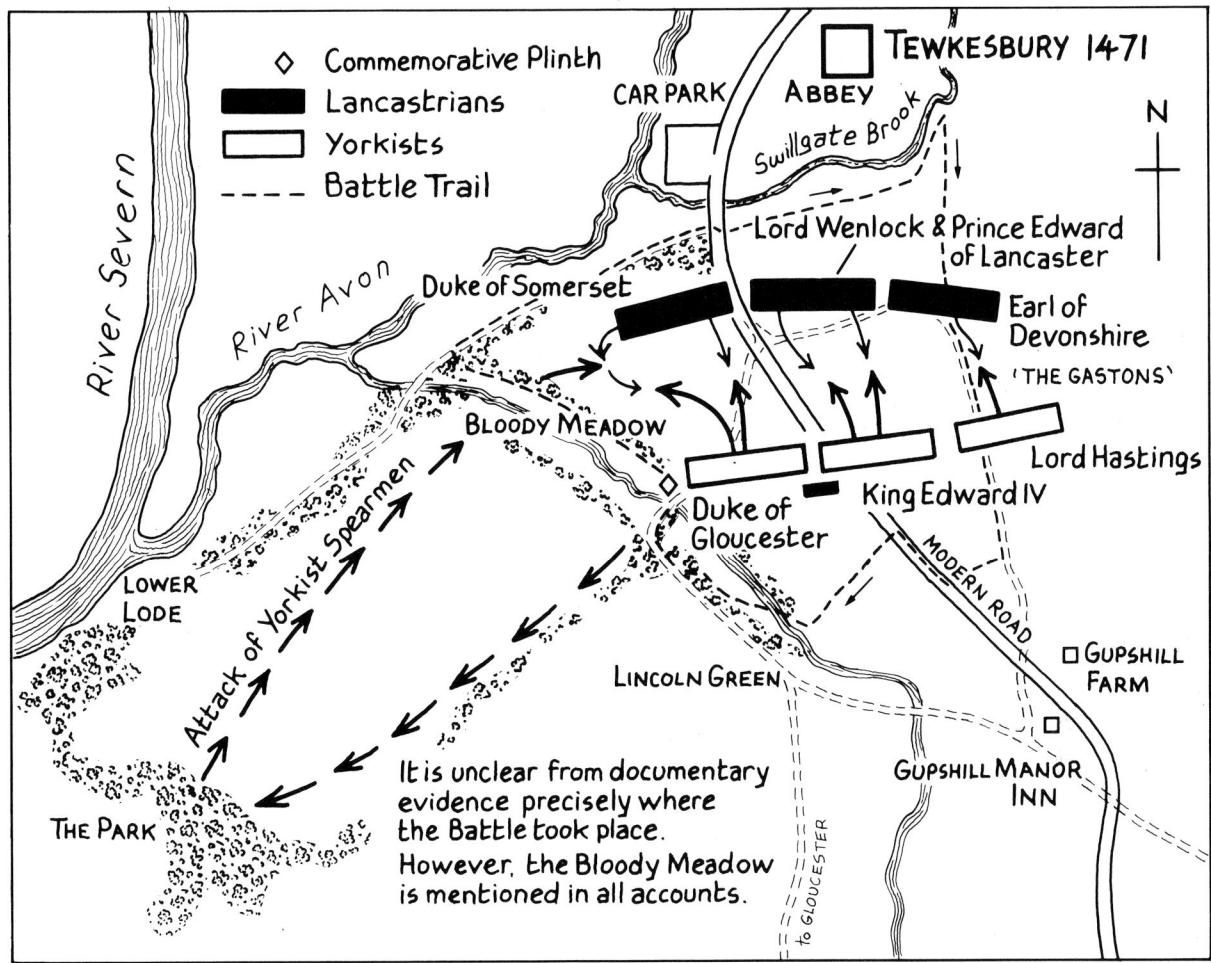

TEWKESBURY 1471

Commemorative Plinth
Lancastrians
Yorkists
Battle Trail

River Severn
River Avon
CAR PARK
ABBEY
Swillgate Brook
Lord Wenlock & Prince Edward of Lancaster
Duke of Somerset
Earl of Devonshire
'THE GASTONS'
Lord Hastings
King Edward IV
Bloody Meadow
Attack of Yorkist Spearmen
Duke of Gloucester
LOWER LODE
LINCOLN GREEN
MODERN ROAD
GUPSHILL FARM
It is unclear from documentary evidence precisely where the Battle took place. However, the Bloody Meadow is mentioned in all accounts.
THE PARK
GUPSHILL MANOR INN
to GLOUCESTER
N

of Somerset was in command and when the tired men reached Tewkesbury, having been denied entry to Gloucester, they were forced to take up positions facing the Gloucester road where Edward's army was close behind. He had started from Windsor, with his brother Gloucester in charge of his left wing and Lord Hastings the right wing. His troops had just won Barnet so morale was high and they were reinforced by Sir Richard Beauchamp of Gloucester, who had locked the gates in the face of the queen the day before. The Lancastrians were about 5,000 to 3,500 Yorkists but old Lord Wenlock, a former Yorkist, was treated with suspicion by the queen's commanders and fighting with his back to the abbey, Somerset was not optimistic about the outcome.

The battle on 14 May started with Somerset advancing while Gloucester appeared to retreat. In fact King Edward had planned this for he had arranged for a party of 200 spearmen, placed on the hill by the present golf club, to descend and attack Somerset's rear. Wenlock could have saved the day by attacking with Somerset but he stood firm and the duke, so angered with his commander, returned and dashed in Lord Wenlock's brains with his mace, supposing Wenlock to be in league with King Edward. The battle was then nearly over and the Lancastrians took to their heels, some cut down by the Abbey Mill, others trapped inside the abbey. The young Prince was caught and executed with about twenty others including Somerset. Queen Margaret was caught in Little Malvern and taken to the Tower where she was imprisoned.

Little Malvern still has the remains of its twelfth century Priory Church founded by the Benedictines. The tower, transept and chancel remain but are incorporated into Bishop Alcock's new church of 1482.

The battle trail, Tewkesbury

THE SITE

I have reckoned on the battle site being near the abbey with the abbey vineyards in the back of the prince's position and the Earl of Devonshire's army on the left wing facing the area called 'the Gastons'. The Swillgate brook is in the rear and the fleeing troops were caught in it and the Avon. The area around Gupshill is equally suitable for this theory and the motte and bailey castle opposite Gupshill Inn is known as Queen Margaret's Camp. The spearmen could have been placed on the little hillock near the present water works but it would not have been high enough for the spearmen to see when to attack Somerset's rear in their very successful ambush.

THE WALK (L)

Starting from Lincoln Green, which is ½ mile (.8km) out of Tewkesbury on the Gloucester road, turn down Lincoln Green towards the golf club. At the end there is the old Gloucester road now a farm track, and opposite is Bloody Meadow where the walk starts. The gate leads to the battle plan which, newly erected and based on Kathie Best's green poster, is on your left in the field. The council has planted willow, whitethorn, redthorn and alder trees in clumps in the meadow and elsewhere on the walk, which was laid out in 1986 so that the trees still have to survive a few more winters before they contribute to the scene.

The hawthorn hedge on the right is well grown and when we made the walk the first part of the meadow walk was wet underfoot after April rain, which at the time of the battle must have hindered the heavily armed Yorkists in their retreat. The boggy ground in the middle of the field would have been impassable for us without Wellington boots so, even in summer, suitable footwear is essential. A small orange-tip butterfly appeared and darted overhead and later we saw a yellow brimstone, both appearing early in the year for butterflies. At the end of the meadow the path goes through a small wood to the lane where turn right and proceed past the pumping station. You are now on the Avon walk (green sign with ship is the symbol here) and if you had turned left you would have come to Lower Lode where the Avon meets the Severn. After the pumping station the road meets the modern Gloucester road, which cross carefully and go through the metal gate into the sports field opposite. In front of you is the back of the abbey, where the old vineyard was situated. Walk down Swillgate brook, in fact wide enough here to prevent a man in armour from crossing, to the large horse-chestnut tree.

The metal post here is without its flag, but consult the map and you will see that you turn sharp right and follow the path to the King George V gates into the Gastons where there is a modern cemetery on the right and a hedge on the left. This leads to Forester's Road to the left and Abbot's Walk where you turn right past the three silver birch trees to the telephone kiosk and the Gloucester road where, if thirsty, you can divert to the left where 500yd (460m) on the right-hand side of the road is Gupshill Inn, built in 1430, which is where Queen Margaret spent the night before the battle. It was her army who camped in the old castle opposite. The inn has a map of the battle and some interesting timber work. It is in very good condition and seems to have been restored in a way that has not spoiled the building.

Suitably refreshed, rejoin the walk which now continues down the Gloucester road to the bus stop (Midland Red) where cross over the stile into the grassy field on your left. This is a ridge and furrow field, and although when we saw it the grass was very long, the ridges can be clearly seen. This was a common type of agriculture in the Middle Ages and there are other examples on battlefields – notably at Radway on Edgehill – which are worth seeing.

The field has a farm at the end with a dairy herd but the path turns right through a wooden V-shaped stile, on the right beside the last new house in the row, and over a wooden bridge then left into the farm meadow. Here the yellow brimstone butterfly greeted us and there were clumps of newly planted trees. On the right some children were playing on a small island in the brook (which appears to have no name on the map). Soon we are back at Lincoln Green where the walk started. If fine it is worth climbing the hill to the golf club car park from where the whole battlefield can be clearly seen. This is where the leader of the 200 spearmen waited, hidden by the trees, until the moment came when Someset's men passed and he and his men had to rush down and attack their rear.

TO SEE NEARBY

Tewkesbury Abbey Note the brass plate in the centre aisle to Prince Edward.

Tewkesbury Abbey

Tewkesbury Museum Open Easter–October, 9am–5pm. Closed during the lunch hour. This has a model of the battle and copies of documents from Trinity Library, Dublin, and the British Museum listing the main Lancastrian losses, mostly by execution, at the battle. There are also coats of arms of the main contestants. Kathy Best's green poster which makes a useful map is for sale (price 95p) as well as a collection of guide books.

Battlefields Mortimer's Cross, Evesham.

BOSWORTH FIELD
22 August 1485

The air was filled with smoke and the crack of cannonfire could be heard as I approached Bosworth Field in September 1987. The army which reached Ambion Hill first, that of King Richard, followed my route, but there the resemblance stopped. In place of the Wars of the Roses struggle the re-enactment that was taking place was a Sealed Knot struggle of 1640. The royalists were doing rather well and actually beating the parliamentarians. On the touch-line – for it seemed to me that Ambion Hill was roped off like a football field – were merry maidens selling Civil War ribbons and buttons. The crowd were enjoying themselves and the cameras were popping all around me.

'Why not have a Bosworth re-enactment of 1485 vintage?' I asked innocently of a huge man directing traffic, in a helmet and tabard which he probably wore for his gardening and car-washing.

'That was last year, mate.'

THE BATTLE

In early August 1485, Henry Tudor landed at Milford Haven with an army of 2,500 mercenaries and supporters. There was slim hope of usurping Richard III, who had an army, on paper at least, of twice this size. The Stanleys however, though promising secret support, did not commit their army. Lord Stanley from Shropshire was fearful that his son, Lord Strange, a captive in Richard's control, would be executed if he supported Henry.

Richard was not slow in gathering an army. The Duke of Norfolk brought 3,000 infantry from East Anglia, Northumberland came down to Leicester with about the same number, and the only notable army leader who joined Henry was the Earl of Oxford, who had learnt to keep his men close to their standards after his disaster at Barnet. Richard's army of about 10,000 camped on Ambion Hill, near Sutton Cheney, to block the invaders who were moving

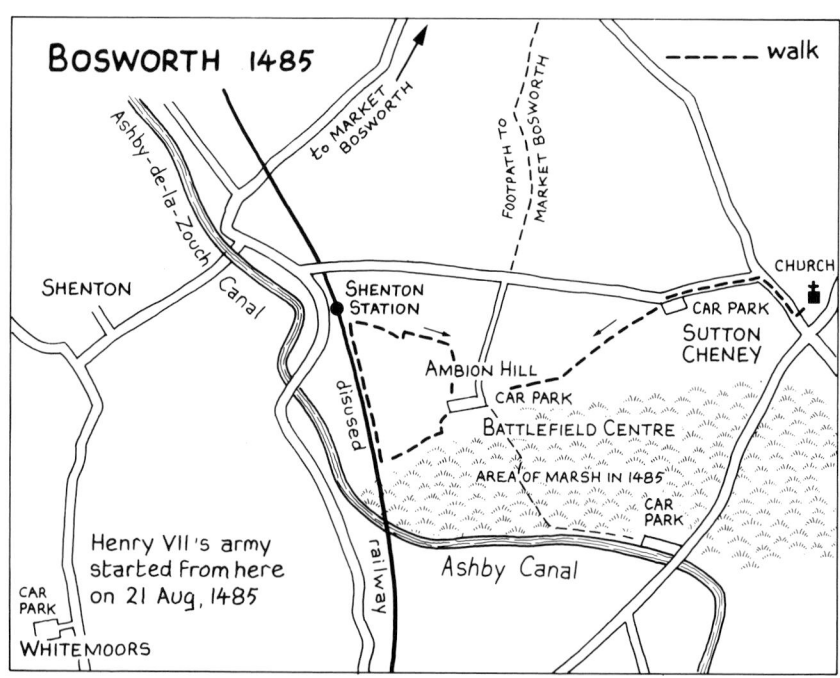

from Atherstone to Whitemoors where they spent the night before the battle. Meanwhile the Stanleys in two groups of about 6,000 men, including mounted archers, were in two camps at Market Bosworth and at Dadlington. It is very unlikely that they were together. Lord Stanley was a declared traitor and Sir William was anxious to keep his hand open, in case Richard was victorious. The fact that he was later executed by Henry indicates that he was untrustworthy.

It was an unusual situation and no battle on English soil has ever started with such a doubtful outcome. Richard had the best position on Ambion Hill, and could see the approaching red dragon banners. His vanguard under Norfolk slowly pushed back the Earl of Oxford's men. The artillery on both sides did little damage but must have created smoke. Suddenly Richard saw Henry's little band isolated, perhaps on the way to get help from one of the Stanleys. He charged down but his horse was bogged down in the marsh and Lord Stanley's men, who had safely negotiated the marsh, surrounded him and cut him down. Norfolk was also killed, but Northumberland escaped without taking part in the battle and Sir William Stanley rescued his son but effectively the battle ended with the death of Richard.

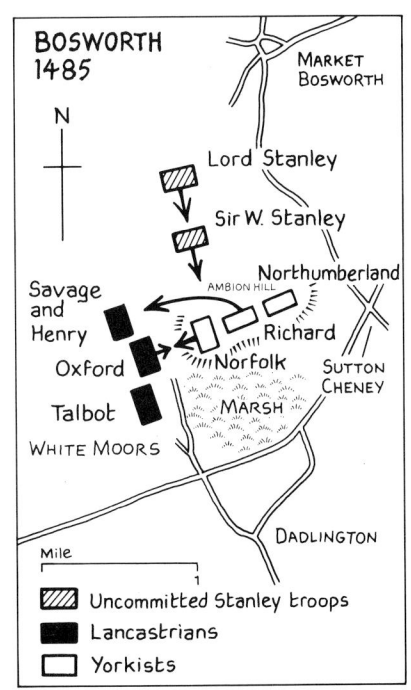

The battle trail and booklet by D. T. Williams (Battlefield Centre) put the two Stanleys in one group to the north and suggest that Richard charged down that side of the hill. This assumes his horse was killed, rather than fell into the marsh, and that it was Lord Stanley, not his brother, who picked up the crown and put it on Henry's head. The commemorative well stands where the king is supposed to have died and there is also a monument at Shenton station. Shakespeare's version, portrayed in *Richard III* and in the film in the Battlefield Centre, is incorrect (the film shows Spanish rocks and sand as the terrain and only one Stanley not two) and very misleading. Surely it is time to make a new video for visitors with a more truthful version, admirable though the museum and general presentation for visitors are.

THE WALK
Sutton Cheney church is the starting point and here the Richard III Society have a plaque and the local ladies have made kneelers with royal arms etc. The footpaths in this area have a footprint on them and are easy to find. The path to Ambion Hill is just off the Shenton road and there is a car park nearby. The route round the battlefield is well sign-posted with battle-plans and flags and takes about half an hour. It has some strong gates, weighted down so that they shut easily, so anyone in a wheel chair or with a child in a push-chair, could have a problem getting round. There are also footpaths to Market Bosworth and to Whitemoors from Shenton station (another park here) and there is a restaurant, museum, shop, toilets and a diorama with the aforementioned video of the film of *Richard III*. When I visited the battlefield in September, 1987 and there was the full-scale Sealed Knot battle of 1640 going on with plenty of artillery and casualties, it was a reminder that Naseby is not far away. On that occasion however the parliamentarians won the day.

Sir William and his Cheshire men were content to stay on the side-line and Lord Stanley, whose son was in Richard's care as a hostage, was unlikely to oppose his brother.

The *Richard III Society* have tried to clear Richard's name. They proved successfully one night in a mock trial on television that the murder of the Princes in the Tower cannot be proved to be at the orders of the unfortunate king. The royal motto *Loyaulte me lie*, 'Loyalty binds me', was unfortunate for Richard. It was lack of loyalty that lost him Bosworth. Henry Richmond was not a particularly likeable person – as a king he has the reputation of being a miser – but he doesn't seem to have been as wily as his successor, for example, at intrigue. The author Paul Murray Kendall in his excellent biography, *Richard III*, paints a picture of a man wronged by history who was intensely loyal to his older brother, a keen soldier who fought at *Tewkesbury* and *Barnet*, who inspired great affection from men like Francis, Lord Lovell, and William Catesby. Who is right – Shakespeare or Kendall? Probably the arguments will continue for ever, but there seems to have been a plot at Bosworth to be disloyal to the king. It worked.

TO SEE NEARBY
Kirby Muxloe Castle Open under English Heritage, and home of Lord Hastings, whom Richard executed earlier in his reign.

Naseby (see page 145).

(pp 98–9)
*Ambion Hill and
(inset), King Richard III
(National Portrait Gallery)*

RICARDVS · III · ANG · REX ·

STOKE FIELD
16 June 1487

Sometimes known as East Stoke, the battle of 16 June came about because Lord Lovell, one of the survivors of Bosworth, and Robert de la Pole, Earl of Lincoln, assembled an army in Dublin with Lambert Simnel, a 10-year-old who claimed to be one of the lost Princes in the Tower. Lincoln, who had a strong claim to the throne as a nephew of Edward IV, employed 2,000 German mercenaries under Martin Schwartz. Having landed at Fowdrey Castle, Lancashire, the rebels made for the Midlands and were at Southwell on 14 June while the king, supported by Lord Stanley (now Earl of Derby) and his son, the Earl of Oxford, and Lord Pembroke had an army of 12,000 at Nottingham. The Fosse Way was a natural place for the two armies to meet. Lincoln made use of the Trent Hills above the small village of East Stoke. He put his weakly armed Irish on the left, Schwartz in the centre with his crossbow men, and his own troops on the right wing. Outnumbered but fighting for their very survival, the rebels held up Oxford's vanguard for three hours. Finally Robert Brandon – standard bearer to Henry VII – led on the second line and Schwartz was killed. The Irish were cut down in great numbers and many were caught trying to ford the Trent at Fiskerton. The king planted his standard in a 'burrand' bush and Robert Brandon was knighted on the field. Most of the rebels were killed, Simnel was captured and only Lord Lovell escaped by swimming his horse over the Trent (see page 101). The Wars of the Roses were finally over and Henry VII was firmly placed on the English throne.

THE WALK (L)
East Stoke is a few miles out of Newark on the Fosse Way. Follow School Road and the path down to the wall of Stoke Hall. At the end of the wall is a road through to East Stoke Church. It is approached by slippery steps up from the road and at once there is a monument to Lord Pauncefote, first British Ambassador to the United States of America. There is a new monument to the battle dead just outside the porch. It mentions Schwartz, Lincoln and Lord Geraldine (also known as Fitzgerald) and 3,000 dead. The inside of the church is worth seeing; there is a picture of Scott's last expedition as one of the owners of Stoke Hall was present on it, and a picture of Henry VII.

From the church the track goes down a slope to, on our visit, a large heap of sugarbeet. Behind the heap was a gate and a footpath to the river. Both sides of the path were ploughed up, and with the November weather – fog and damp – setting in early, we were unable to find the burrand bush monument which is on private land. The path ends at the junction of the navigation river and the river proper, where there is a much larger footpath leading almost straight up the slope to the Fosse Way. This is the fisherman's route but to see Red Gutter, return the way you have come but take the edge of the field next to the green area marked Stoke Wood on the Ordnance Survey map. Red Gutter is a gap in the wood leading up the hill. It is well protected by a barbed-wire fence so not visible all the way up. Going on to the gate, there were pheasants about and in summer it must be a good place for wild flowers.

The other route up to the Fosse Way follows roughly the line of Lincoln's army and then back to East Stoke village via Humber Lane and the Pauncefote Arms.

Fiskerton Ferry (no longer running) is at the end of the lane past the church and is a pleasant place for a picnic.

The burrand bush stone at Stoke (Maj R W Naesmyth of Posso RA)

MINSTER LOVELL AND LORD LOVELL

One of the mysteries of the Wars of the Roses is what became of Lord Lovell. He was one of Richard III's closest supporters, Governor of Wallingford Castle and Chamberlain of the Household as well as a soldier of some experience. After Bosworth he fled abroad but returned with Lambert Simnel to take a leading part in the Battle of Stoke. Some reports, possibly by Lovell or his friends, said he had been killed at that battle or in escaping from it. Francis Bacon, however, states he swam over the Trent on his horse and escaped to Minster Lovell, where he had prepared a special bolt-hole in a cellar. Only his butler knew of it and brought him food at regular intervals. One day the butler failed to come and Lord Lovell died of starvation.

In 1737 a letter was written by William Cowper, Clerk of Parliament, to Francis Peck an antiquary of the time:

'On 6th May, 1728, the present Duke of Rutland related in my hearing that, about twenty years before [1708] upon laying a new chimney at Minster Lovell, there was discovered a large vault or room underground, in which was the entire skeleton of a man, as having been sitting at a table, which was before him, with a book, paper, pen etc, etc,: in another part of the room lay a cap; all moulded and decayed. Which the family and others judged to be this Lord Lovell, whose exit hath hitherto been so uncertain.'

The cellar or vault has never been excavated, but the south-west tower – according to A. J. Taylor, Chief Inspector of Ancient Monuments and author of the official guidebook to Minster Lovell – was built by Francis, Lord Lovell, and has a 'massive foundation' including a wall to prevent water seeping in from the River Windrush. Perhaps the British Heritage archaeologists will have a new dig and rediscover the hidden room that was the last resting place of Richard III's loyal servant?

Minster Lovell Hall before it fell into decay

SHAKESPEARE'S BATTLES

The first battle that occurs by implication in *I Henry IV*, is *Pilleth*, and it is left to the Earl of Westmoreland to bring the news to his king:

. . . the noble Mortimer
Leading the men of Herefordshire to fight
Against the irregular and wild Glendower,
Was by the rude hands of the Welshman taken,
A thousand of his people butchered.

But to comfort the king there is news a few lines further on of the battle against the Scots at *Homildon Hill*, which was only a few months later in 1402. Here Sir Walter Blunt, 'new lighted from his horse, stain'd with the variation of each soil' has brought good news at last:

The Earl of Douglas is discomfited:
Ten thousand bold Scots, two and twenty knights,
Balk'd in their own blood did Sir Walter see
On Holmedon's plains. Of prisoners Hotspur took
Mordake the Earl of Fife, and eldest son
To beaten Douglas: and the Earl of Athol,
Of Murray, Angus and Menteith.

Brave Hotspur however rebels against his king and the scene is set for the *Battle of Shrewsbury* the following year:

The trumpet sounds retreat; the day is ours
Come brother, let us to the highest of the field,
To see what friends are living and who are dead.

Prince Henry, later Henry V, kills Hotspur but the former prisoner, Douglas, who had allied himself with Hotspur, flees. However he is captured, but is spared by Prince Henry:

Go to the Douglas, and deliver him
Up to his pleasure, ransomless and free:
His valour shown upon our crests today
Hath taught us how to cherish such high deeds
Even in the bosom of our adversaries.

In *Henry V*, made famous by the film with Sir Lawrence Olivier, we have *Agincourt*. The failure of this king was to leave only an infant successor:
Henry the Sixth, in infant bands crown'd King
Of France and England, did this King succeed;
Whose state so many had the managing,
That they lost France and made his England bleed.

Tomb of King Henry VII and Elizabeth of York at Westminster Abbey (Woodmansterne)

We now have the War of the Roses with the various characters appearing and disappearing on the stage of Shakespeare's history. The *First Battle of St Albans* for once is reasonably accurate and young Clifford removes the body of his father, slain by young Richard of York:

Meet I an infant of the House of York,
Into as many gobbets will I cut it
As wild Medea young Absyrtus did.

a prophesy he was to fulfil at *Wakefield*. The Duke of York also kills Warwick:

So, lie thou there;
For underneath an alehouse' paltry sign,
The Castle in St. Albans, Somerset
Hath made the wizard famous in his death.
Sword, hold thy temper; heart be wrathful still:
Priests pray for enemies, but princes kill.

Now we go to the most famous of all battle scenes, that of King Richard III at *Bosworth*. Alas it is not accurate, but it is certainly stirring stuff, especially King Richard's oration to his army:

What shall I say more than I have inferr'd?
Remember whom you are to cope withal;
A sort of vagabonds, rascals and runaways,
A scum of Bretons, and base lackey peasants,
Whom their o'er-cloyed country vomits forth
To desperate ventures and assured destruction . . .
Fight gentlemen of England! fight, bold yeomen!
Draw, archers, draw your arrows to the head!
Spur your proud horses hard and ride in blood;
Amaze the welkin with your broken staves!

Richmond is left to unite the two roses by marrying the heiress, Elizabeth of York:

We will unite the white rose and the red.
Smile heaven upon this fair conjunction
That long have frown'd upon this enmity!
What traitor hears me, and says not amen?
England has long been mad, and scarr'd herself;
The brother blindly shed the brother's blood,
The father rashly slaughter'd his own son,
The son, compell'd, been butcher to the sire:
All this divided York and Lancaster,
Divided in their dire division,
O, now let Richmond and Elizabeth,
The true succeeders of each royal house
By God's fair ordinance conjoin together!

FLODDEN
9 September 1513

The unspoilt battlefield at Flodden is not hard to find. Stand on top of Piper's Hill and ahead you can see the ridge of Flodden Hill. The Scots burnt their camp before withdrawing to meet the English army. The smoke blew back into their faces, so there was a wind on that day in September. The noise of the Scottish cannon booming out at Ford Castle and the tramp of thousands of feet as the English took up their positions, the clatter of men deploying and letting their bill-shafts fall onto the ground – it was a noisy start to the battle. In the rear is the Tweed valley and Coldstream.

Today it is all so peaceful and only three hundred and seventy five years ago it was so different. The lanes were not much narrower then than they are today. They were choked with men struggling to get up to their positions. The area covered by the battle was at least 3 miles (5km) wide, so communications would have been very difficult. No one would know that Argyle and Lennox had been defeated by Stanley until the smoke cleared and they could see Stanley's banners on the hill. Once I took part in an Army Cadet 'battle' and, as signals officer, was responsible for laying the telephone cable between the command post and the hill where our forward troops were supposed to be.

Thomas Howard, eldest son of the Earl of Surrey, commanded the van-guard at Flodden. He was a sailor and always wore his Admiral's whistle round his neck. He wore a red velvet skirt during the battle which must have confused both friend and foe, and after the battle he was created Earl of Surrey while his father became Duke of Norfolk. He was one of the leaders of Queen Mary's Catholic army, and died in 1544. He was forty at the time of Flodden.

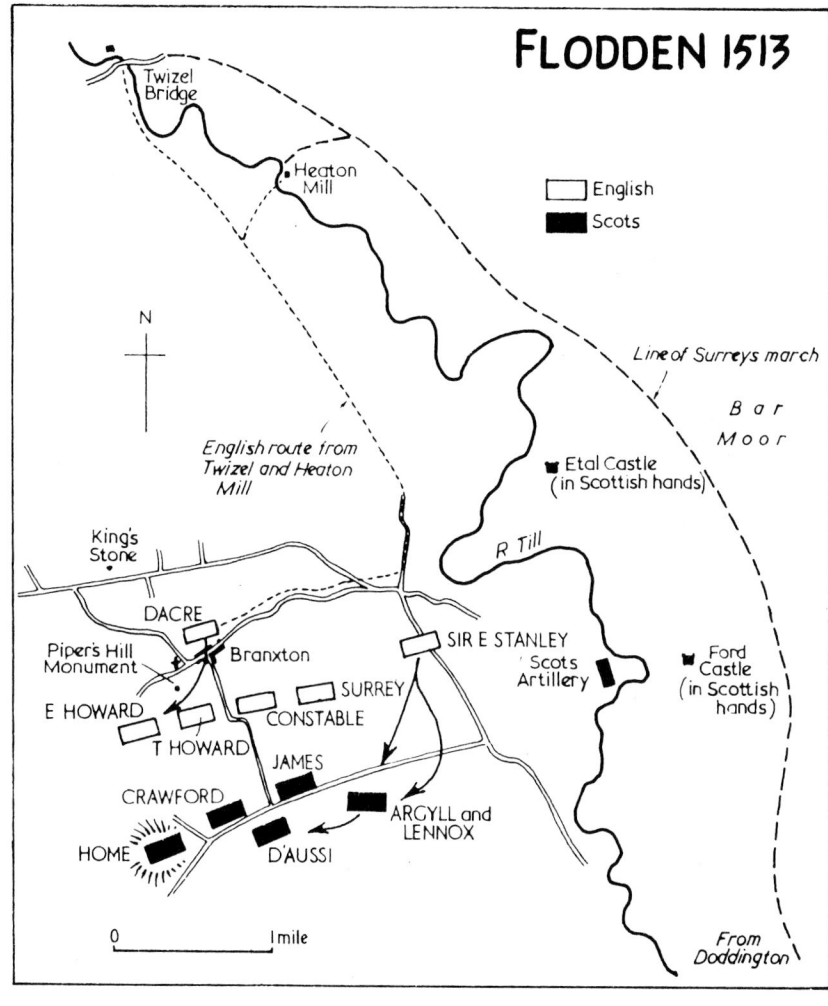

Piper's Hill monument

King's Stone, Flodden

On reaching the hill I was promptly captured by the enemy, who could then speak directly to our commander – an unusual and confusing episode in military communications.

The events which led to Flodden began when Henry VIII took his army to France in 1513, and Louis XII asked James IV of Scotland for help. The Scots king, flattered and supported by some French arms and the Count D'Aussi with a few French knights, had a large army of 60,000 men with 5 huge cannon firing 60lb shot; Robin Borthwick, James's gunner, had 7 field pieces. James had no cavalry other than Lord Home's borderers, but his army was always keen to fight the English and, having crossed the border at Coldstream, it invested Etal, Norham and Ford castles before camping on Flodden Hill. At Ford Castle, King James was entertained by Lady Heron, who tried to detain him until the English army arrived. In fact the 70-year-old Lord Surrey, a veteran of Bosworth, was at Wooler with 26,000 men including a detachment of naval captains and their companies under his brother Thomas Howard. Another member of the family, Edmund Howard, commanded the right wing and Lord Dacre commanded the horse. Lord Stanley was present with his men and a detachment of archers. The Scots had spears and two-handed claymores, but the English had bill-hooks and lighter swords.

Surrey decided to move up to occupy Branxton Hill and prevent the Scots from retreating back to Scotland. It was a dangerous move as one group under Admiral Howard had to cross the Till at Twizel Bridge (the old bridge still stands and must be similar to that crossed by the English, two abreast); Lord Surrey with the main force crossed at Heaton Mill ford. Both Etal and Ford castles were avoided as being in Scottish hands. James turned his army round and occupied Branxton Hill before Surrey got there, but he was unable to get his artillery re-sited before Surrey's army, in five groups, positioned itself in front of Branxton village with Lord Dacre in reserve. A lucky shot from the inferior English artillery killed Borthwick. James, who horrified his men by fighting on foot, had his centre held up by the English billmen. On his left Lord Home with Huntly's Highlanders captured some of the Cheshire men, but Heron's Northumberland men beat them off and they retired to a hill with their horses and took no further part in the battle. Sir Edward Stanley, arriving late, found that Argyle and Lennox were the only two Scottish contingents in front of him. Attacking via Marden Farm, Stanley's archers cleared the Scots from the hill and then he attacked them from behind. In the centre King James was killed by a billhook and the battle was over.

The 'Flowers of the Forest' pipe tune was composed in honour of the Ettrick archers, who were all killed except for one man who returned home to Selkirk. Stanley was made Lord Monteagle, Surrey became Duke of Norfolk and the Admiral was created Earl of Surrey in his stead. Some 1,700 English were killed but four or five times that number of Scots, and the Abbess of Coldstream had cart-loads of wounded to care for.

THE WALKS (L, S, M)

There is a car park at Branxton and a short walk up the footpath to the monument, a large granite cross on Piper's Hill, where the English right wing formed up. Branxton church is worth looking at as it has monuments to both Scots and English regiments and the door of the church is inscribed to the memory of a soldier who died of wounds received in the Korean War.

There is a long walk from Twizel Bridge to Etal Castle, but this is some 5 miles (8km) from the scene of action and the walk up to the monument and to the church takes some time as the hill is steep and it is not possible to stray from the path as the local farmer ploughs every field. There is a route of medium length however by taking the track beyond the monument to Branxton Stead and then up Branxton Hill, where turn diagonally left by the farm and pick up the hill tarmac road down to Branxton village again. Marden Farm is on your right when you descend the hill and it also has a connecting footpath with the village.

TO SEE NEARBY

Ford, Etal and *Norham* castles. The first is used by Northumberland Education Department and has mostly been rebuilt; Etal is a picturesque ruin and Norham is a much larger ruin on the road to Berwick. Etal Manor grounds are open on some Sundays during the year and are renowned for their autumn crocus display. Heaton Mill is also open to the public. It is a very pleasant area for walkers and, even late in the year, on a fine day the views are spectacular.

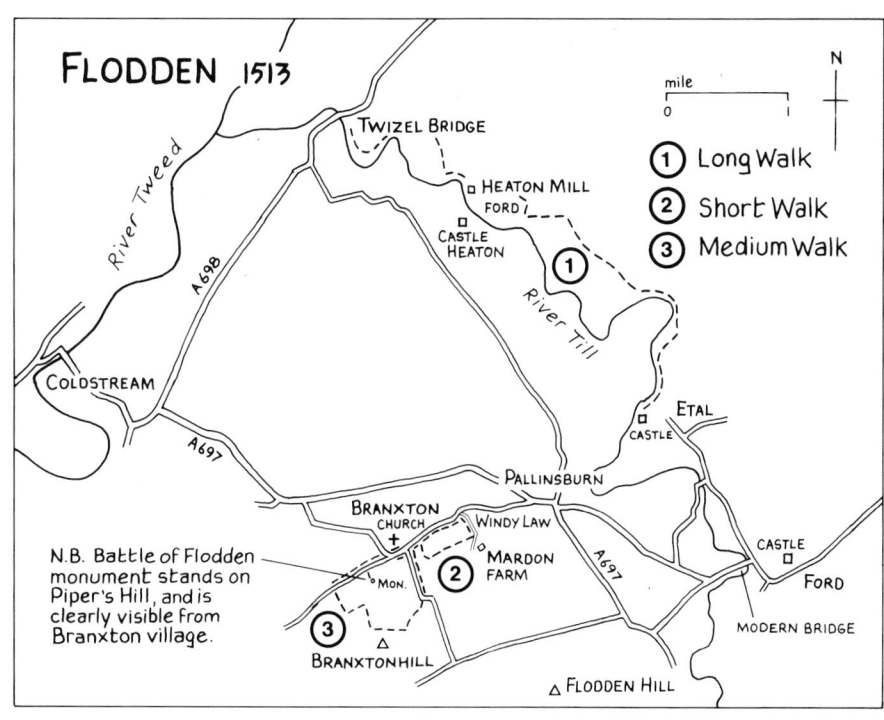

THE SEALED KNOT

The Society of Cavaliers & Roundheads

The Sealed Knot has a magazine and copies can be obtained from the Edgehill Museum, Farnborough Hall Stables, Farnborough, Warwicks.

Sealed Knot re-enactment of the Battle of Sedgemoor in 1985

What is the Sealed Knot? Is it a secret society to bring back parliamentary control and do away with the Crown? Is it a special group of actors who go round trying to break each other's heads with pikes and wooden swords? Is it a men's club? It is none of these things. It was founded in 1968 by Brigadier Peter Young DSO, MC, FH, and by 1971 had become a limited company. It is non-profit-making and in fact makes money for charity. Created to stimulate interest in the Civil War, it re-enacts Civil War battles (not always at places where they were fought – see Bosworth, page 00) between March and October. Sometimes it strays outside its age and re-enacts Sedgemoor for example; but it takes care to get the uniform, equipment and character of its armies as correct as possible. Even its camp-followers have to dress up and Monmouth's cavalry seemed to be remarkably female in its 1985 tri-centenary re-enactment.

To take one particular regiment – the Earl of Northampton's Banbury garrison, a Royalist group based at Banbury Castle. It has four main groups: pikemen, dragoons, musketeers and artillery. Membership often consists of young families, the man joining, say as a pikeman, paying £10 subscription that includes his wife, as a camp-follower, and two children under eighteen. Some women prefer to dress as men and fight too, others look after the wounded, bring water onto the field or help in other ways. At the Battle of Cheriton re-enactment some years ago, a wounded pikeman was collected by two ladies in a baby Austin (1930 vintage) and taken to Winchester hospital. He insisted on bringing his pike which conveniently fitted up through the sunshine roof.

The Society has a long record of self-sufficiency. One doesn't stay at the best hotel and turn up for breakfast with musket and baldrick. But at the re-enactment of Marston Moor a complete Cavalier regiment, who had joined in twentieth-century 'mufti', emerged from the train at York in uniform and lined up on the railway station to the astonishment of railway staff and normal passengers alike.

Most members attend five or six musters and some mini-musters. In winter there are banquets, social gatherings, display and training days organised by individual regiments.

A word of warning – although one doesn't have to turn up at musters, you soon find that there is more to the Knot than you imagined and that even a mini-muster like the one held at Basing House (see page 129), involves considerable training so that people are not injured. The re-enactment of Sedgemoor involved both the Knot and the Army and a complete re-design of uniforms. The whole event (fought twice on successive days) was a triumph and the ground shook when the cavalry passed by. The ambulance men and women, dressed with a St John's cross on their seventeenth-century hats, worked hard and one rider who fell was carted off to hospital – in a Range Rover not a horse and cart – and will be unlikely to forget the experience. The hardest things was persuading Monmouth to lose and as a spectator I counted many rebels who rose up and fought on regardless of how many times they were 'declared dead'.

The Sealed Knot has a magazine and copies can be obtained from the Edgehill Museum, Farnborough Hall Stables, Farnborough, Warwickshire.

Members purchase their own uniform at about £25, but some prefer to make it according to Sealed Knot specifications. Wellington boots and 'smocks' are not allowed. The following details are given:

Pikemen will require a helmet, pikes supplied by the Regiment. Dragoons will require a helmet or felt hat, sword and baldrick; pole arms are supplied by the Regiment. Dragoons will require a helmet or felt hat, sword and baldrick; pole arms are supplied by the Regiment. Musketeers will require a felt hat and musket. Muskets cost anything between £80 and £150 depending on the type chosen.

Camp-followers will require a dress of seventeenth-century design which can be obtained or made up as per patterns.

Transport and a tent are required to attend musters.

PINKIE
10 September 1547

German armour of the 16th century (Wallace Collection)

The death of Henry VIII provided no change in policy as regards Scottish affairs. Young King Edward VI was proposed as a suitor for the unmarried Mary Queen of Scots. The castles of St Andrews and Broughty on the east coast of Scotland were in English hands and by September 1547 the situation was so bad that Protector Somerset decided to carry out his 'rough wooing' by moving an army of 17,500 men from their gathering point at Newcastle to Scotland. It was well equipped and included 15 cannon, 200 mounted arquebusiers (horsemen with early types of firearms) under a Spaniard, Gambosa, as well as archers and hackbuteers. The latter were an early form of musketeer and their heavy guns had hooked-butts, and were called hackbuts eventually. Lord Clinton's well-directed fleet provided additional artillery and supplies as long as the English kept near the coast.

Arran, the Scottish Protector, had 25,000 men but, as at Flodden, few were horsemen, and only Lord Home with his border contingent, whom he placed on the right wing of his army, were present when the battle started. Arran fortified Inveresk, taking up his position to block the Edinburgh road with his left wing at Musselburgh. He had Lord Arran's archers next to him in the centre and Angus and the Highlanders on the road nearest the sea.

On 9 September the Scots horse charged a body of English horse and Lord Home was wounded and his son captured. On the 10th the battle started and Somerset, who had placed his army on Falside Hill with Vane and Grey's horse on his right wing, his infantry in the centre and Bryan's cavalry on his left, had a commanding view of the Scots. Angus's men had 18ft (5m) pikes and held off Grey's charge, many horses and men being killed. Gambosa saved the day by attacking Angus with his arquebusiers and directing the cannon on the Scots squares. The Scots now retreated and Clinton's ships added to the toll by firing at the Roman bridge at Musselburgh. Lord Fleming and the Masters of Buchan, Ogilvy, Erskine and Livingstone (all sons of earls) were all killed here. The English lost few men, the most important being Shelley, commander of the Boulogne Horse.

Somerset's 'rough wooing' achieved nothing for Mary married the French dauphin, Francis, and the English were forced to give up all their Scottish possessions in the Treaty of Boulogne (1550).

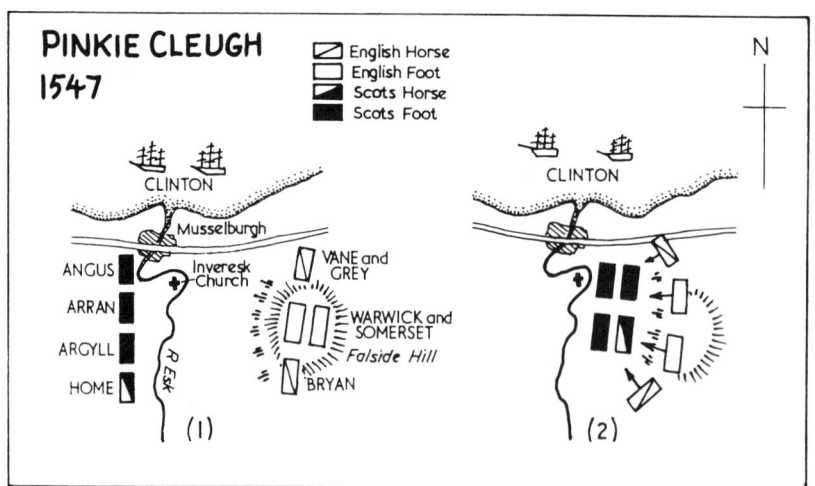

THE BATTLEFIELD TODAY (S)

Falside Castle, Pinkie

There is no monument to Pinkie (which is the name of the burn that the English troops crossed en route for the Scots position). Falside Hill is worth a climb from the roundabout just off the A1. The castle at the top is a private house, but as a tower it would have been useful for Somerset's viewpoint. The old bridge at Musselburgh is now used for pedestrians only and the nearby town Carberry, where Mary Queen of Scots surrendered to the Confederate Lords in June 1567, now belongs to the Church of Scotland and has a candle factory. Although Scotland seems to disown the battle of Pinkie, there is a monument at Bunbury, Cheshire to Sir George Beeston, who died at the age of 102 and fought 'contra Scots apud Muselborrow'.

EDGEHILL
23 October 1642

Whether viewed from Kineton or from its summit, Edge Hill is a great bluff of a hill standing proudly out of the Warwickshire landscape. It was an ideal position for King Charles. He apparently found a local squire out hunting the day before the battle.

'Why aren't you in my cavalry, man, instead of partaking in such a trivial sport when the nation's future is at stake?'

'Yes Your Majesty', said the unfortunate man. The following day his body was one of the many found lying on the field of battle.

Charles I had raised his standard at Nottingham in August 1642 and with his cousin Prince Rupert in command of the cavalry, he moved to Shrewsbury where he gathered his infantry together until he had about 12,000 men, one quarter of whom were cavalry. There was a shortage of arms and some of his artillery had incorrect ammunition, but he was able to march slowly towards London with only Lord Essex and the London trained-bands to stop him. Essex had an army of about 10,000 but less cavalry and very few men with experience of action. On 22 October the first action of the Civil War took place at Powick Bridge when Prince Rupert drove off Fiennes's horse that was attempting to intercept a cavalry-escorted convoy of silver plate for the king's funds. Essex occupied Worcester but Charles bypassed him and camped at Edgecote, site of a battle in the Wars of the Roses, posting his scouts on the top of Edge Hill, where they could keep a watch on Essex's army, now at Kineton.

The battle that took place on 23 October was the first large-scale action of the Civil War. First Charles took his army down off the hill to face Essex at Radway. With Rupert on the right, the Earl of Lindsey in the centre and Lord Wilmot on the left, he had a well-balanced force. His artillery was grouped together in the centre and not far away the royal standard was guarded by Sir Edmund Verney. The parliamentarians had Essex in the middle, Ramsey's horse on the left facing Rupert and Fielding with a mixture of dragoons and

Civil War pot helmet (York Castle Museum) *and Civil War basket handled sword* (York Castle Museum)

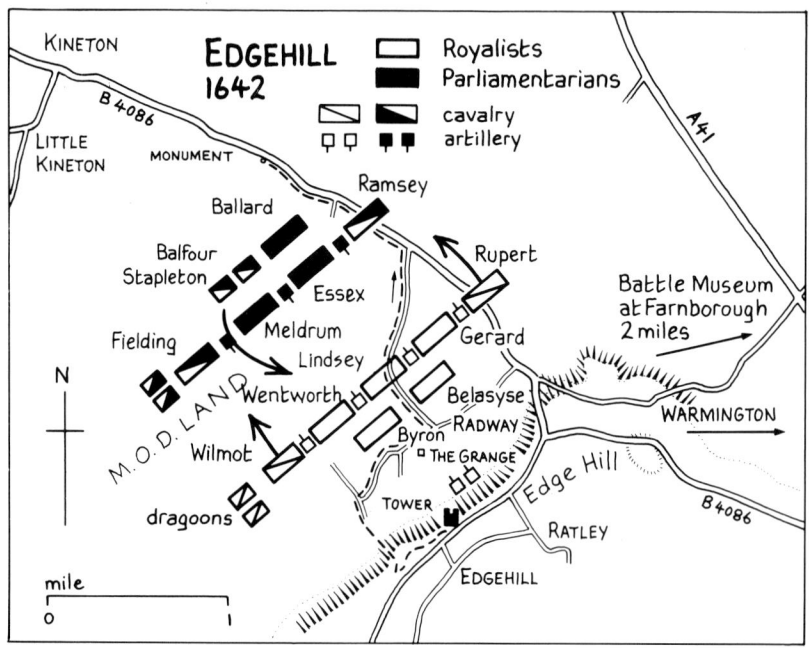

The King's view at Edgehill

horse on the right. In The Oaks were two reserves of horse under Balfour and Stapleton.

The royalist horse on both wings charged, breaking up the horse of both Fielding and Ramsay and chasing them off the ground. The infantry remained fairly static but Stapleton and Balfour, finding that most of Byron's reserve of horse had charged with Rupert, attacked the royalist guns, cut their traces and then wheeled round to attack Verney and the standard. Verney was killed and Lindsey mortally wounded. Fortunately Rupert arrived back in time to save the royalists from defeat and the standard was rescued by Sir John Smith, who was to lose his life at Cheriton in 1644.

The following morning the approach of reinforcements under John Hampden strengthened Essex, who remained on the field. Charles withdrew but the way was open to London and only the trained-bands at Turnham Green prevented the king from getting there.

THE WALK (L)

Starting from the folly, known as Edgehill Tower, built by Sanderson Miller in the late eighteenth century and now an inn, the footpath goes behind the inn and down steeply to the field below, where there is a seat. The monument in the field to your right is nothing to do with the battle. It is a local monument to a man who fought at Waterloo erected by his naval friend. The path goes through a muddy drop into a field and then into a lane leading to Radway green. Here follow the road round past the Grange, where there is a duckpond and attractive garden, but the lawn was used as a helicopter pad when I was there. There are many riders on a Saturday morning using the local stables and, if it was not for the fact that the battlefield is out of bounds to the public as it is army property, Edgehill could make a very interesting walk.

The little church, replacing the old one that was dismantled in the last century as unsafe, has a monument to Captain Kingsmill killed during the battle, erected afterwards by his widow. It badly needs repairing as at some time a local collector removed his helmet and revealed an ugly spike used, unsuccessfully, to hold it down.

The walk continues now along the road to the B4086 to the small cylindrical monument, which on my visit had a wreath placed there by the Thomas Ballard Regiment of the Sealed Knot Society.

TO SEE NEARBY

Edgehill Battle Museum is in the stable block of Farnborough Hall (National Trust) about 5 miles away. It has interesting photographs, relics and a second-hand bookstall.

Cropredy Bridge (see page 130).

Broughton Castle Home of Lord Saye and Sele, who fought for parliament in the battle and whose castle was occupied by the royalists along with Banbury Castle, which no longer exists.

BRADOCK DOWN
19 January 1643

Church gates at Bradock. The parliamentarians had their defences in the field opposite

The start of the Civil War in Cornwall saw the main landowners as royalists but, until they captured three ships at Falmouth belonging to the parliamentary navy, they were very short of arms and ammunition. The Plymouth forces under the Earl of Stamford were solidly for parliament and, under the command of Colonel Ruthven, a Scottish professional soldier, set out in January 1643 towards Lostwithiel. Hopton had his headquarters at Boconnoc House, home of Lord Mohun, and when Ruthven dug in at Bradock Church, he positioned his two small drakes (small cannon) on his left wing behind some gorse with Arundel's horse nearby. In the centre was Grenvile and the infantry and on the right Hopton's horse. Lord Mohun had a small reserve by the house. Ruthven's men were astonished by the fire from the two drakes and early on 19 January the royalists attacked along their line. Ruthven's men put up little resistance, many were captured and Ruthven himself plus a few horses escaped to Saltash where a boat took them into Plymouth. Mohun followed up with his reserve and the parliamentary artillery was all captured intact. Cornwall was cleared of parliamentarians until Essex's ill-fated expedition.

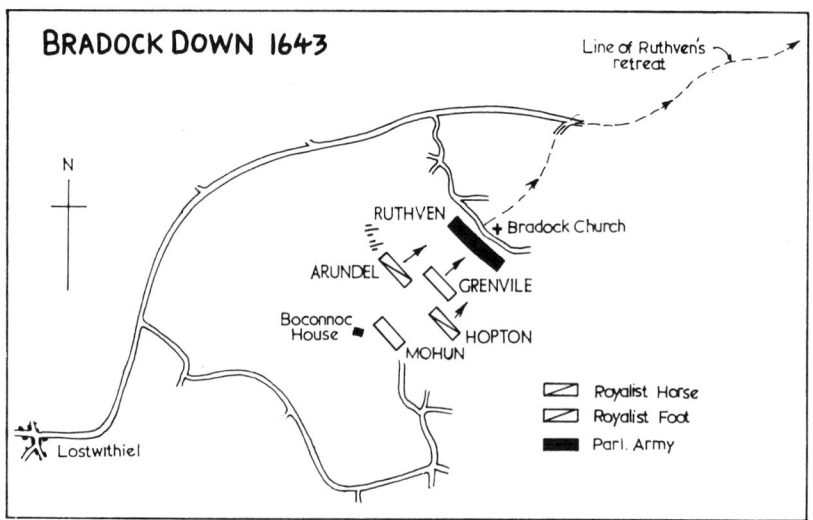

THE BATTLEFIELD TODAY (S)
Bradock Church is easily found by taking the lane off the main A390. The obelisk is nothing to do with the Civil War and Boconnoc Park is private, though the church is open and on the way to it is the flat area where Ruthven's men were drawn up facing south down the hill. There is no monument and it is supposed the dead were buried in one of the many tumuli in the area, one of which is quite near the obelisk. The gardens of Boconnoc Park are occasionally open during the summer and their rhododendrons are worth seeing in full flower. This makes a pleasant outing coupled with a visit to *Lanhydrock* (National Trust) (see *Lostwithiel* page 135).

STRATTON
16 May 1643

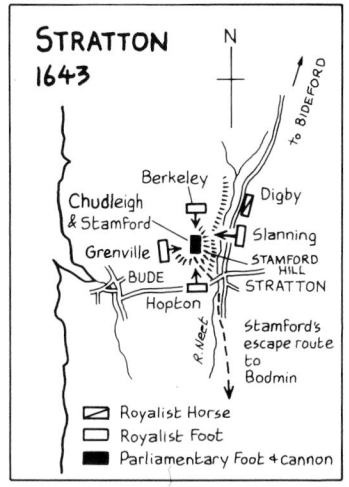

After the royalist victory at Bradock Down, Hopton still required further reinforcements before he could attack Plymouth, which was supplied from the sea. The parliamentary commander in Cornwall early in 1643 was James Chudleigh, and on 25 April Hopton was defeated in a skirmish with Chudleigh at Sourton Down near Tavistock, losing 1,000 muskets and all his correspondence. Stamford now took over from Chudleigh and moved to north Cornwall with an army of 6,800 where he occupied a hill near Stratton commanding the main route between Devon and Cornwall on the north coast. Hopton's army was a mere 3,500 but he was in friendly territory.

The Cornish infantry now came into its own. Hopton moved to Stratton in May and, based at the Tree Inn, divided his army into four groups. Sir John Berkeley commanded the north group, Sir Nicholas Slanning the east, Sir Bevil Grenvile the west and he himself the south group. Digby's horse blocked the road to Bideford and the first attack on the hill was unsuccessful due to Chudleigh's artillery. The royalists were short of ammunition and Hopton gave the order to attack with pike and sword at 3pm. Stamford now escaped to Bodmin with his parliamentary horse, leaving Chudleigh and the infantry on the hill. In spite of a brave fight, Chudleigh was captured along with his guns. Hopton turned these on the remaining parliamentarians, who surrendered. Not only did Hopton capture the artillery, 1,700 prisoners including Chudleigh who became a royalist, 70 powder barrels and £5,000, but also the muskets he had lost at Sourton. It was a great victory and Charles I issued a proclamation at Oxford praising his army. A copy of this can be seen in the church.

THE WALK (M)

Starting at the square in Stratton, look at the church which has the proclamation and one or two other relics of the battle, then cross into Maiden Street and down to the Tree Inn where there is a memorial high up on the wall, that is easy to miss. Perhaps more monuments should be high up to avoid graffiti and damage. Carry on down Bridge Street, round the corner and up Poundfield Lane. This crosses the main A39 road and climbs up towards Stamford Hill. There is a wicket gate leading to the top of the hill, where there is a strange sugarcane-like monument to the battle in a field with, when I was there, a horse that took a keen interest in my sandwiches. The top of the hill is very small and Chudleigh must have been cramped so that an attack was all he could do to avoid being either starved to surrender or attacked on all four sides at once. One of his attackers, Antony Payne, was a 7ft (2m) giant and came from the Tree Inn, where his portrait can be seen along with some scythes said to have been used in the battle.

Plaque on the Tree Inn (D.S.)

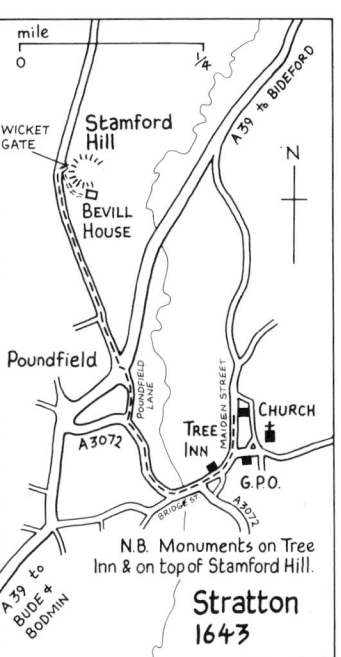

Stratton battlefield and monument (D.S.)

LANSDOWN HILL
5 July 1643

So near Bath, yet out in the country, Lansdown is the end of the ridge. There is a sudden drop until the next hill, Freezing Hill, where Grenvile started his attack. Position yourself behind the stone wall at the area marked 'Gate' on the map and you can imagine the position taken up by Waller in the twilight. His men manned the wall with their muskets and pikes. Fires were lit and kept burning all night so the royalists were deceived. No one saw Waller's retreat and the wall in the morning light was much the same. The pikes and some of the muskets were there but no one behind them. A simple ruse and one that worked.

After Stratton the Cornish army had moved up to Bradford-on-Avon, where Hopton, reinforced by Prince Maurice's cavalry, had an army of 4,800 with 21 guns. Waller, with the remnants of Chudleigh and Stamford's force, and reinforced by Heselrige's 'lobsters', so-called because they were so heavily armed with plate armour, had more foot but slightly less cavalry. He was, however, well supported by cannon, which he used to advantage by occupying Bath and taking up a strong position facing north on Lansdown Hill.

On 5 July Hopton, positioned on Freezing Hill, was out of cannon shot but his first venture to attack Waller was repulsed by 1,000 cavalry and only Maurice's idea of putting infantry with the horse checked the Roundheads so successfully that Grenvile asked to lead the infantry in a suicidal frontal march on the guns. With horse on either side of them and musketeers attempting to encircle Waller, Grenvile attacked. They must have been too low for the guns to hit them until the final 100yd (90m) when the guns opened up and the slaughter was terrible. Some of the horses fled as far as Oxford thinking the day lost. Grenvile was mortally wounded but his servant put young Grenvile on his shoulders and took the lead, so that the Roundheads were pushed back to a defensive wall that must have been near or even the same one that stands today 300yd (275m) behind the monument. When darkness fell Waller retreated on Bath leaving camp fires and pikes and standards in the air to deceive Hopton. In his moment of victory Hopton was blinded by an exploding ammunition cart so that Lansdown remains a drawn battle, though like Newbury I the royalist army remained in control of the field.

THE WALK (L)

Part of the walk takes place on the Cotswold Way so it is well signposted. Starting from the centre of Bath, there is a Badgerline bus to take you up Lansdown Hill as far as the racecourse. Here take the turning that combines the road to the golf course and to the racecourse. It has a triangular (locked) gate but the wall is easy to climb on the left and seems to have had a stile that is now broken. A track leads down to the 6th tee with a wood on the right-hand side. The track dips suddenly but on the right in the wall is a well-made stone stile. Over this and you are on another tee, but the path carries on over a wooden stile and into a large field hugging the left-hand side of the wall. There was a clump of harebells in a dip, that from a distance looked like bluebells. In the nettles a few small tortoiseshell butterflies and, suddenly, three heavily laden Cotswold Way walkers pushed past. The path suddenly turns right by the trig point in the corner of the field. Ahead is a wireless mast and the headquarters of No 12 Observer Group. Through a gate and the nettles give way to a macadam lane that leads out onto the main and busy Lansdown Hill–Bath road. Turn right here and almost immediately cross the road, over a stone

Stone stile on the Landsdown walk. Note the stonework is only partially mortared

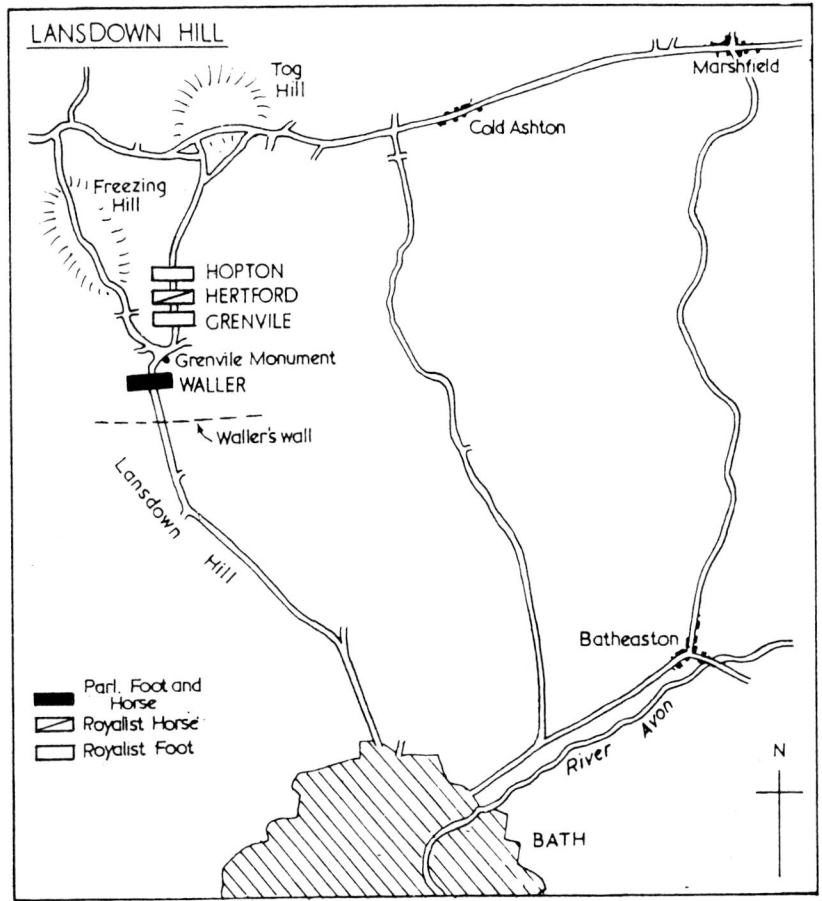

LANSDOWN HILL

Tog Hill
Marshfield
Cold Ashton
Freezing Hill
HOPTON
HERTFORD
GRENVILE
● Grenvile Monument
WALLER
Waller's wall
Lansdown Hill
Batheaston
River Avon
N
BATH

Parl. Foot and Horse
Royalist Horse
Royalist Foot

and wood stile, and there some 200yd (180m) from the road is the Grenvile monument repaired in 1955. The new notice in memory of D. W. Stratford is not correct. Grenvile did not attack alone. His friend Slaning took the musketeers round the flank and there were some of Carnarvon's horse with him. On the back there are some strangely flowery verses by minor poets Cartwright and Llewellen and on the other side an apt description of Grenvile: 'In a word a brighter courage and a gentler disposition were never married together'.

Past the monument there is another stile and the path gets damp and covered in nettles. There are glimpses of nearby Freezing Hill with its earthworks, much older than 1643. Then after some chestnut trees the path comes to a field and goes down the left-hand side under the wall to the corner, where the Cotswold Way drops sharply to the left. Turn right and through a gate to a diagonal track across a field. Your way takes you back to the Lansdown–Bath road and by following this to the left past two fine clumps of beech, to your starting point.

The walk took about 45 minutes and flowers discovered during July were vetch, harebell, knapweed, large thistles, ragwort and cranesbill. Apart from tortoiseshells, there was a small meadow brown butterfly, very few birds but lots of sportsmen around – cyclists, horse riders, golfers (including a learner who needed an 'L' as he was a danger to walkers) and some picnickers. The walk must have been about 3½ miles (5.6km) but could have been longer if one had wanted to descend Hanging Hill to Beach Farm and up the hill to the earthworks on Freezing Hill. Personally I like to keep to ground as flat as possible so as not to break one's stride.

TO SEE NEARBY

Dyrham Park (National Trust) There was a minor battle here at Hinton Hill in AD 577 when the Saxons beat the Britons. Inside the fine seventeenth-century house are some arms, including four 1680 muskets used for defending the house in Monmouth's time.

ROUNDWAY DOWN
13 July 1643

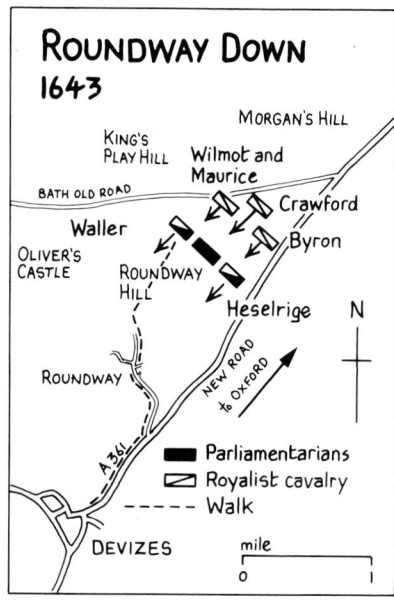

ROUNDWAY DOWN 1643

MORGAN'S HILL
KING'S PLAY HILL
Wilmot and Maurice
BATH OLD ROAD
Crawford
Waller
OLIVER'S CASTLE
Byron
ROUNDWAY HILL
Heselrige
ROUNDWAY
NEW ROAD to OXFORD
N
A361
DEVIZES

■ Parliamentarians
▱ Royalist cavalry
----- Walk

mile
0   1

No better place can be imagined for a cavalry action than Roundway. Lord Wilmot's rush to Oxford for reinforcements and his triumphant return with Prince Maurice, Crawford and Byron, was a great success. This was the zenith of royalist fortune – Waller was truly defeated and it is easy to see where Heselrige's 'lobsters' fell down the steep hill. The ground is still covered in horseshoe tracks, for the area is popular with riders.

Lansdown Hill was a check on Waller, but the royalists, with Hopton's injuries, were in a bad way as they had little ammunition. Bed-cord was used at Devizes, where Hopton camped, to make match for the musketeers. Lord Wilmot went to Oxford for help, having arranged to fire a cannon to alert the Cornish foot they were approaching. With 1,800 horse under Sir John Byron, Crawford and Prince Maurice, Wilmot hurried back from Oxford to find that Waller was waiting for him on Roundway Down. Heselrige's heavy horse was on his right wing, his foot was in the centre and his own horse on the left was double the number of Wilmot's horse. However before the enemy's forlorn hope reached their ranks, Wilmot charged and both cavalry wings turned and fled. Heselrige fought bravely but his horse was forced back down the slope and many were killed.

Bassett led the Cornish infantry up the hill, having heard the signal cannon, and challenged Waller's abandoned infantry. Wilmot captured Waller's cannon and threatened to shoot the enemy's infantry unless they surrendered. This was the greatest royalist victory of the Civil War and only Waller and a handful of his cavalry escaped to Bristol and Gloucester.

TO SEE NEARBY

Devizes Museum This has a fine library, where there is information on the battle as well as examples of weapons of Alfred's time that might have been used at Edington.

Littlecote Park, Newbury Colonel Popham from Littlecote took part in the battle and was one of the parliamentarians to escape with Waller. Littlecote today is open to the public and has a fine collection of Civil War armour as well as being used by the Sealed Knot and other groups as a site for battle re-enactments.

THE WALK (M)
Leave Devizes by the London Road and walk past the Police Station taking the road to Roundway village. Carry on through this to Roundway Hill, where the track ends and there is a large stand of fir trees. The open ground ahead is Roundway Down and the battle must have taken place here and to the left, for Waller managed to escape by riding along the ridge until it was safe to descend and retreat towards Bristol.

There is another viewpoint from Morgan's Hill opposite the North Wiltshire Golf Club, but this means a detour as there is no footpath across the down.

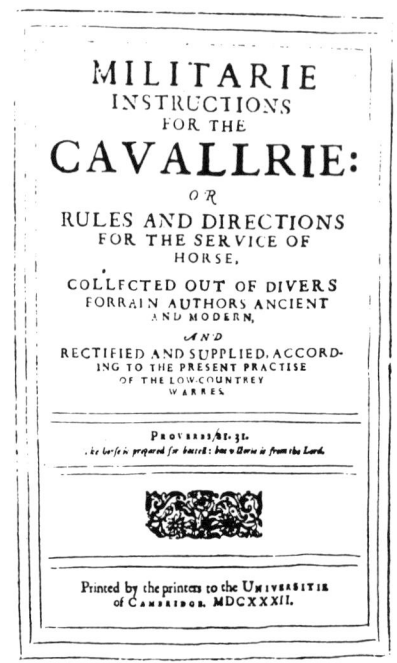

MILITARIE INSTRUCTIONS FOR THE CAVALLRIE:

OR

RULES AND DIRECTIONS FOR THE SERVICE OF HORSE.

COLLECTED OUT OF DIVERS FORRAIN AUTHORS ANCIENT AND MODERN,

AND

RECTIFIED AND SUPPLIED, ACCORDING TO THE PRESENT PRACTISE OF THE LOW-COUNTREY WARRES.

PROVERBS XXI. 31.
the horse is prepared for battel: but victorie is from the Lord.

Printed by the printers to the UNIVERSITIE of CAMBRIDGE. MDCXXXII.

Title page from an early cavalry Manual (National Army Museum)

NEWBURY I
20 September 1643

The first battle of Newbury came about when the royalists withdrew their blockade of Gloucester and allowed the Earl of Essex to relieve the town with an army of 15,000, many of which were London trained-bands under General Skippon. The king had Rupert's horse and that of Sir John Byron, as well as Nicholas Byron's and Lisle and Wentworth's infantry. He had a large, mixed artillery battery but was light in ammunition. Essex's army was reduced by almost a third after leaving men in Gloucester and his horse was beaten by Rupert at *Aldbourne Chase*. The way was open to Rupert and he occupied the Wash Common area of Newbury, blocking Essex's route. With the arrival of Essex next day the royalists were in position down the Andover road and Essex remained on the ground to the left and right of Wash Common Farm. His artillery at Round Hill commanded the only high ground.

The king's troops moved up in the morning and blocked the hedges of Dark Lane (now no longer) and their artillery fired across the common from Battery End. Rupert's charge was held in check by the trained-bands, who fought bravely all day. Falkland was killed in Byron's charge across the field near Dark Lane. The battle lasted until dark with Essex concentrating his forces on Round Hill, which the royalists failed to capture. The king withdrew in the dark, his ammunition exhausted, and the way was open for Essex to return a hero to London.

Falkland memorial, Newbury

Aldbourne Chase where Rupert won a cavalry skirmish before Newbury

LORD FALKLAND

As his monument is the main sight at Newbury, the career of this remarkable young man should be looked at in detail. His father, Sir Henry Cary of Aldenham Hall, near Watford, married Elizabeth, daughter and heiress of Sir Lawrence Tanfield of Burford. Lord Tanfield's monument can be seen in Burford Church together with an effigy supposed to be their grandson.

Lucius Cary was born about 1610 and inherited his father's title and estates in September 1633. He was a scholar and friend of Cowley, Ben Jonson and Suckling. When he volunteered to fight against the Scots at Newcastle in 1639, his friend Cowley wrote:

Great is thy charge O North be wise
and just,
England commits her Falkland to
thy trust,
Return him safe; learning would
rather choose
Her Bodley or her Vatican to lose.

Lucius returned safely and entered parliament as member for Newport in 1640. He made speeches on episcopacy and on the Ship Money bill. In January 1641 he became a Secretary of State and member of the Privy Council. He was present at the raising of the standard at Nottingham and at Edgehill. At Newbury he was in the front rank of Lord Byron's regiment, and charging through a hedge received a musket ball in the stomach which killed him instantly. His body was not found until the following day and Prince Rupert wrote to Essex saying, 'We desire to known from the Earl of Essex whether he have the Viscount Falkland, Capt. Bertie and Sgt. Major Wiltshire prisoners or whether he have their dead bodies'. One of Falkland's servants was sent to fetch his master's body and it was buried at Great Tew Church in Oxfordshire.

There were other notable people killed at Newbury, but Lord Falkland was the essence of seventeenth-century aristocracy, rather like Sydney at Zutphen, and his death was a great loss to the king.

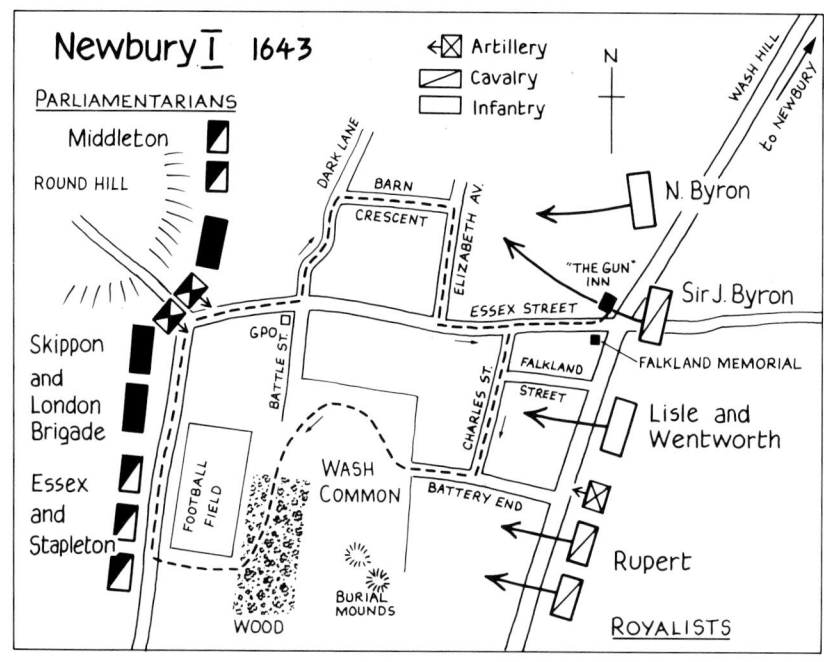

THE WALK (M)

Newbury I occupies an area mostly covered in houses today. Start at the Gun Inn, walk across the road to see the Falkland Monument with lines from Burke on the reverse:

The blood of man is well shed for our family,
for our God, for our Country, for our kind.
The rest is vanity. The rest is crime.

S. R. Gardiner calls him the 'noblest of the King's supporters a prophet whose vision of peace was too pure and too harmonious to allay the discords of his own day'. From the monument carry on down Essex Street, then turn left down Charles Street, right into Battery End and you are in the recreation ground. Here are the two great burial mounds with their Victorian stones, which were put there at the time of the Diamond Jubilee in 1897.

Over the common and into the wood on the other side – firs and oaks with a mass of leaves in September. Through the wood and one meets the football field and the attractive Wash Common Farmhouse. Here turn right and back to Essex Street where there is a footpath opposite the Post Office at the end of Battle Street. Take this footpath, which passes close to a house and garden and is, in fact, Dark Lane; but the field on the left where much of the battle was fought is private. Alas, the path soon stops at Barn Crescent (a few years ago it went right down to the other side of the field). Turn down the crescent and back down Elizabeth Avenue to Essex Street and the Gun Inn; time about 30 minutes.

WINCEBY
11 October 1643

One of the lesser known battles of the Civil War was fought at Winceby, a small hamlet east of Horncastle on the road to Old Bolingbroke. The royalist governor of Newark, Sir John Henderson, with Widdrington, his second-in-command, set out to relieve Bolingbroke Castle, besieged by Cromwell's horse recently returned from Hull where they had been reinforced by the horse of Sir Thomas Fairfax. The parliamentary scouts were very efficient and soon spotted the royalist force making for Bolingbroke. Lining the top of Winceby ridge, Cromwell charged the enemy before they had time to form up properly. Cromwell's horse was killed under him and it was Fairfax who won the day by first moving to the right and then to the left across Cromwell's front to attack Savile, who commanded the royalist right and had got out of position. Savile's men were trapped in a field with high hedges and a gate that opened the wrong way. He was captured and many of his troopers killed. In Slash Hollow a large stone by the road is where the battle took place. In spite of being knocked down, Cromwell remounted and his second charge, supported by Fairfax, routed the royalists – who retreated to Newark losing supplies and 1,000 prisoners – securing Lincolnshire for parliament.

THE BATTLEFIELD TODAY (S)
Slash Hollow is easily found below Winceby petrol station. There is little change to spoil the scene today. In spite of there being a Nature Reserve nearby there is no obvious battlefield walk.

Old Bolingbroke Castle is now a substantial ruin in the hands of English Heritage and well worth a visit. It stands on flat land below the church, and the church tower is probably the best place to take photographs. Famous as the birthplace of Henry IV, it is a pleasant place off the main road and both Winceby and Bolingbroke Castle would make pleasant stops on a cycle ride from Lincoln.

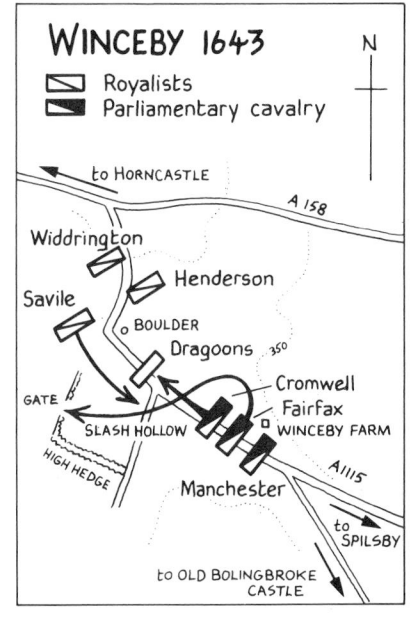

Winceby battlefield

NEWARK
21 March 1644

The royalists garrisoned Newark at the start of the Civil War with a governor. The town became one of the best fortified towns of the war. On one side the Trent, on the other the city walls, and the defenders built two star forts or sconces, one of which, the Queen's Sconce, still survives, if in rather a battered and uncared for form. The town had been fortified before at the time of the Pilgrimage of Grace (1536) and the defenders improved these fortifications, rebuilding them where necessary. After Winceby, the new governor, Richard Byron, was nearly isolated and in March 1644 Meldrum pressed an attack on the Spittal, situated near the King's Sconce. Byron sent for help from Prince Rupert and in March the latter assembled an army at Bridgworth, using Tillier's newly arrived troops from Ireland and the survivors of Lord Byron's cavalry, recently defeated by Fairfax at Nantwich.

Meldrum's army was situated on the Island, the area between the Devon and the Trent, north of Newark. By 20 March Rupert's army of 6,000 was past Balderton and camped on Beacon Hill, having circled round Newark to approach Meldrum from the north east. Dividing his horse into three groups, he took command of the right wing, Sir Richard Crane the left and Gerard the centre. Lord Loughborough commanded the reserve and Tillier, who arrived late, was instructed to attack Meldrum's bridge of boats at Winthorpe over the Trent. Byron took a large force of horse and infantry to attack Muskham and the parliamentary troops from Norfolk fled burning the bridge behind them. The royalist cavalry charged three times to dislodge Thornhagh and Rossiter's cavalry. The attack was successful, though Rossiter managed to capture Gerard. The hard-pressed parliamentary commander, Meldrum, surrendered next day, being short of food. Rupert allowed his army to march away, officers keeping their swords, but he captured their baggage train and 3,000 muskets and ammunition. All outposts at Gainsborough, Lincoln, Sleaford and Crowland were overrun and Newark held out until 1646 when Lord Belasyse, the then governor, only surrendered at the request of the king.

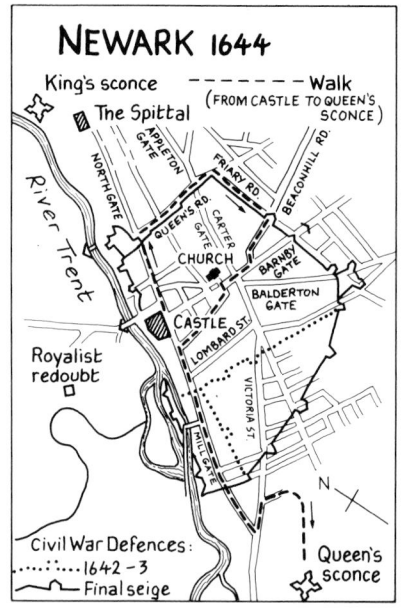

THE WALK (L)

Starting from the castle, where King John died, cross Beastmarket Hill to The Ossington, dating from 1881 and a coffee shop today. Turn left into Bargate and cross the road into Slaughterhouse Lane. This is the town wall area and a small piece of reconstructed town wall with a plaque can be seen on the corner of Northgate. Carry on down Northgate and turn right into Queen's Road. Turn right into Friary Road, then right again to the church, St Mary Magdalene, one of the largest parish churches in the country. It was badly damaged in May 1646 by the parliamentary army and only the glass in the east window of the south choir (fourteenth century) remains from before this date. Outside the church there are some fine buildings to see in Market Square. Note the Ye Olde White Hart, a fine example of early domestic architecture, and in Stodman Street the Governor's House (now two shops – Ernest Rick clothiers and Ye Old Governor's Tobacco Shoppe) where the Newark governors lived during the siege. Sir Richard Willis, one of the last, was dismissed for siding with Prince Rupert in his quarrel with the king in October 1645 following the loss of Bristol.

Follow on down Stodman Street into Castle Gate which leads to narrow Mill Gate, where there is a small museum that has siege relics and some of the

Newark siege coins. Mill Lane leads into Victoria Street, where there is a children's playground in Boundary Road that has the Queen's Sconce in the middle of it. It has four angle bastions that could hold two cannon, with space for a regiment of foot to camp in the centre. The pits round the outside kept out cavalry and there were other pits filled with spikes in the Bannockburn calthrop tradition. The King's Sconce in Malt Kiln Lane north of the town is no longer visible, but drawings of other works can be seen in the publication *Newark on Trent, the Civil War Siegeworks* (HMSO, 1964).

The walk can be completed by returning to the centre down Victoria Street, Beaumond Cross and Carter Gate back to Market Square. Return to the castle, where the best view for photography purposes is across Trent Bridge on the Island. There is a water bus in summer for tourists.

BASING HOUSE

Originally a motte and bailey castle, Basing is not built in an obvious place for a castle. It had a shell keep, unusual for a motte of Norman date. The visible remains are of the mid-sixteenth century and date from the Paulet's inheritance; Sir William Paulet, first Marquess of Winchester, crenellated the house in 1531. It was built of brick with five towers, only one of which can be seen today. The fifth marquess fortified the house for King Charles and the architect, Inigo Jones, was one of the royalists who took shelter there.

In 1644 Colonel Norton besieged Basing and a message reached Oxford that the marquess could only hold out for a further ten days. Colonel Gage offered to lead a relieving force. Two hundred and fifty horse were assembled, made up of servants and volunteers, and equipped with a number of packhorses carrying supplies of food and ammunition. Gage asked the marquess to make a sally when he approached to draw off the besiegers.

Proceeding on a Monday via Wallingford and Aldermaston, where some parliamentary soldiers were captured, on the Wednesday his troops arrived before Basing. With white scarves on their right arms and using the watchword 'St George', they attacked Norton's horse and reached the entrance of the house, where they were quickly admitted by the marquess.

Gage unloaded his ammunition – 12 barrels of powder – then left for Basingstoke where he found wheat, malt, bacon, cheese, butter and 100 sheep. His horse returned to Basing, beat off the enemy, some of whom took refuge in the church where they were captured. Gage spent the rest of the day getting the carts into the house, together with another 14 barrels of powder. At midnight on the Thursday, Gage passed silently over the Kennet by a ford, then over the Thames by another ford a mile from Reading, and reached Wallingford. Gage reached Oxford the following day, having lost 11 men with about 40 wounded but bringing in at least 100 prisoners. It was a gallant feat and Gage should have been promoted. Instead he was killed trying to break down Culham Bridge at Abingdon later in 1644. King Charles had knighted him and 'sustained a wonderful loss in his death, he being a man of great wisdom and temper'.

Basing finally fell to Cromwell on 15 October 1645 after a seven-day siege. Heavy artillery broke down the walls and a fierce attack captured the house. Inigo Jones was led out wrapped in a blanket and all the contents were looted. All the Catholic books, rosaries and pictures were placed in a waggon and taken to London for a public bonfire. The road to London was now open and Cromwell dismantled the house so completely that very little remains to be seen today.

Gates of Basing House

CHERITON
29 March 1644

Cheriton is a confusing battlefield. To understand it you must put yourself in Waller's position. He camped at Hinton Ampner and put his artillery on the road facing his enemy, and only by looking from this viewpoint can you understand the royalist action. They wanted to clear the wood on their left flank first and had they not been forced to attack piecemeal due to the nature of the ground with its hedges and lanes the outcome could have been different.

My first visit to Cheriton was shortly after the battle had been re-fought by the Sealed Knot. There were a few wounded men sitting by the road after this and, as explained on page 108, the casualty ward at the hospital must have raised a few eyebrows at the sight of a bleeding pikeman, with pike, walking down their corridor.

Early in 1644 the king at Oxford received fresh supplies of arms from abroad and Hopton's army, reinforced by the aged Earl of Forth, guarded the road to Winchester which was threatened by Waller who had already captured Alton. Forth moved to Alresford before Waller and on 28 March the two armies faced each other between Alresford and Hinton Ampner. Each army was about 10,000 strong with little to choose between them. Waller had spent the night at Hinton Ampner House and arranged his artillery on the site of the modern road. He put his horse in two divisions in the field below and a part of his foot into Cheriton wood. The map shows the position of the sides after Appleyard had cleared Leighton's men from the wood. It was a strange thing to do – the artillery were ineffective as they would have shot up their own men. The royalists occupied the ridge above, but the only route down was by a sunken lane. Hopton sent Colonel Appleyard with musketeers and pikes to clear the wood. This he did, but before advantage could be taken of this success, young Sir Henry Bard had charged on the other wing, where his horse were quickly surrounded and cut to pieces. The same thing happened to

(pp 126–7)
The Sealed Knot musketeers in action
(Dodgson)

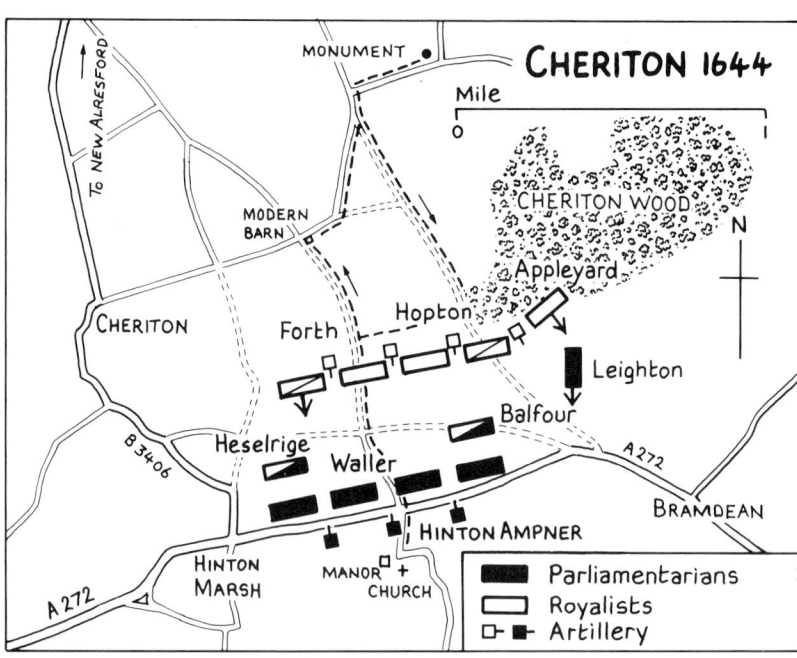

Edward Stawell, who was captured. Heselrige, who had spied a gap between the royalist foot and horse, moved forward and Forth was compelled to retreat. Among the killed were Lord John Stuart and Sir John Smith, who had rescued the colours at Edgehill. Waller was triumphant but his horse did not follow up the victory and Forth and Hopton retreated in good order to Basing House, setting fire to Alresford on the way.

Cheriton battlefield today

THE WALK (L)

Start from Hinton Ampner Church; Hinton Ampner means 'the high farm of the almoner' (of St Swithun's Priory). Inside the little church are the Stawell tombs and the church door erected in 1643, the year before the battle. Hinton Ampner House nearby is open under the National Trust.

Down the path to the main road (A272 Petersfield to Winchester); a few miles to the left is the hollow where General Eisenhower addressed the troops before D-Day in 1944, called Cheesefoot Head on the Ordnance Survey map. The path goes straight opposite the road to the church and passes a few cottages before entering the lane. Carry on between two high banks, which are a mass of blackberries, hips and other autumnal display in September. There is a pronounced rise, followed by a dip which must have been the ridge occupied by Hopton and Forth. Carry on along the farm track until you come to a modern barn and the lane to North End. Turn right here and up the hill where a path forks off to the right; avoid this and carry on up the hill, where turn right and the new monument is on the left. It was erected in 1973 and had some faded wreaths on it. Retrace your steps a little, then the path back goes straight down the drove to the corner of Cheriton Wood (Forestry Commission and mostly closed to the public as it is used by a shooting syndicate). Here turn sharp right; you are now on a bridleway and end up at the top of Hopton's ridge where you are back on the narrow lane to Hinton Ampner.

CROPREDY BRIDGE
29 June 1644

The Oxford canal at Cropredy. Battlefield walk goes down right hand tow path

The defeat of Hopton at Cheriton meant the king was forced to abandon his garrisons at Abingdon and Reading. Oxford was nearly surrounded so Charles decided to make a break out and head for Worcester. He had hoped to meet Rupert there after the latter had relieved York. Reaching Banbury, Charles moved towards Daventry closely followed by Waller. For a day the River Cherwell separated the two armies, Waller having about 6,000, including some artillery commanded by James Wemyss, which slowed him down. However he captured Cropredy Bridge before Charles could get there. The royalists, numbering about 7,000, were strong in cavalry, both Charles and the Earl of Cleveland having troops of horse, with the Earl of Brentford commanding the foot. Waller sent Middleton with his horse to capture the ford at Slat Mill, Colonel Birch to hold the bridge while he attacked the royalist van at Ayle's Bridge on the road to Chipping Warden. The Earl of Northampton, only a teenager, led the royalist cavalry against Middleton and drove him back over the river, Cleveland took Waller in the rear and captured

CROPREDY BRIDGE

Coventry
Mollington

Daventry ↑ Chipping Warden

Ayle's Bridge

(Royalist vanguard)

WALLER

Wardington

Cropredy
BIRCH

CLEVELAND

Cherwell

N

MIDDLETON
Slat Mill

BRENTFORD
AND CHARLES

Banbury ↓   ↓ Banbury

Parl. guns
Parl. Horse
Parl. Foot
Royalist Horse
Royalist Foot

Wemyss and his guns. Only Birch held out for a time on the bridge and Waller escaped with difficulty, his army mutinous and demanding their back pay. Charles was left with a clear road to the West. It was to be his last victory.

THE WALK (L)

Cropredy Bridge has been rebuilt since the one held by Birch and the latest bridge dates from the 1930s. There is a plaque on both sides. The football field is the best place to take photographs but the gate to it is sometimes locked. From the gate cross the road to the shop and take the steps down to the canal path; follow this to the footbridge where cross over into Red Lion Street. There is a gate into the churchyard and until recently there was some armour there that had been dug up on the river bank. Leave the church by the other path and go down Station Road turning left by the school, then into a field that leads to a canal bridge. Cross this and turn left back to the shop. It is a pleasant walk lasting about an hour depending on how long you spend in the church. The Brasenose Inn is worth a visit and near it the 'cup and saucer', a stone trough and bowl of unknown date. Cropredy is within easy cycling distance of Edgehill and if you include Edgehill Museum at Farnborough, the three sites make a good circular route. Another way of visiting Cropredy is by boat along the Oxford Canal. Holiday barges can be hired at Aynho basin.

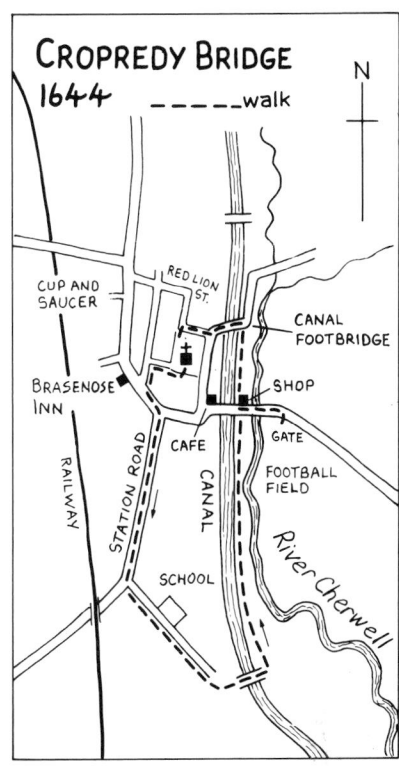

Cropredy Bridge – rebuilt in the 1930s

MARSTON MOOR
2 July 1644

The largest battle of the Civil War took place outside York where the Marquis of Newcastle was besieged by three parliamentary armies: the Eastern Association under Manchester; the Scots commanded by Alexander Leslie, Earl of Leven; and the Fairfaxes who had defeated royalist forces at Nantwich, Cheshire, in January and at Selby in April. However Prince Rupert had rescued Newark where he beat Meldrum in March (see page 122). So help was on its way and, with a force of about 8,000, Rupert was joined by Goring and Lucas on 1 June with 5,000 horse and 800 infantry. Starting from Lathom House he crossed the Pennines and was at Knaresborough Castle by 30 June. The parliamentary army moved to Long Marston to block the road to York, but Rupert moved to Boroughbridge, Overton and Poppleton where he seized a bridge of boats guarded ineffectively by Manchester's dragoons. York was relieved on 1 July. Rupert determined to give battle at once and reluctantly Newcastle and Eythin, in charge of the foot, had to agree, though the foot took a long time to get to Long Marston.

Sir Bernard de Gomme has left an accurate picture of the troops drawn up for battle and this can be seen in the British Museum. On the left the parliamentarians had Cromwell and the Scots cavalry under David Leslie, then Crawford and Manchester's foot in two lines, then Lumsden and Baillie's foot with Fairfax's foot behind and on the right wing Thomas Fairfax's horse and the rest of the Scots horse. Opposite Cromwell was Byron's horse with Goring on the left wing and Newcastle's infantry, commanded by Eythin and Tillier, in the centre. Rupert kept his horse and that of Blakiston in the rear. The royalists were outnumbered by about 8,000; the parliamentary army was about 27,000 men.

Basket-handled sword from York Castle Museum (c. 1640)

Cavalier sword from York Castle collection. Note picture of King Charles I in the basket work

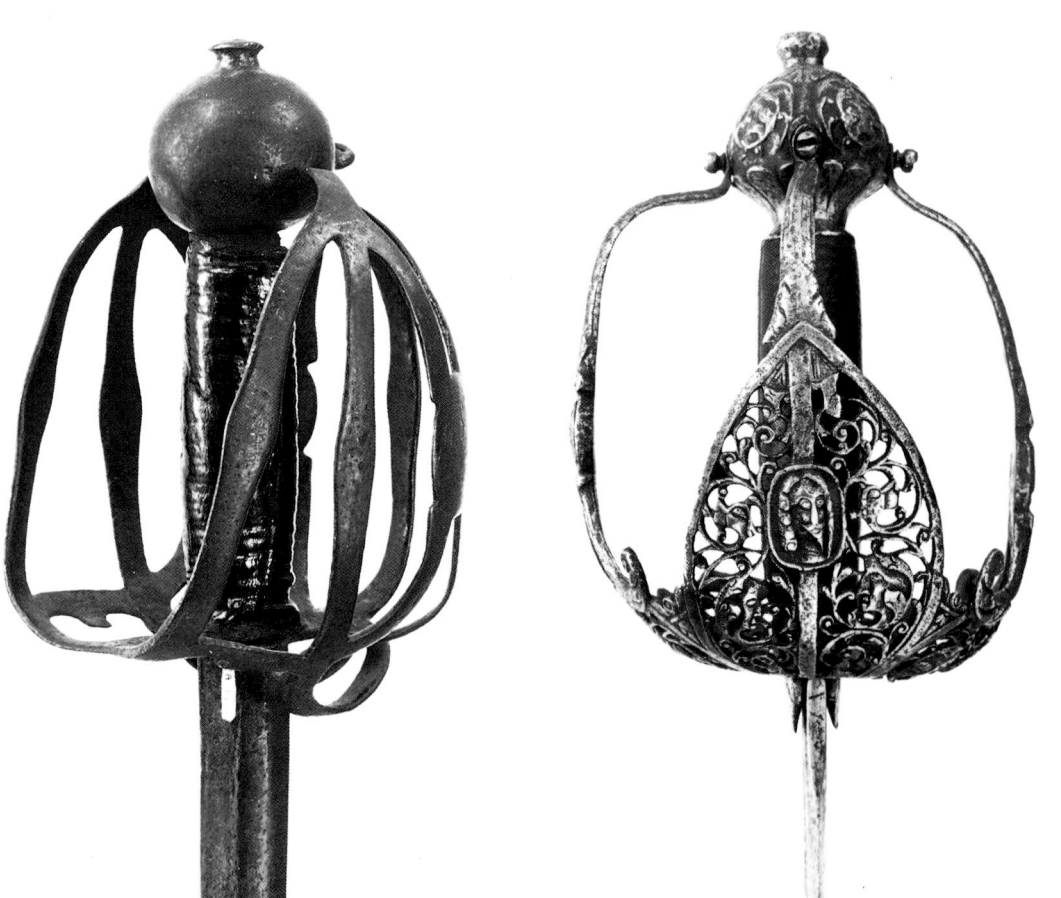

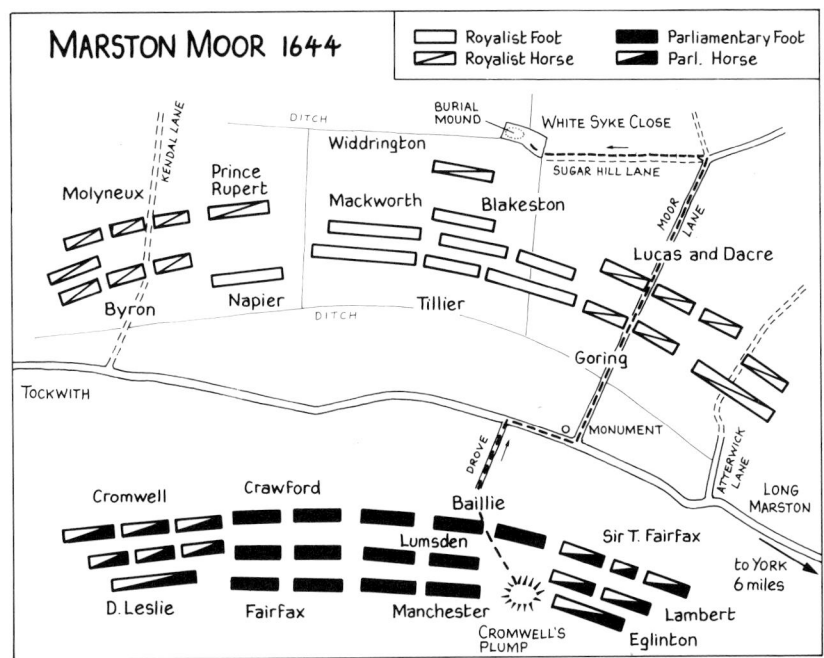

MARSTON MOOR 1644

Legend:
- ▭ Royalist Foot
- ▨ Royalist Horse
- ▬ Parliamentary Foot
- ◤ Parl. Horse

Map labels: DITCH, BURIAL MOUND, WHITE SYKE CLOSE, Widdrington, KENDAL LANE, Molyneux, Prince Rupert, Mackworth, Blakeston, SUGAR HILL LANE, MOOR LANE, Lucas and Dacre, Napier, Tillier, DITCH, Byron, Goring, TOCKWITH, MONUMENT, DROVE, ATTERWICK LANE, LONG MARSTON, Cromwell, Crawford, Baillie, Lumsden, Sir T. Fairfax, to YORK 6 miles, D. Leslie, Fairfax, Manchester, CROMWELL'S PLUMP, Eglinton, Lambert

The battle started with a short artillery duel, but the enemy advanced on Rupert's lines at about 7pm when many of the royalist officers had retired to their carriages for dinner. On the left Goring chased most of the Scots horse off the field. On the right Cromwell was wounded but his men pushed back the royalist horse. In the centre the fight was long and fairly even until Cromwell returned to the action and, much later, the Whitecoats were forced into White Syke Close, where many were cut down and the survivors eventually surrendered. Rupert was unhorsed and hid in a beanfield, Goring was finally pushed back by Fairfax and although many ran away before knowing the outcome of the battle, the parliamentarians won a great victory. York was captured a few days later and Newcastle fled abroad. Rupert fled to Lancashire with the remnants of his cavalry and the parliamentarians split up, the Scots going home.

It was a triumph for Fairfax and Cromwell, but it was also a costly victory and only the king's victory at *Cropedy Bridge* which had taken place on 29 June prevented an Allied attack on Oxford.

THE WALK (M)

Marston Moor is about 7 miles (11km) west of York and the monument stands beside the B1224 to Tockwith. There is an easy stroll up the drove opposite the monument and then across the field to Cromwell's Plump, a group of three trees ringed by a fence marking the highest point of the slope. Here stood the Scots horse and later Goring's horse after it had advanced and driven off the Scots. Opposite one can see the royalist positions, now well-cultivated farming land. Returning to the monument take the lane, known as Moor Lane, which runs from the monument for about ¾ mile (1km) until it divides, where climb the gate on the left and you are now in what is left of White Syke Close. Here on my visit there were calves grazing and one well-grassed mound, which is about all one can see of the burial mounds today. There was a family of partridge scurrying about and it was very peaceful in early September. It looked a good place for blackberries and there were blue scabius and ragged-robin flowers in the ditch. The armies must have covered a very wide area but unfortunately there are no footpaths, so a circular walk is not possible.

LATHOM HOUSE

One of the most gallant events of the Civil War was the defence of Lathom House, home of Lord Derby near Ormskirk, Lancashire, against Fairfax's army in two sieges. A large rambling building with nine towers, one of which had a clock and was known as the Eagle Tower, Lord Derby left it in 1643 leaving behind Lady Derby, the children and a garrison of 300 men, 12 horses and a good supply of food and ammunition. He went over to the Isle of Man to see to his property there and, when he left, Lathom was not threatened by the parliamentarians.

However Fairfax arrived in March 1644 and arranged for Colonel Rigby to besiege the place. The besiegers had some heavy cannon, including a large mortar that did some damage – knocking down the clock and also breaking Lady Derby's bedroom ceiling. A sortie led by Captain Rawsthorne and including the twelve horse, captured this mortar and dragged it inside the house's two lines of defences.

Captain Chisenhale led another sortie and captured one of the engineers, who was able to give information on the parliamentary mining plans, so that the next attack was defeated. The defenders were organised so that half were on duty while the other half rested. All went well and in reply to Rigby's summons to surrender, the countess sent the following reply:

'Tell that insolent rebel he shall neither have persons, goods nor house, when our strength and provision is spent, we shall find a fine more merciful than Rigby, and then if the providence of God prevent it not, my goods and house shall burn in his sight; myself, children and soldiers rather than fall into his hands, will seal our religion and loyalty in the same flame.'

On 27 May Prince Rupert, having captured Liverpool, relieved the house and escorted the brave countess and her family to the boat for the Isle of Man. Colonel Vere was put in command of the house and the second siege started after Marston Moor. It lasted until December 1645, when Rigby commented on the 'smell and taste of their garments' being noticeable when his envoy visited Vere. On 3 December the royalists finally surrendered due to shortage of food and marched out, officers keeping their swords, to Aberconway. Lathom was completely destroyed and there is nothing there today.

Parliamentary helmet (York Castle Museum)

LOSTWITHIEL
2 September 1644

The victory of Cropredy Bridge in June 1644 and the entry of Essex into the West Country gave Charles 1 the great chance to block up the parliamentary army in pro-royalist country. Essex relied on his fleet for supplies so when he reached Cornwall he occupied Lostwithiel, as its small port at Fowey could be reached from Plymouth with supplies. Grenvile's army of 2,400 came up and stopped his further advance and the king with about 14,000 prevented any return. Essex had a mere 10,000 and was short of food and the wet weather had deprived his men of dry shoes and clothing. Morale was low, and only Balfour's horse succeeded in breaking out and reaching Plymouth in the early hours of 31 August.

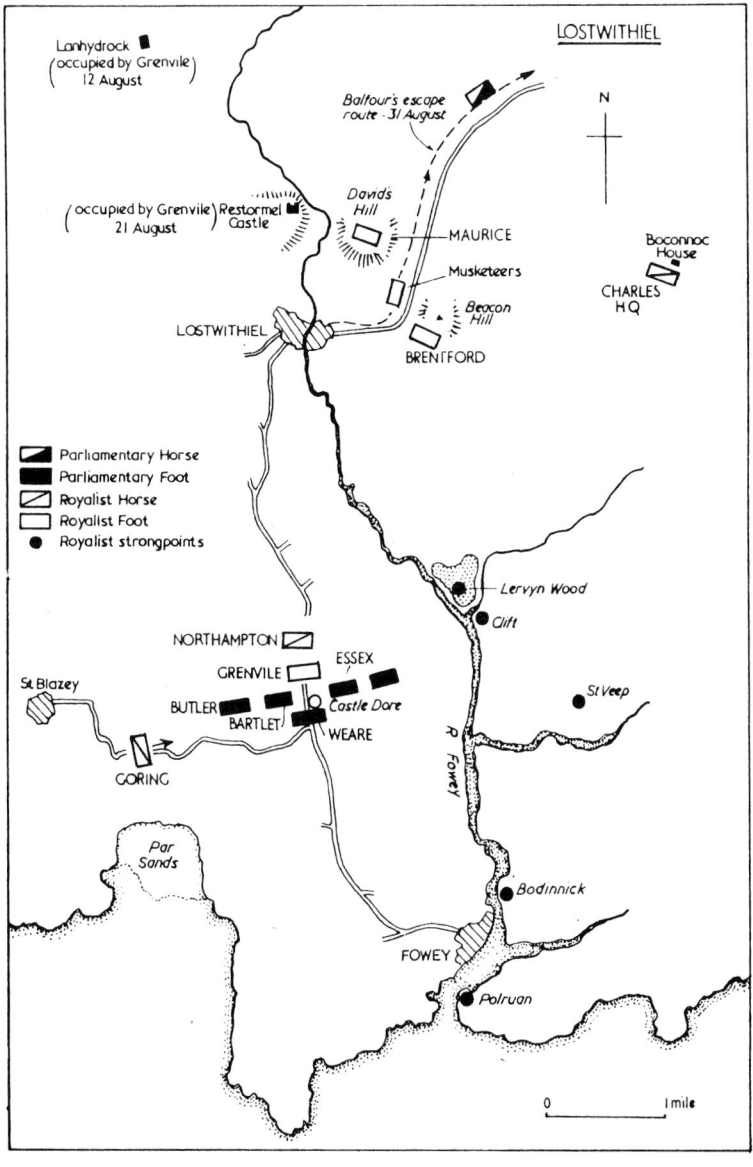

Restormel Castle

Grenvile captured Lanhydrock House, home of Lord Robartes who had commanded parliamentary infantry at Newbury, then moved on Restormel Castle. Castle Dore was the last place to surrender and Skippon, who took over after Essex left by boat, finally surrendered 6,000 men. It was a great royalist triumph. Unfortunately the king was too lenient with his prisoners and, though they were marched to Portsmouth, Skippon and others quickly escaped to rejoin the colours and play a major part in the final battle at Naseby.

THE WALK (L)

As the Battle of Lostwithiel took place in several unconnected areas round the town, the walk we have selected is Sir Richard Grenvile's route between Lord Robartes's House, Lanhydrock, and the Norman castle of Restormel; but we will make the walk in reverse. This 3 mile (5km) walk took Grenvile's men nine days but the walk below took three hours, allowing at least forty minutes at Lanhydrock, which is a good place for a break, and has a restaurant.

Leaving the car park at Restormel go down the road to the farm. There is no sign, but it is a public road to the front of the farm's very neat and tidy garden and round to the road leading to Restormel Waterworks. The road has a grassy bank and it is in shade most of the way. At one stage – this was late July – I had to stand in the ditch as the flail tractor went past cutting the beech hedge mercilessly. There were a few fishermen about, otherwise no one to be seen. In fact my companions on the walk were a tortoiseshell butterfly, a hawk and numerous very shorn-looking sheep.

The waterworks loomed ahead as the metal road comes to an end. The path now goes through two fields, the first had barley and the second, protected by rough hedges, was a mass of wild flowers. I found bird's-foot trefoil, vetch, honeysuckle, pink campion and marjoram. The beech hedges gave way to a rust-red coloured gate and through this I found myself in a wood. Ahead was a dried-up stream-bed full of stones, old branches and sand. It turned into a path on the left and taking this way I soon turned right again and through a clearing to, in about 100yd (90m), another red gate into a clearing. Later I read that a Victorian Lord Robartes wanted carriage drives between all his property so this is one of them and it makes a good footpath. The walker is now in a wood with tall beech trees, fir and some silver birch. There are rhododendrons, for which Lanhydrock is famous, and at last a bright blue hydrangea beside a seat. Here I had my picnic and nearly left my camera behind as, standing up, one can just see the house on the left above the trees.

There is another gate and then you are in the barton of the house by the carriage house and plant nursery. The entrance is on the left and the first room you come into has a portrait of John Robartes MP who fought for parliament at Edgehill, Newbury I and then came back to Cornwall as field marshal with a small army as most of Cornwall was royalist. Ousted by Grenvile he escaped to Plymouth with Lord Essex and became governor of the town during the siege. He fell out with Cromwell and took no further part in proceedings of state, spending his time planting trees on his estate and completing his house. Finally he became a royalist and Charles II created him Lord Radnor. This explains why Lanhydrock is in such good condition in spite of a disastrous fire in 1881.

After the visit to the house and church, go out of the park down the drive past the car park to the left. Then turn right past the Estate Office and keep right to come out on the road opposite the cricket ground, in use as I went past. The last Lord Robartes was a keen cricketer and his study has some ancient MCC photographs including one of a team on a ship for the Far East including Wisden and a man called Diver. The latter was unusually dressed so

Lostwithiel Church was used for stabling for the parliamentary horses, who were given water to drink in the font. It was also used for prisoners, two of whom escaped by climbing up into the tower and pulling the ladder up after them. Enraged enemy troops tried firing muskets at them and finally let off a barrel of gunpowder which destroyed the interior of the church but did not harm the two men in the tower.

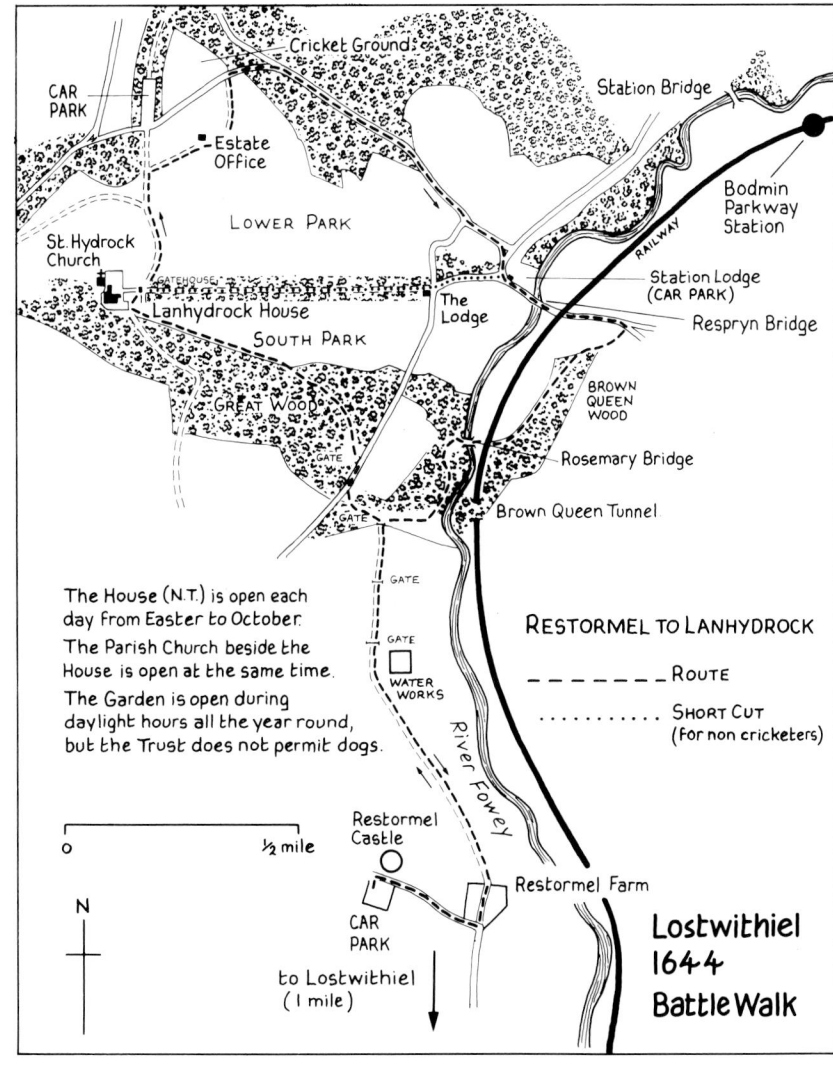

The House (N.T.) is open each day from Easter to October.
The Parish Church beside the House is open at the same time.
The Garden is open during daylight hours all the year round, but the Trust does not permit dogs.

RESTORMEL TO LANHYDROCK

– – – – – – ROUTE
· · · · · · · · · SHORT CUT (for non cricketers)

Lostwithiel
1644
Battle Walk

Lostwithiel – St Nectan's chapel. It lost its tower in the battle by cannon fire and has never been restored

could have been the ship's diver, but some cricket historian will no doubt put me right.

The road goes right downhill to Cutmadoc and eventually Respryn Bridge, a favourite spot for fishermen and children, rather narrow yet accessible for cars but not for large lorries. Cross the railway and at Waterlake Cottage fork right. Note the old cross in the cottage garden. On the right is a metalled track leading to Brown Queen Farm. Take this and when you reach the No Entry (my map showed a footpath) sign turn right to a stile. This was placed here by the Community Programme squad in 1980. The path leads through a wood downhill to a narrow tunnel leading under the railway. There is then a stile leading to a CP footbridge across the River Fowey, which is about 30ft (9m) wide at this point. It is well constructed but easy to miss and at one point I had thought of removing my trousers and wading across, but the map and a notice saying 'Rosemary Bridge, const.1980' reassured me that this was not necessary. Who Rosemary was we are not told but it is possible she was one of the girls on the Community Programme who helped build the bridge. You are now in Higginsmoor Wood and the path follows the river until there is a fork right leading to the dried-up stream-bed, which follow, minding the holes, until it crosses a real stream by means of a granite bridge. On the left you will see the red gate you came through two hours ago. You are now on the road for home.

The walk was 6 miles (9.6km) but it could have been shortened by following a route to Respryn Bridge direct via the South Park road from Lanhydrock. But this means you don't see the cricket field and this would be a pity, especially during a Test Match, as sure enough one of the spectators was able to give me the latest score.

TO SEE NEARBY

Battlefields   Bradock Down, Stratton.

NEWBURY II
28 October 1644

The second Battle of Newbury should not be confused with the first. The leaders were different (Essex and Prince Rupert being absent) and the ground was very different. Charles's army set out from Oxford to relieve the hard-pressed Colonel Boys at Donnington as well as Basing House and Banbury. He was closely watched by the parliamentary committee, headed by the moderate Earl of Manchester, Waller, Skippon and, of lesser importance, Cromwell. Charles fortified Shaw House to protect the road from Reading, Speen to protect the road from the West and Colonel Boys had thrown up considerable earthworks at Donnington Castle, which can still be seen.

Cromwell and Balfour with some cannon and foot went round Newbury via Hermitage, Chieveley, North Heath (where they spent the night) and Boxford where they crossed the river Lambourn to attack Prince Maurice's men at Speen. Meanwhile Manchester waited until 5pm when it was dark to attack Shaw. The attacks were beaten off and Manchester lost 500 men. During the night Charles withdrew to Oxford via Chieveley leaving his cannon with Colonel Boys. Later Prince Rupert relieved Donnington and the cannon were safely brought back to Oxford. It was a drawn battle but left the town of Newbury in parliamentary hands.

Oliver Cromwell by Samuel Cooper
(National Portrait Gallery)
Donnington Castle showing the royalist earthworks in the foreground

OLIVER CROMWELL

The Cromwell family came to fame at the time of the Reformation and Thomas Cromwell was the minister whom Henry VIII put in charge of the dissolution of the monasteries. Oliver was the fifth child of Robert Cromwell, Member of Parliament for Huntingdon and a wealthy man who married Elizabeth Steward of Ely, a wealthy widow. Educated at Dr Peard's Puritan school in Huntingdon, Oliver went to Cambridge (Sidney Sussex College) at the age of sixteen. His favourite book was Raleigh's *History of the World*.

His father died leaving him a farm to run and he married Elizabeth Bourchier in 1620. It was natural he should take his father's place in parliament and become the leader of the anti-royalist faction. He seems to have had no military training and took to it naturally. C. H. Firth in his biography *Cromwell*, published in 1901, sums him up as 'No English ruler did more to shape the future of the land he governed, none showed more clearly in his acts the plain heroic magnitude of mind'.

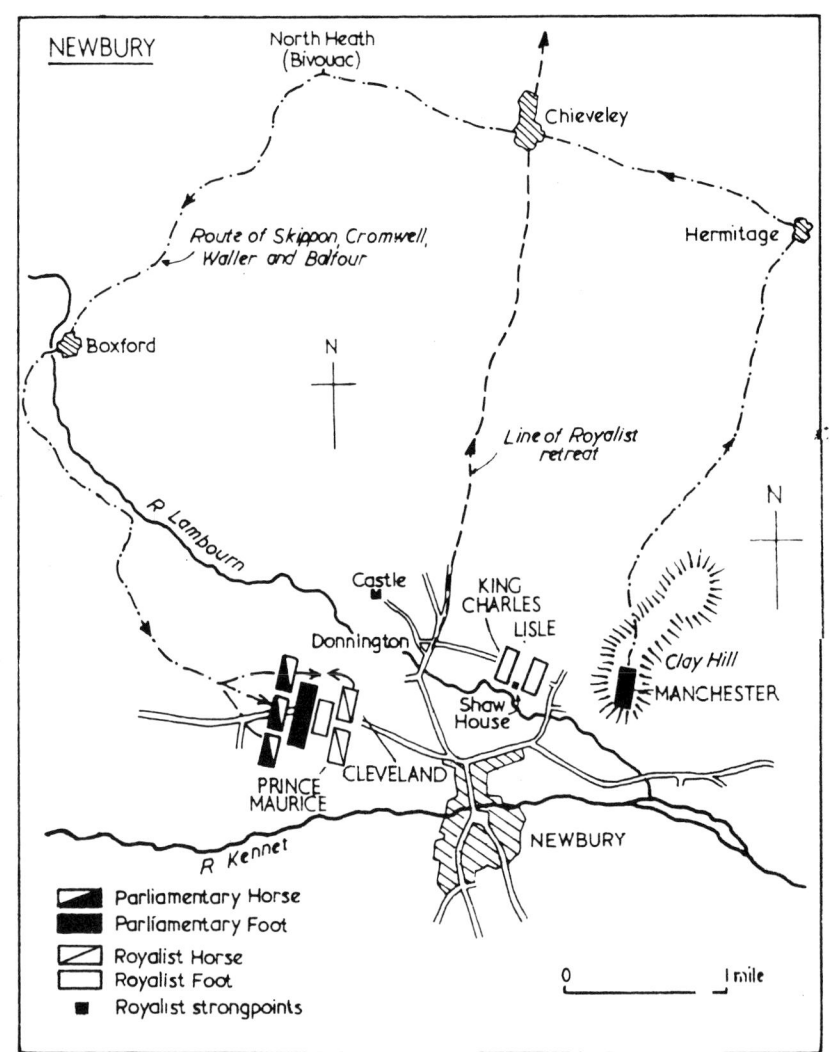

NEWBURY

North Heath (Bivouac)
Chieveley
Route of Skippon, Cromwell, Waller and Balfour
Hermitage
Boxford
N
Line of Royalist retreat
N
R. Lambourn
Castle
KING CHARLES LISLE
Clay Hill
Donnington
MANCHESTER
Shaw House
PRINCE MAURICE
CLEVELAND
NEWBURY
R. Kennet

◣ Parliamentary Horse
◼ Parliamentary Foot
◪ Royalist Horse
▢ Royalist Foot
■ Royalist strongpoints

0   1 mile

THE WALK (L)

This is a two-hour walk which needs a fine day; it is well signposted. Start at Donnington Castle (follow the Watermill Theatre signs from Newbury centre and the Ministry sign to the castle, ignoring the Private sign leading to the house as the castle car park is to the left of this and is free but closed at 6.30pm). The footpath goes to the left of the earthworks through a wood with oak, sycamore, beech and even young elms present. In early May we found bluebells and celandines. At the end of the wood is a new stile where turn sharp left downhill with a cattle field on the left. At the foot of the hill turn right towards some new houses and you will find an inn called the Blackbird on the Boxford road. The small road has to be taken to get over the River Lambourn which is fast flowing and remarkably clear.

The footpath continues left over a stile and goes beside the river, where you may see ducks, swans and some unusual reeds. There were yellow flags, not yet out, and some buttercups. Later in the day we found kingcups, much rarer, growing in clumps on private land.

The path then passes a fish farm and continues to a 'blasted oak' tree then to two rows of young beech beside a stile where we saw a tortoiseshell butterfly. Sitting on the stile here there is a fine view back to the castle. The footpath comes out opposite 40 Grove Road near the Speen notice. The guns from Donnington must have just reached this spot and Cromwell, who was strangely subdued this time, was probably outgunned. The walk now carries on via the footpath back to Donnington village. Stop at the almshouses (built 1393); note the attractive garden and, inside the doorway, the plaque to Charles Howard, Earl of Nottingham, who refounded them by letters patent in 1601. They were untouched during the battle and have been well looked after since. The road to Shaw is on the right, going past two schools and over the main Oxford road to a large field on the left with a footpath sign. On the right is Shaw House, now a school, and we asked the caretaker for permission to look at the old earth walls inside. Some skeletons were dug up in 1822 when glasshouses were being erected.

The footpath goes through the gate opposite and diagonally across the field (sheep when we were there but it is used for the local steam fair) and through a tunnel under the A34. Turn sharp right and carry on along a rough farm track which runs parallel with the road. This ends at the farm where turn sharp left to a small, overgrown stile that leads out onto the road by some large chestnut trees. Opposite is the golf course, but the footpath carries on to the right though it is not easy to find. In fact after walking 200yd (180m) down the road we found a bridleway sign and went up Snelsmore House drive, beautifully looked after with benches on the right and mixed fir and chestnut trees. The walk carries on past the house into a wood, full of nettles and fallen branches. Cross over the next road and into Cromwell's Glen, clearly marked; on the left at the foot of the slope is a stile with a notice saying you 'At your own risk'. Walk this way. No musket shots ring out and the wood here is a mass of bluebells. We disturbed a rabbit and noticed some wild cherry about to blossom.

Finally there is a sign just saying 'Path' and you come out into a field where the path carries on past the cricket club, across two stiles, one of which was broken, and past a very modern house to a small lodge where suddenly you are back at the Donnington Castle poplar-lined drive. There was a large white horse in the field and we sat in the sun eating our sandwiches attended by the castle jackdaws. It had taken almost two hours and apart from two men with dogs we had the walk to ourselves.

TO SEE NEARBY

Littlecote Park, Hungerford. Has a fine collection of Cromwellian arms and armour. Open daily April–October.

See also *Newbury I* (page 119).

Newbury District Museum has models of both Newbury I and II.

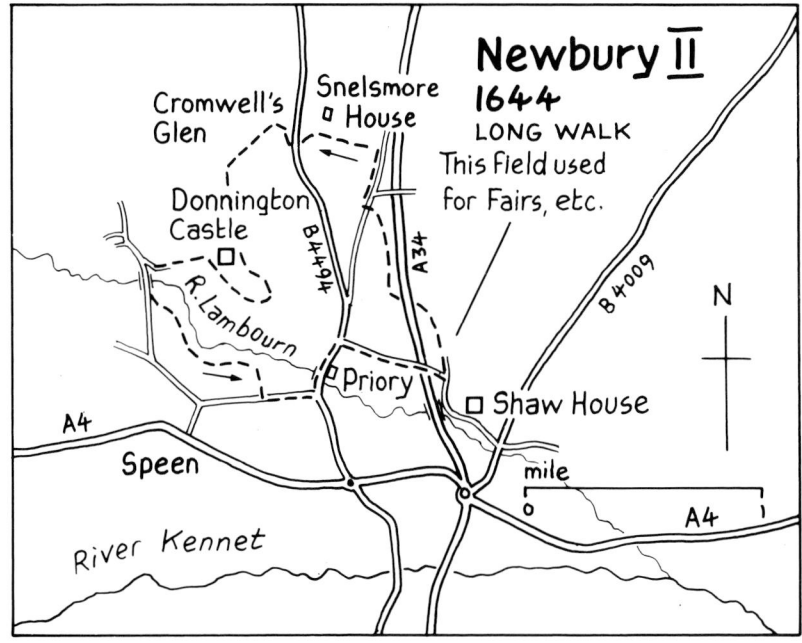

Charles I (W. Scott)

AULDEARN
9 May 1645

No hero of the seventeenth century stands out so clearly as James Graham, Marquis of Montrose. John Buchan wrote about him, Sir Walter Scott had his sword in the Abbotsford Armoury and there is a monument to him in St Giles's Cathedral, Edinburgh. Yet his reputation hangs entirely on eighteen months campaigning, and as Buchan points out he was no ordinary Cavalier. He started as a member of the Scottish Covenant and remained a true Presbyterian. He took part in the Scottish army occupation of Newcastle in 1639 and as a youngster amongst so many plotters, the chief of whom was Argyll, he realised that the country was likely to become a dictatorship so he decided to seek out the king at Oxford and offer him his services. Like a 'sea-wind in a stifling room' his enthusiasm won over the king and his council. He was made lieutenant-general of all royal forces in Scotland and his friend Antrim was sent to Ireland for reinforcements.

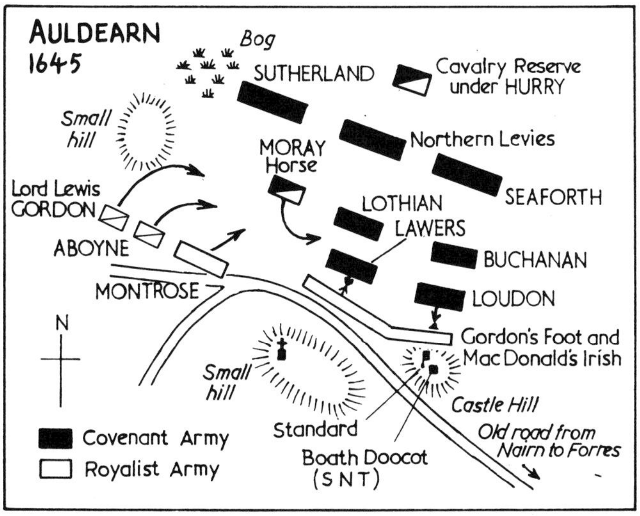

The amazing period of victories began. One man was to step forward with his clan to serve Montrose in most of his victories with a bravery that won many allies as well as actions. This was Alasdair Macdonald, known as 'Colkitto', as he was originally from Colonsay island and could fight equally well with either hand. *Coll keitach* the Gaelic became Colkitto whose 2,000 ragged followers were from Ireland and had been sent over by Antrim to join Montrose. With the help of Graham of Inchbrakie, the Robertsons and Stewarts, armed with bows and arrows, ancient swords, a few muskets but little ammunition and at first only three lean horses, Montrose's army had to make do with stone throwing in their first action. However they had speed and surprise on their side. His enemies soon came to fear him for they never knew from which direction he would appear next.

King Charles received a letter from his confident lieutenant-general:

Give me leave after I have reduced this country to your Majestry's obedience and conquered from Dan to Beersheba, to say to your Majesty then, as David's general said to his master, 'Come thou thyself, lest this country be called by my name.

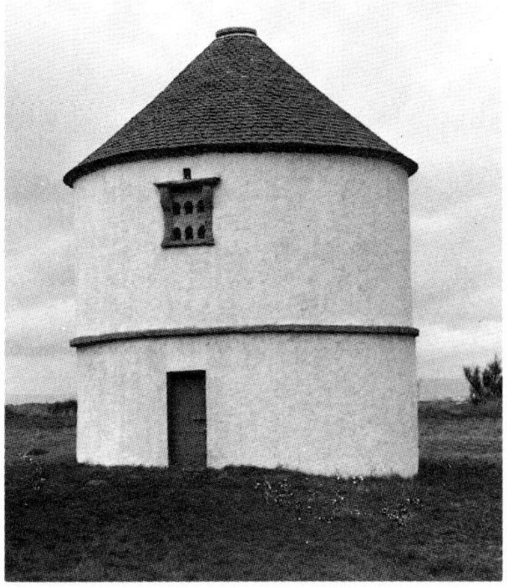

The Boath Doocot that stands on the hill where Montrose had his standard (National Trust for Scotland)

In September 1644 Montrose defeated Lord Elcho at *Tippermuir* near Perth. He then turned up at Aberdeen, which fell to his sword. In spite of the winter weather his little army crossed the mountains to *Inverlochy*, near Fort William, where they defeated Argyll's Campbells. The slaughter here may have instigated the Campbells' later revenge at Glencoe (see page 168). Argyll escaped by boat. Short of supplies, Montrose entered Dundee, where a new character enters the scene. Colonel Hurry, once one of Rupert's men, had joined the Scottish general Baillie as a cavalry commander.

On 8 May Montrose was at Auldearn, a small village between the valleys of the Findhorn and Nairn. He had a small army of 2,500 men but he was joined by the Gordon horse and Lord Aboyne's horse, which he placed on his left wing. The Gordon foot and Irish he placed on the right with his standard on the top of the Boath Hill, where the Doocot now stands. He himself with his foot was just out of sight of the approaching Hurry, who had nearly 4,000 foot and 400 cavalry. Hurry's men were bunched up because of a bog on their right wing but they attacked the Irish, believing Montrose was with them. Sorely pressed the Irish gave way, but Montrose gave the order for his horse to charge the enemy horse. The Moray men turned the wrong way and collided with the Lothian regiment. The northern levies fled and Hurry tried unsuccessfully to stop the general retreat. Drummond, commanding the Moray horse, was tried and shot as a traitor in Inverness. The news reached England and Leven withdrew his army to the north west to stop Montrose from crossing the border. The importance of the battle is in its tactics of a weak right wing and encircling left, a plan used by Cumberland at *Fontenoy* and on a grand scale by Napoleon at *Austerlitz.*

THE BATTLEFIELD TODAY (S)

Follow the National Trust of Scotland signs to the Boath Doocot; on top of the hill is a viewpoint with a battle plan. Roads have changed since the battle which makes it confusing.

TO SEE NEARBY

Culloden and, before you get there, *Cawdor Castle*, where the original French muskets captured at Fishguard (see page 186) hang on the staircase wall.

NASEBY
14 June 1645

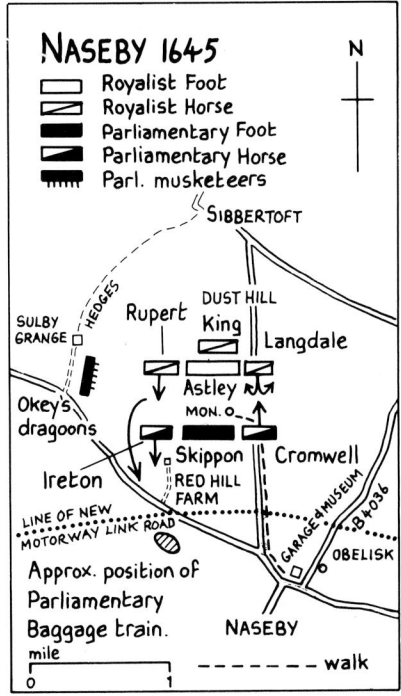

NASEBY 1645 N

- ☐ Royalist Foot
- ⊟ Royalist Horse
- ■ Parliamentary Foot
- ◤ Parliamentary Horse
- ▥ Parl. musketeers

SIBBERTOFT

HEDGES
SULBY GRANGE
DUST HILL
Rupert King Langdale
Okey's dragoons
Astley
MON. O.
Ireton
Skippon Cromwell
RED HILL FARM
GARAGE & MUSEUM
LINE OF NEW MOTORWAY LINK ROAD
B.4036
OBELISK

Approx. position of Parliamentary Baggage train.

NASEBY

mile
0   1

– – – – – walk

While Montrose was winning every battle in Scotland for the king's cause, the royalist army sacked Leicester in May 1645. No less than 140 cart-loads of spoil were taken to the garrison at Newark and Rupert, over-confident with the king and about 9,000 experienced troops, moved slowly south to Market Harborough anxious to draw Fairfax away from Oxford. This they succeeded in doing in spite of the fact that the parliamentary army, with Cromwell commanding the horse, was 13,000 strong, though many of them were untried newly called-up members of the New Model Army. Langdale's horse were anxious to return north and there was some friction in the royalist camp. However Rupert seized the high ground above Naseby and placed his own regiment on the right wing, Astley's foot in the centre and Langdale on the left. In reserve he had Howard's horse, his own foot and the king's bodyguard.

Fairfax meanwhile had occupied Red Hill above Naseby, with broken ground on his right where Cromwell stood, Skippon, back from Lostwithiel without a scratch, took command of the foot and Ireton the left wing. According to the de Gomme map (see Marston Moor) of the battle, both sides had 10 heavy cannon. At the start Rupert charged Ireton and scattered his detachment but, as at Edgehill, his detachment was out of the main scene of action and not capable of a second charge when it returned. Cromwell drove off Langdale, whose horse were outnumbered, and in the centre Aston got the better of Skippon until Cromwell intervened. The royalist infantry was abandoned and the king, prevented by the Earl of Carnwath from leading his reserve to attack Cromwell, withdrew to Leicester with the horse. Rupert's blue-coated infantry fought on, but elsewhere the royalist foot surrendered in great numbers. The most decisive battle of the Civil War was over.

THE WALK (M)

There are no footpaths at Naseby and, although at present unspoilt, the southern end of the battlefield is to have a motorway link road over it shortly. This will spoil it; but if there is no turning off point into Naseby itself, the main part of the farmland that is Naseby will be untouched. The museum is at the back of the garage in the upper part of a barn and seems to be closed on Saturdays. From here walk out of Naseby on the Sulby road then turn right at the bottom of the hill towards Sibbertoft. The grass verge on the left is wide enough to walk on and after about a mile (1.6km) there is a stile on the left with a concrete base. Through here and keeping close to the hedge you come to the Cromwell monument, erected in 1936 and supposedly marking the place from where Cromwell started his charge. In fact he was further to the right. It is a very peaceful spot with hawthorn hedges and it is a pity that one cannot do a round walk returning by the Sulby hedges where Colonel Okey lined up his parliamentary dragoons.

The parish church is worth a visit. It houses the table round which the King's rearguard were drinking when disturbed by Ireton. There is a legend that Cromwell was secretly buried in the churchyard when his tomb was desecrated at the Restoration. No one has yet to prove this legend as true and as Oliver's funeral cost £60,000, a huge amount at that time, it is unlikely that his tomb could have been easily disturbed.

TO SEE NEARBY

Fitzgerald Obelisk Another monument standing on private land just off the road to Clipston, erected by Lord Fitzgerald, a local landowner.

Battlefields Bosworth Field, Northampton.

(pp 146–7)
Looking for one's husband. Re-enactment of Battle of Naseby (J. Dodgson)

(2) 5

Sr. beinge comanded by you to this service, I thinke my selfe bound to acquaint you with the good hand of God towards you, and vs. wee marched yesterday after the Kinge whoe went before vs from Daventree to Haverbrowe, and quartered about six miles from him, this day wee marched towards him, Hee drew out to meete vs. both Armies engaged, wee after 3. howres fight, very doubtfull, att last routed his Armie, killed and tooke about 5000. very many officers but of what quallitye wee yett knoe not, wee tooke alsoe about 200. carrages all hee had, and all his gunns, beinge 12. in number, whereof 2. were Demi canon, 2. demie Culveringes, and (I thinke) the rest Sacres, wee pursued the enimie from three miles short of Haverbrowe to nine beyond, even to sight of Leicester whether the Kinge fled. Sr this is none other but the hand of God, and to him aloane belongs the Glorie, wherein none are to share with him, The Generall served you with all faythfullnesse and honor, and the best commendations I can give him is, that I dare say hee attributes all to God, and would rather perish then assume to himselfe, which is an honest, and a thrivinge way, and yett as much for bravery may bee given to him in this action as to a man. Honest men served you faythfully in this action, Sr they are trusty, I beseech you in the name of God not to discorage them, I wish this action may beget thankfullnesse and humilitye in all that are concerned in itt, Hee that venters his life for the libertye of his countrie, I wish hee trust God for the libertye of his [illegible], and you for the libertye hee fights for, In this hee rests who is

your most humble servant

Oliver Cromwell

June 14th 1645.
Haverbrowe.

LANGPORT
10 July 1645

After Naseby, the only large royalist army in the field was Goring's West Country force, which was besieging Taunton. Three times they were close to taking it, but Blake in Taunton Castle said he had three pairs of boots left and would eat two of them before he surrendered. Goring positioned his army at Langport as his spies said that the New Model Army was approaching in July 1645. The Parrett defended two sides of the town, the walls another and breastworks were thrown up so that it became a well-fortified area. The royalist horse was surprised at Isle Abbots by Massey who commanded some of the parliamentary horse, and Fairfax moved to Long Sutton. Goring sent most of his artillery to safety at Bridgwater, keeping two heavy guns on the Somerton road with his musketeers defending the ditches. Fairfax and Cromwell went up the narrow lane by Uphill windmill (so it is recorded in Cromwell's correspondence) and turned left to the Wagg ford (now a bridge), strongly held by Fairfax. Using his artillery to advantage, Goring silenced the two royalist guns and Cromwell left Major Bethel's horse to lead the charge over the ford. Closely followed by Colonel Desborough, the royalists were forced back and the parliamentary musketeers drove off the royalist musketeers. All was confusion in Langport. The town was set on fire and Goring withdrew to Bridgwater leaving most of his infantry as captives. Some men made a stand at Aller and others climbed Burrow Mump. A few days later Bridgwater surrendered.

Fairfax (National Portrait Museum)

THE WALK (L)

Taking a tip from Colonel Burne in *More Battlefields of England* I climbed Huish Episcopi church tower to see the battlefield. In fact a better view is obtained on the crest of the hill going to Somerton. Leave Huish church and

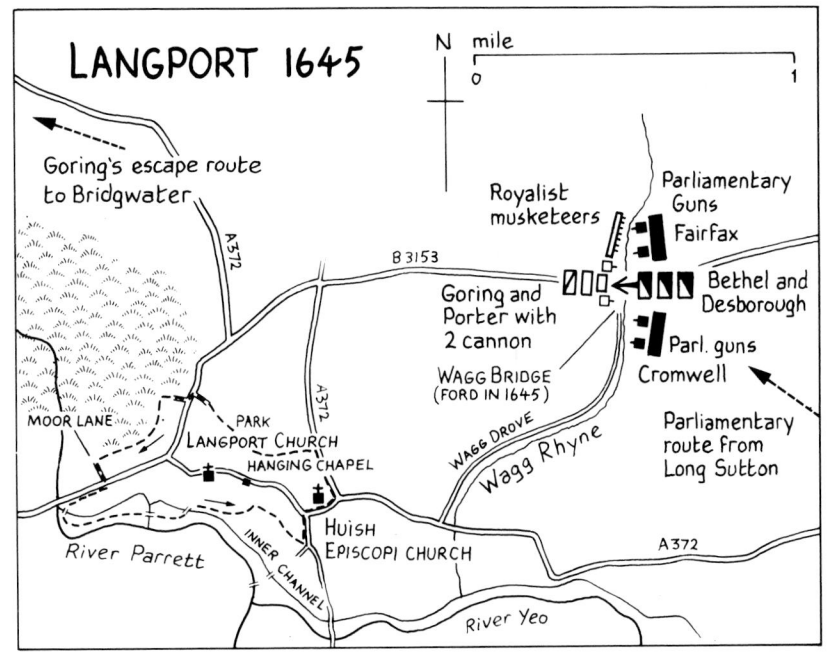

The Cromwell letter telling Parliament news of Naseby

walk down past the school until the gap in the hedge where there is a footpath with a hawthorn hedge on the left and houses on the right. This meets the path from the Hanging Chapel. Here turn right into the park, which cross over to the school. On the right is the old railway station. Cross over the main road here and turn down the footpath between the Do-it-Yourself shop and the bicycle shop. There is a footbridge at the end over a rhine (Somerset rhines are usually 8ft (2.4m) wide and deep, so that anyone jumping them needs to be very fit). You are now in swamp land but it was dry in July and there is a pleasant grassy walk along the backs of gardens until you come to Moor Lane. Take the footbridge here past a carpenter's shop into Bow Street. Turn right into the Lang Port (the planner of the town must have been a Scot) and go as far as the River Parrett crossing. Do not cross the bridge but take the turning left before the bridge and then right over a footbridge onto the river bank. This is a public area with seats for the fishermen. Carry on to the back of the town car park where there is another bridge with a dry ditch on the left and the river on the right. There is a third bridge over the ditch into a field where there was a clump of white willow trees shining in the sunshine as if they had been polished. Suddenly a heron was disturbed and with a few powerful strokes was airborne above us, its long legs flat out behind like an Olympic swimmer's. The path goes behind the retirement home garden, surely the finest grown vegetables in the town, across a dilapidated stile and into the lane leading back to the impressive tower of Huish Episcopi church.

View from top of Huish Episcopi church

Burrow Mump. Fortified and used as a refuge after Langport and as an observation post by the King's troops at Sedgemoor

KILSYTH
15 August 1645

The interesting thing about Kilsyth is that it was probably Montrose's greatest victory and yet it was too late to affect the English Civil War. Charles had already lost Naseby and Goring had been defeated at Langport, so the Kilsyth campaign was an isolated incident. After another victory at *Alford* in July.

Montrose had been strengthened by 1,400 Highlanders and Irish as well as a small body of horse under Patrick Graham. Baillie had 6,000 foot and 800 horse so Montrose was outnumbered. He heard that Baillie was expecting recruits from Glasgow so he positioned himself in the village of Kilsyth, between Stirling and Glasgow very close to the Antonine Wall (see below). The main road was blocked by Montrose with his right wing at Woodend and with his left at Riskend (now a quarry). He had the Gordon and Ogilvy horse behind in reserve and his Macleans occupied some cottages on the left wing near the Colzium Burn. Baillie tried to outflank him as the hill above Colzium is much higher and the Macleans, without orders, charged him. Montrose, seeing the dent in his line, rather like Hopton at Cheriton, ordered his Ogilvy horse forward and they charged the Covenanters' right wing cutting the enemy line in two. Montrose now ordered the advance and the Fife Levies retreated in their hundreds. Baillie and Argyll escaped with most of the cavalry but the Irish, who had not forgotten the slaughter of their camp-followers in Methven Wood a few days before, cut down the stragglers and many were

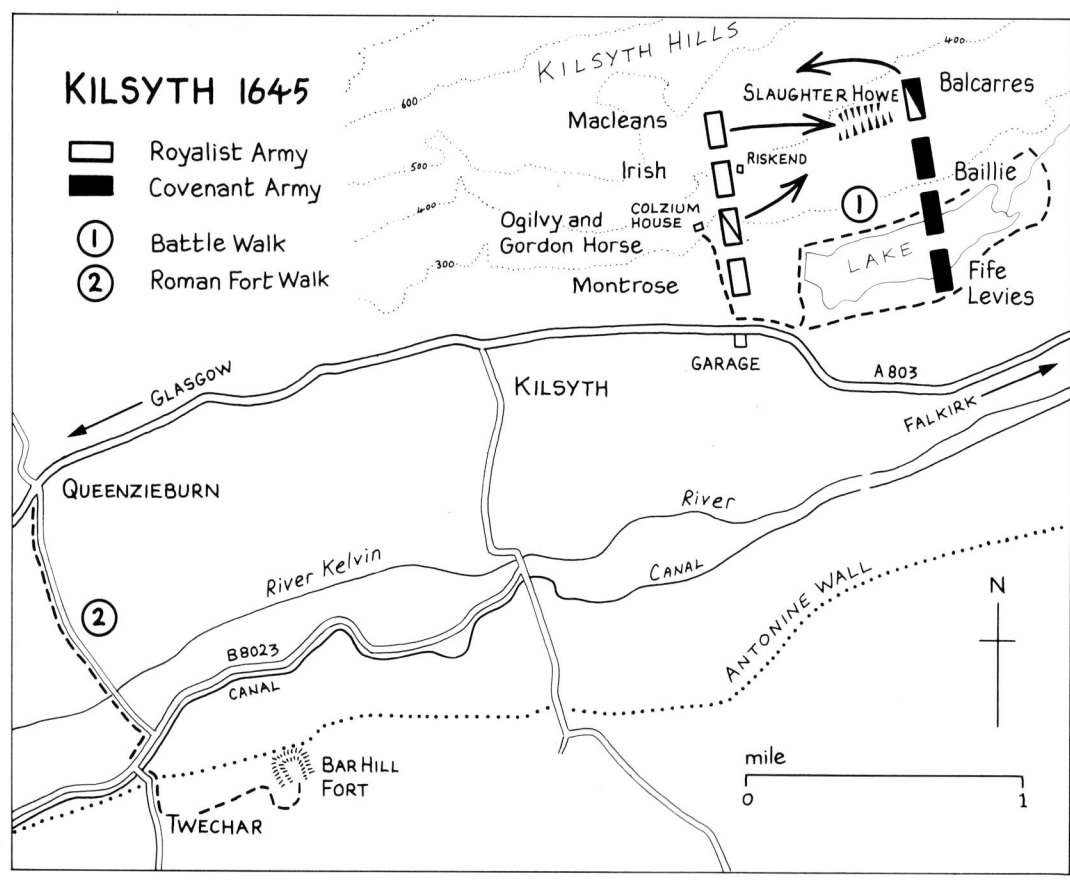

killed. Montrose lost six men of note, but Philiphaugh (see page 154) was not long away.

THE WALKS (M and M)

The A803 is the best starting point for a walk. Take the turning opposite the garage on the left-hand side of the road heading into Kilsyth and enter the Colzium-Lennox park. This is beautifully looked after and has a clock theatre as well as fine trees and plants. The battle monument is in the shape of a curling stone and is next to the clock theatre on the main lawn.

Coming back down the drive turn left along the old road to the path leading sharp left up to the small lake. Beside the muddy track on the site of the battle, were two swans floating majestically in the reeds. The footpath goes clockwise round the lake and back to the A803.

The nearby Antonine Wall, a Roman Wall the frontier between Forth and Clyde cAD80, consisted of a wall of sods on top of rocks, except in the east where clay was used. On one side there was a road and on the other a ditch. There were twenty forts for the garrison, mostly on high spots, one such being Bar Hill near Kilsyth. Rough Castle, the best of the forts, is near Bonnybridge a few miles west of Falkirk. To get to Bar Hill take the lane from Queenzieburn, 1 mile (1.6km) beyond Kilsyth, cross over a disused railway, under what was once a railway bridge, turn right and then left over the Forth & Clyde Canal to Twechar. The footpath starts by a war memorial (remarkably well looked after) and leads past a farm (very noisy dogs) through a red metal gate. The track goes to the top of the hill, then take a gate to the left to a plantation of young oaks. The fort is here and outlines in the grass show where the two main buildings stood. The view over Kilsyth valley is excellent. This was a mining area and suffered from bad housing but today, although partly derelict, it has some surprising gardens, like Colzium, and a good hotel.

SIR JOHN HURRY

There are few more interesting characters in the Civil War than Sir John Hurry, who crops up on both sides of the border, first of all fighting against the king, then for him, then for the Covenanters then finally for Montrose.

Hurry was a native of Aberdeen. He had an adventurous spirit and went south in 1640 where he joined the army of the Earl of Essex. On learning of a treasure of £21,000 being conveyed to Thame, he deserted and joined the royalists at Oxford, where he led the royalist expedition with Prince Rupert into Oxfordshire that ended at the skirmish of *Chalgrove Field* and the death of John Hampden. He returned to Oxford where he was knighted by the king.

In August 1644 he was taken prisoner in Lancashire and once more changed sides. This time he returned to Aberdeen only to be made commander of the force that the Covenanters raised to attack Montrose at *Auldearn*. After this defeat he seems to have been dropped by the Covenanters and next appears in the north of Scotland as Montrose's major-general when the latter returned to Scotland from Denmark. No doubt Hurry decided that he would rather fight for Montrose than for the ever-arguing collection of priests and townsfolk who constituted the Estates that controlled the forces against him.

The Battle of *Carbisdale* in the north east of Scotland was a disaster. Hurry commanded the vanguard which was overwhelmed and he was taken prisoner. Montrose was captured a few days later. The prisoners were well treated and young Napier, a boy of sixteen, recorded later in his life seeing 'Colonel Hurry, a robust, tall, stately fellow with a long cut on his cheek'. He was drinking heartily with his fellow prisoners but this must have been his last happy day. Montrose was hung on the scaffold in Edinburgh on 21 May 1650 and Hurry followed his master's fate shortly afterwards.

PHILIPHAUGH
3 September 1645

Newark Castle where the prisoners were slaughtered after the Battle of Philiphaugh. It is still said to be haunted

After his victory at Kilsyth, Montrose occupied Glasgow but his army soon dwindled away until it was below 1,000 men. He decided to go into the Borders with the hope of gaining fresh recruits. General Leslie, one of the victors of Marston Moor, set out from Hereford to Scotland via the east-coast route and by September was at Gladsmuir, near Prestonpans, with an army of 6,000 experienced troops, mostly horse. Montrose was camped on the junction of Ettrick and Yarrow Waters. His scout, driven out of Sunderland village on the other side of the river from Selkirk, was ignored, and Leslie achieved complete surprise at dawn with a party of dragoons under Agnew

LORD OGILVY'S ESCAPE AFTER PHILIPHAUGH

The prisoners captured after Philiphaugh included young Lord Ogilvy, whose horse had performed so well at Kilsyth. The Covenanters at St Andrews condemned him to death and he was imprisoned in St Andrews. There he pretended to be sick and asked for permission for his mother and sister and wife to visit him on the eve of his execution. He persuaded the guards to withdraw when the three women entered his cell. Then he quickly changed clothes with his sister and she put on the nightcap he had been wearing and got into the sickbed. At eight o'clock in the evening the three walked out past the guards and Ogilvy mounted a horse and made for Menteith in the Highlands where he had friends. The three women were brought before Argyll but, as they were related to the Hamiltons and Lindsays, who had power in the government, there was nothing he could do.

attacking Montrose's Irish from the other bank of the Yarrow Water and Leslie himself attacking Montrose from Selkirk. His army was routed and only a few horse and he himself escaped to Carbisdale; it was his final battle and defeat. In May 1650 he was executed in Edinburgh and his monument stands in St Giles's Cathedral close to that of his old adversary Argyll. Scotland's greatest soldier was dead.

THE WALK (M)

There is nothing to see at the battle site but there is a walk from the entrance to Bowhill House, along a track to Newark Castle which stands high above Yarrow Water. Here Leslie brought the Irish women and camp-followers after the battle and imprisoned them in the still discernible castle forecourt. Today it is covered by long grass and weeds, and some say they are aware of an uncomfortable feeling and unearthly noises at dusk. The day after the battle Leslie killed all the camp-followers.

TO SEE NEARBY

Bowhill House This is open to the public during summer and has a fine collection of arms and some pictures of the Duke of Monmouth. The owner is His Grace, the Duke of Buccleuch and Queensberry KT.

Traquair At Innerleithen nearby. Montrose was refused entry here on his escape but it has long been a Stuart house and the gates are kept permanently shut until the next Stuart monarch takes the throne.

Battle monument This stands in the garden of a private house next to a tennis court and permission has to be obtained to see it. Perhaps there should be another monument by the junction of the two rivers.

PHILIPHAUGH 1645

Line of Montrose's escape — PEAT LAW — LINGLIE HILL — Agnew — A 707 — Leslie — SELKIRK — Douglas — EARTHWORK — Irish — Montrose — NEWARK CASTLE — Yarrow Water — BOWHILL — River Ettrick — N

- - - - walk
□ Royalist Army
■ Covenant Army

DUNBAR
4 September 1650

The monument, Dunbar, which is now hidden beside the vast cement works

After the execution of Charles I, the Scots accepted young Prince Charles as Charles II, though he was made to sign the Solemn League and Covenant professing he was a Presbyterian. But Cromwell, just back from Ireland, had an army in the field and on 22 July had crossed into Scotland with 20,000 men. The Scots were not slow to raise an army of 30,000 under David Leslie. Edinburgh was well defended and the land between Musselburgh and Dunbar, where Cromwell brought in his supplies by ship, was laid bare of any cattle or other food for his men or horses. Cromwell found that, as at Philiphaugh, Leslie could move with great speed, and the retreating Roundheads found the Scots army on Doon Hill looking down on Dunbar and blocking their route to the border. On 3 September, urged on by his preachers, Leslie moved his army down the hill, with his left by Spott House and his right near the present cement works.

Cromwell attacked the Scots right wing with six cavalry regiments under Fleetwood, Whalley and Lambert, and Monk's infantry in the centre. Some of his cavalry got behind the Scots, and Cromwell's own regiment poured through the gap. The Scots had extinguished their match and had trouble firing their muskets in the rain; they fought bravely but without success. Cromwell's experienced troops cut them down and over 5,000 surrendered. They were marched to Durham, many dying en route of starvation. Some 2,000 were shut up in the cathedral at Durham, where they damaged the monument to the victor of Neville's Cross, Lord Neville, so that today only the trunk of his body remains on his tomb. 'The Lord hath delivered them into our hands' wrote Cromwell after his victory, and only 200 wretched captives survived to be sent to Virginia. The following year the Scots were beaten yet again at *Inverkeithing* and Charles, with hopes of support from England, took the road to disaster at *Worcester*.

TO SEE NEARBY

Dunbar harbour is worth a visit as are the old castle ruins. Cromwell built the 'new' harbour, now known as the 'old' harbour. Also worth seeing are the *Miller Park* and *Tantallon Castle*. Battlefields *Prestonpans* and *Pinkie*.

THE BATTLEFIELD TODAY (S)

The battlefield is ruined by the massive cement works; the battle monument stands beside the old A1. To find it you have to take the slip road, off the A1 after the Dunbar turn-off, marked 'Cement Works and East Barns'. On the left-hand side by a hawthorn bush, where the road turns right and runs in front of the works, is the monument, a large stone with the words 'Here took place the brunt or essential agony of Dunbar' and on the pedestal the two army watchwords 'The Covenant' for the Scots and 'The Lord of Hosts' for Cromwell.

The harbour, Dunbar

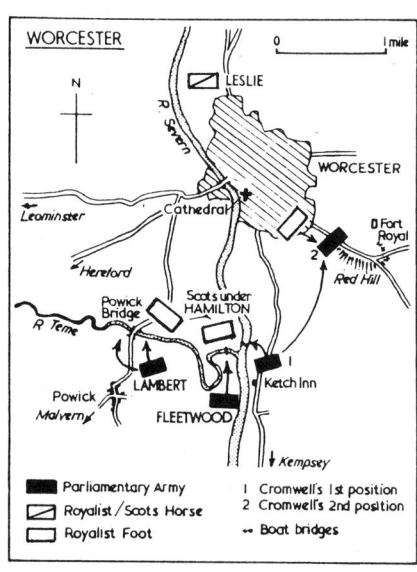

WORCESTER
3 September 1651

The Scottish army that young Prince Charles took over the border in 1651 was some 13,000 strong, but it lacked spirit. The Scots under Leslie were tired and the army rested at Worcester to await reinforcements from Wales. The city was well fortified with Fort Royal defending the London Road, Castle Hill the river, and gun emplacements near St Martin's Gate, Frog Gate, Fore Gate and Pitch Croft with a bridge over the river Severn (further up stream than the present bridge) and a gun emplacement on the west bank.

There were Scots defending Powick Bridge on the Teme and Hamilton's men defending the junction of the Teme and the Severn (opposite the Ketch Inn). The battle started with Generals Fleetwood and Lambert attacking Powick and the former floating a bridge of boats down to the Teme–Severn river junction to give Cromwell, who was in charge, the opportunity to switch men from one river bank to another. Charles led an attack on Perry Wood in person and some of Cromwell's cannon were captured, but the result was never really in doubt with Leslie's cavalry remaining inactive. The Duke of Hamilton was wounded on the steps of the Commandery, Red Hill fort was captured and Prince Charles with a few followers escaped from a building in New Street (now a restaurant) and through St Martin's Gate to the days of hide-and-seek that led to his escape to France from Shoreham.

THE WALK (L)

The centre of Worcester makes an easy and most interesting walk. Start from the *Commandery* in London Road. Here there is a museum (open Tuesday–Saturday) with a fifteen-minute slide and sound show in the Great Hall. Immediately above the Commandery is Red Hill where indentations in the park are all that remains of the star fort. Go back down London Road and across the busy City Walls Road to Friar Street, where there are some attractive jettied houses. Carry on to New Street where Prince Charles's house can be

Sidbury gate monument, Worcester

The Commandery
This was the headquarters of the royalists during the battle. It is now a museum and the start of the walk

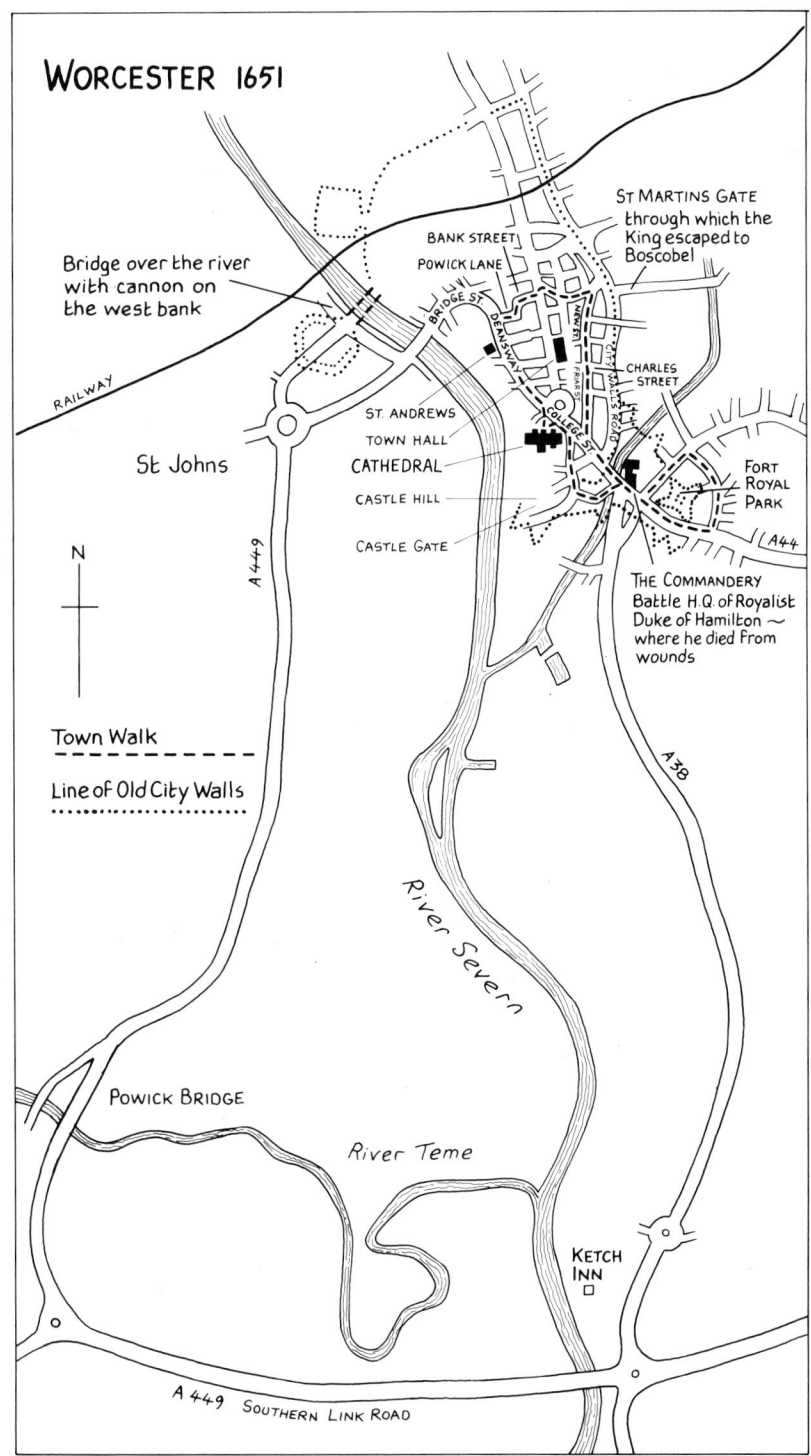

WORCESTER 1651

Bridge over the river with cannon on the west bank

RAILWAY

St Johns

N

A449

Town Walk - - - - - -

Line of Old City Walls ....

River Severn

POWICK BRIDGE

River Teme

A 449 SOUTHERN LINK ROAD

KETCH INN

BANK STREET
POWICK LANE
BRIDGE ST
DEANSWAY
COLLEGE ST
NEW ST
FRIAR ST
SIDBURY ROAD

St MARTINS GATE through which the King escaped to Boscobel

CHARLES STREET

ST ANDREWS
TOWN HALL
CATHEDRAL
CASTLE HILL
CASTLE GATE

FORT ROYAL PARK

A44

THE COMMANDERY Battle H.Q. of Royalist Duke of Hamilton ~ where he died from wounds

A38

seen at the end on the right. Note the inscription 'Love God, Honour Ye King' on the doorway. Some accounts say Charles leapt from a window onto his horse below, but others say he escaped through the back door when Cromwell's men burst into the front one. Turn left across High Street to St Andrew's Church tower by the river. This is merely a tower and garden now, the body of the church was demolished when unsafe. Carry on past the college to the cathedral. After the cathedral cross over the road and return to the Commandery where there is a tea shop on the canal bank (easily missed).

TO SEE NEARBY

Friar Street Museum

Ketch Inn with views over the Teme and Severn river junction where the parliamentarians had their bridge of boats.

Powick Bridge, where Prince Rupert had a cavalry action in the weeks before Edgehill and forced by Lambert in the Worcester battle.

Battlefields Tewkesbury and Evesham.

CHARLES II's ESCAPE ROUTE AFTER WORCESTER
(September 1651)

The building in New Street, Worcester, where young Prince Charles lodged and which still has 'Love God, Honour ye King' above the doorway, is now a restaurant. From here Charles left with Lords Wilmot and Derby, Charles Giffard and others riding north via Stourbridge to *Whiteladies Priory* (English Heritage, open to the public) where Charles, accompanied by Richard Penderel, hid in a wood. Later he went to Hubbal Grange, now a ruin, and making for the Severn got as far as Madeley where he spent the night in Mr Wolfe's barn. All Severn crossings were guarded so Charles returned to *Boscobel* and on Saturday 6 September spent the day in an oak tree with Colonel Carlis. (*Boscobel House*, Shifnal, is also an English Heritage property, open to the public.) The oak tree can still be seen, though not the original one.

Escorted by Penderel and his brother-in-law, Francis Yates, Charles made for *Moseley Old Hall* near Wolverhampton (National Trust property open to the public). Here Charles spent the night in a secret room, while next day parliamentary soldiers searched the grounds. The following day dressed as a manservant Charles accompanied by Jane Lane, sister of Colonel Lane a local royalist, left for Bentley Hall. They travelled on horseback, Charles sharing a horse with Jane. At Bromsgrove the king's horse cast a shoe and he had to take it to the blacksmith, a very anti-royalist character. Then proceeding to Wootton Wawen they found the inn occupied by hostile cavalry. Without halting they left for Stratford upon Avon and Long Marston, where they halted for the night at Mr Tomes's house. (This is now a guest house and *Goodrest Farm* near Bromsgrove, where he halted for a rest, still stands). On 11 September the party continued to Chipping Camden and on to Cirencester where they halted at the *Crown Inn*.

They carried on next day to Chipping Sodbury and Bristol heading for Abbotsleigh House. Lord Wilmot, who had gone ahead, stayed at *Dyrham Park* (National Trust and open to the public) while trying to find a ship to take Charles to France. After three days at Abbotsleigh, alas demolished, Charles went into Somerset and passed through Bruton, Castle Cary and Yeovil to Francis Wyndham's house at Trent. This is not open to the public but is believed to be haunted. Jane Lane headed home and Charles and Juliana Coningsby, niece to Lady Wyndham, pretending to be a runaway couple, left for Charmouth. Here they stayed at the Queen's Arms, awaiting a boat from Lyme Regis, which did not turn up. From Charmouth they went to Bridport where they stopped at the *Old George*, now an antique shop but still carrying an inscription. From here, scared by the presence of so many parliamentary troops, Charles went to the *George* at Broadwindsor, now a business house, for the night. Staying once more at Trent, Charles awaited better news from Wilmot who was in Sussex making plans. On 6 October he left for Wincanton

and Mere where they had lunch at the *George*, now the *Talbot Inn*. They went to Hyde's house, *Heale* near Salisbury, passing Stonehenge. (*Heale House*, property of Major and Lady Rasch, is not open to the public but has a fine garden open on Tuesdays in summer.)

Passing through *Mottisfont Abbey*, Hants (National Trust and open to the public), Charles went to Hambledon to the house of Thomas Symonds, relation of Colonel Gunter, another royalist whom Wilmot had asked for help. The three men went to Brighton on 14 October and once more stopped at a George Inn, now no longer. On the following day they went to a little hovel cottage in Southwick Green, before being led to safety on board the coal boat *Surprise*, master Mr Tattershall. At 8pm the boat sailed for France and next day landed at Fécamp from where Charles and Wilmot went to Rouen and Paris to meet Queen Henrietta Maria, Charles mother. Nine years later Charles was back in England as King Charles II. Lord Wilmot, who had led the cavalry charge at Roundway Down and had planned Charles escape, was made Earl of Rochester.

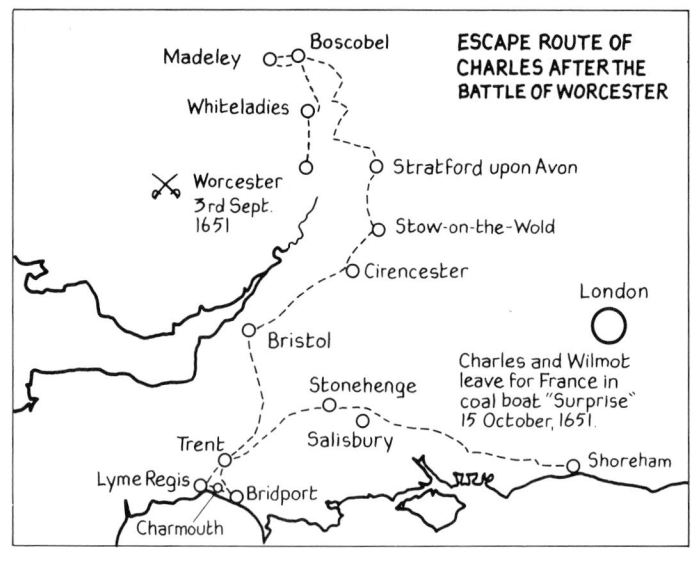

ESCAPE ROUTE OF CHARLES AFTER THE BATTLE OF WORCESTER

Madeley · Boscobel
Whiteladies
Worcester 3rd Sept. 1651
Stratford upon Avon
Stow-on-the-Wold
Cirencester
Bristol
London
Charles and Wilmot leave for France in coal boat "Surprise" 15 October, 1651.
Stonehenge
Trent · Salisbury
Shoreham
Lyme Regis · Bridport
Charmouth

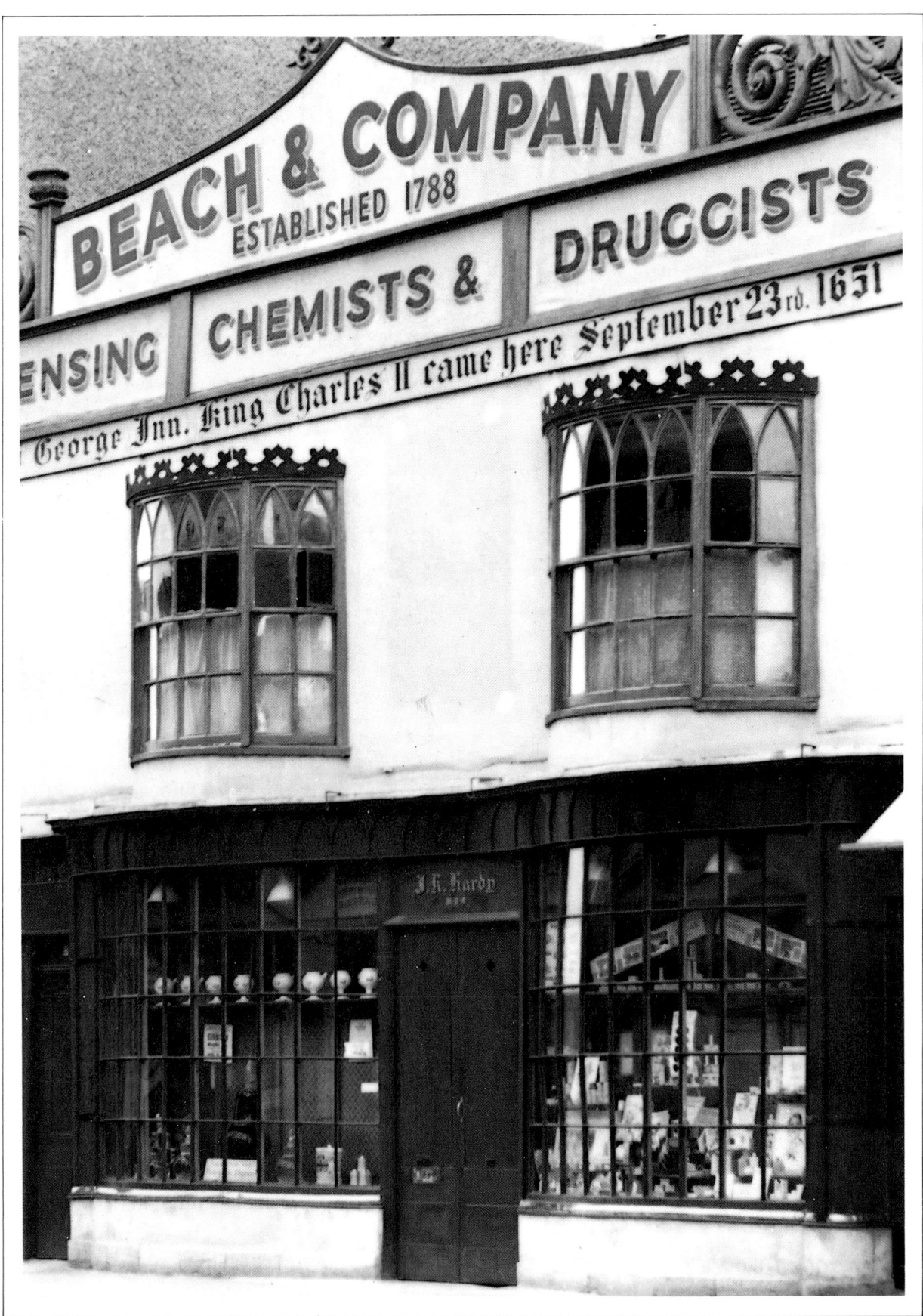

The Old George, Bridport (Bridport Museum)   161

SEDGEMOOR
6 July 1685

When considering Sedgemoor, it is important not to try to place it as a late Civil War battle, for if there were any old antagonists fighting, they were more likely to be sons of Blake's defenders of Taunton and Bridgwater than the fathers. Sedgemoor is an isolated incident – the last pitched battle on English soil – though Clifton Moor, usually dismissed as a skirmish, can also make this claim (see page 180).

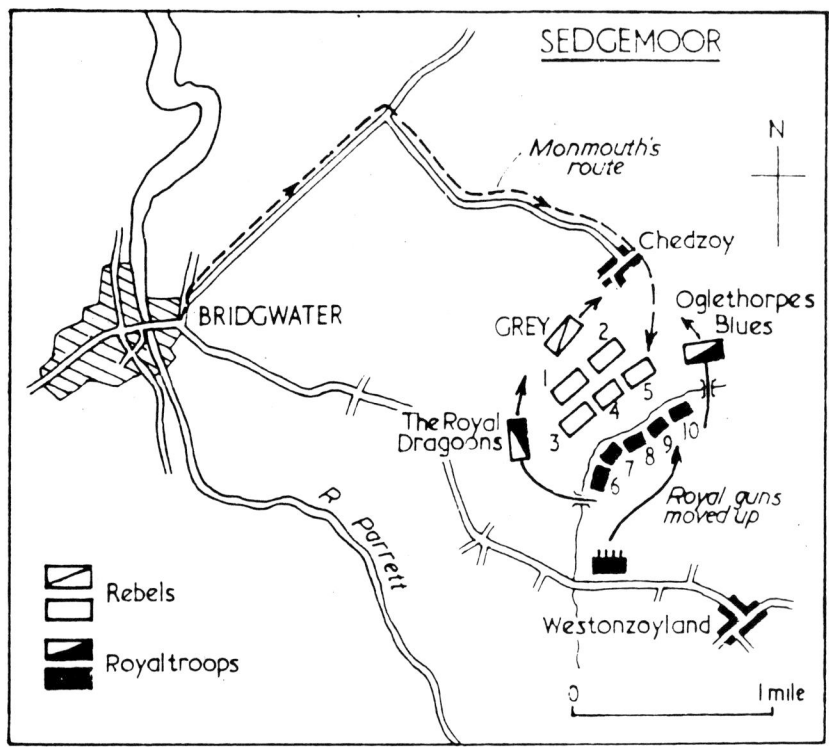

(see page 180)

The Duke of Monmouth landed at Lyme in June 1685 with a handful of followers, some rather out-of-date weapons, no horses, and no military supporters of any consequence. He faced a royal army, recently reinforced by the Tangier garrison under the command of Colonel Percy Kirke, John Churchill's cavalry and Lord Feversham, who was a capable if not brilliant commander. Monmouth gathered his army remarkably quickly from the many discontented weavers in the Taunton area along with men from Dorset and Devon. Exeter was in government hands so he decided to march to Bristol and, proceeding via Glastonbury, he reached Keynsham bridge, where he was surprised by a royal cavalry patrol and lost heart. One of the royal captives persuaded him that Bristol was too hard a town to capture and he was also given news of fresh support in Wiltshire and in the Mendips. Bath refused him entry but he turned on his pursuers and fought a small action at *Norton St Philip*, where the Duke of Grafton, leading the dragoons for James II, was forced to retreat losing not only his horse but quite a few men as well.

Retreating to Wells, where Lord Grey drew his sword in the cathedral to

Captain Dummer of the royal Artillery wrote a brief but interesting account:

July 5. We marched into the Levell . . . Rebels said (to be) in their march towards Bristoll . . . We securely went to sleep, the Foot in camp, and the Horse in Quarters at Weston and Midlesea, saving some Outguards of Horse upon our Right and Left. July 6. At 2 A Clock this morning (securely sleeping) our Camp was Rous'd by the near approach of the Rebells; a dark night and thick Fogg covering the Moon; supiness and a preposterous Confidence of ourselves with the Undervaluing of the Rebells . . . had put us into the worst circumstances of surprize . . . Thus we rec'd the Alarme from Sir Francis Compton . . . with his single Party of 150 Horse and Dragoons . . . From this Alarme there seems to be 2 minutes distance to a Volley of Small Shott from the Body of the Rebells Foot, consisting of about 6000 (but All came not up to Battell) upon the Right of our Camp, followed by 2 or 3 Rounds from Three Pieces of Cannon brought up within 116 Paces of the Ditch Ranging our Battallions. Our Artillery was near 500 Paces distant, and the Horses Drivers not easily found through confusion and darkness. Yet such was the extraordinary cheerfulness of our Army, that they were allmost as readily drawn up to receive them, as a prae-informed expectation could have posted them, tho' upon so short and so dangerous a warning. Six of our nearest Gunns were with the greatest diligence imaginable advanced, three upon the Right of the Scotts, and three in front of the King's first Battalion; and did very considerable execution upon the Enemies. They stood near an hour and a halfe with great shouting and courage, briskly fyring; and then throwing down their Armies, fell into Route and confusion. The number of the Slaine with about 300 taken, according to the most modest computation might make up 1000,

The Duke of Monmouth (National Portrait Gallery)

we losing but 27 on the spott and having about 200 wounded. A victory very considerable where Providence was absolutely a greater Friend than our own conduct. The Dead in the Moor we buried and the Country people took care for the interment of those slain in the Corne Fields.

TO SEE NEARBY

Middlezoy Church Brass to French officer.

Taunton Castle Museum, used by Jeffreys as a courtroom.

Lyme Regis and *Bridgwater* museums.

Somerton New monument (by the library) commemorates three rebels who never returned.

The new monument at Somerton

Battlefield Langport with Burrow Mump (see page 149).

For motorists there is the 'Pitchfork Route' following Monmouth's route from Lyme to Bristol, Bath and back. Contact the Tourist Office in Taunton Public Library for details.

prevent the rebels from damaging the high altar, Monmouth crept back to Bridgwater and started to reinforce it for a siege. The army of Lord Feversham, about 3,500 including no less than 17 guns, camped at Somerton and then made its way to Westonzoyland where tents were put up on the edge of the Bussex Rhine, a windy 8ft (2.4m) wide ditch with only two crossing places. Feversham sent out patrols and then retired to bed on 5 July, leaving young John Churchill on the field.

Monmouth, always prepared to listen to someone else's advice especially if flattering, was introduced to Godfrey, a local farmer who knew the moors well – Westonzoyland being about 7 miles (11km) from Bridgwater over the moors. (His farm at Sutton Mallet is still called Godfrey's farm.) According to Godfrey the king's army was encamped without any protection and could be attacked at night. Monmouth made preparations. Horses had rags tied to their hooves, his four cannon were greased – one that squeaked was left behind – his men given the password 'Soho' and accompanied by Lord Grey his battalions under Foulkes, Basset, Wade, Holmes and Matthews led off in single file in a three-hour march to Westonzoyland. They left at about 11pm

TWO LUCKY REBELS – THE HORSE DEALER AND THE PREACHER

The aftermath of Sedgemoor is usually filled with stories of Judge Jeffreys and the Assizes, with bloodthirsty accounts of the number of rebels executed, so it is interesting to dwell on the luck of those who escaped.

Francis Scott, a horsedealer from Hambridge, sold some horses to Monmouth and, either because he wasn't paid for them and wanted to get them back after the battle, or for another reason, he enlisted in the rebel army. Captured and imprisoned in Westonzoyland Church he determined to escape. Using a nail or sharp instrument he picked the lock in the little north door – the church accounts record the repair of the lock later – and waiting until dark and when the guard was asleep he crept out and made his way home, hiding in a cornfield during the day. The guard must have woken up shortly after this as Scott was the only rebel to escape from the

arriving at 2 o'clock in the morning. All went well except for a careless musket shot that was heard by a sentry who raised the alarm. However the Bussex Rhine seemed to surprise Godfrey, and Lord Grey, who could have created havoc if his men had been given flaming torches, failed to find the upper plungeon (bridge) so they galloped off down the rhine to be fired on by every royal soldier who was up and awake. They fled towards Chedzoy, later pursued by dragoons. Wade and Monmouth however positioned the army so that the three small guns could open up supported by the few musketeers available. Meanwhile Churchill had moved Kirke's and Trelawney's regiments to the right wing so they faced Matthews and, helped by the Bishop of Winchester's carriage horses, moved the guns off the road to Bussex farm where, with daylight approaching, they opened up and did considerable damage. Monmouth fled at daylight, his men were rounded up and put in the church. The battle was over but the recriminations went on for a long time and the Westcountry has never forgotten Judge Jeffreys.

THE WALK (L)

This is an attempt to follow Monmouth's route from Bridgwater although only the Bradney to Westonzoyland path is recommended as the motorway and traffic in the area make it difficult for walkers to enjoy the first part. Start at St Mary's Church, Bridgwater, where Monmouth is supposed to have climbed the tower, using a spy-glass still in the museum, to see the king's army at Westonzoyland. Cross the Parrett bridge and take the turning left to the A38 Bristol road over the railway and motorway. In Bawdrip take Bradney Lane to Peasey Farm. Round the back of the farm is a path to the banks of King's Sedgemoor Drain but, depending on weather conditions, there is also a drove leading straight down in the same direction. We followed the latter and cut through to the drain bank when the drove suddenly ended. One place

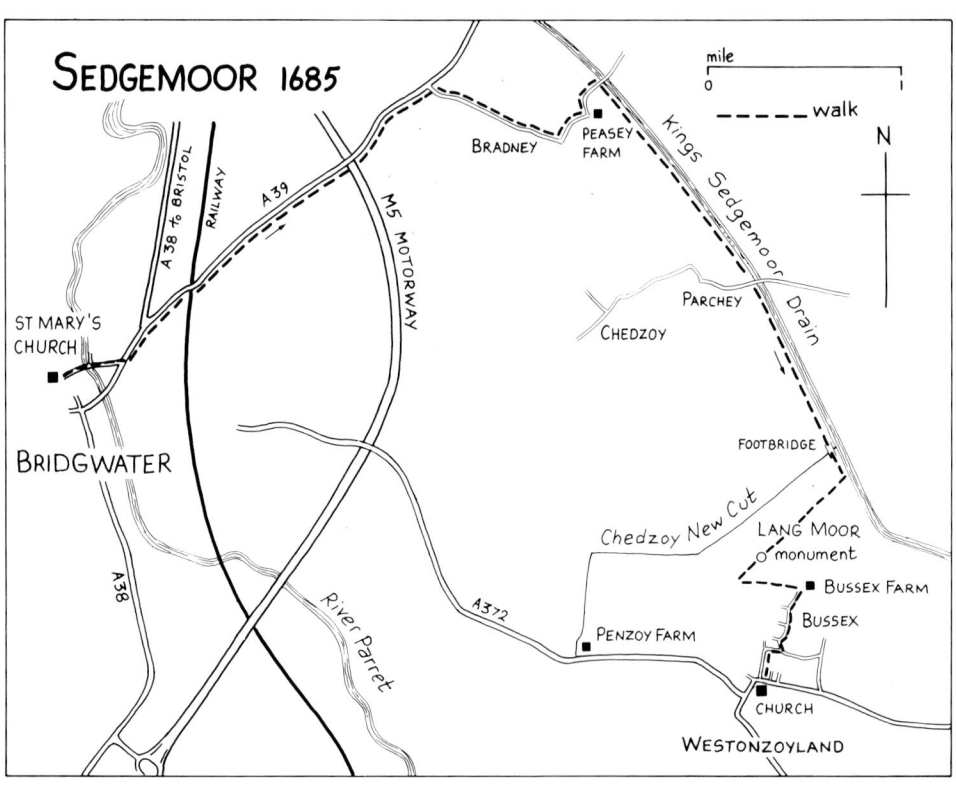

requires a long jump and it might be useful to carry a light ladder for non-jumpers. On the opposite bank (the drain is at least 20ft (6m) wide) is Pendon Hill, where Monmouth looked down on the battlefield after his escape and which, on a fine day, is a good viewing point for photographers, birdwatchers etc. Parchey Bridge is ahead and the path carries on over the stile to the right of this. Carry on until you come under the overhead electricity wires (they sing to you in the wind), when turn off right to where there are a few trees to pick up Lang Moor Drove. It is possible to get lost here, but if you aim for the gates there are usually bridges across the rhines. The Trevelyan monument, erected in the 1920s, stands between two tall white willows. The inscription reads: To the glory of God and in memory of all those who doing the right as they gave it fell in the Battle of Sedgemoor 6 July 1685 and lie buried in this field or who for their share in the fight suffered death, punishment or transportation.

Pro-Patria

Trafalgar 1805 Plassey 1757 Quebec 1759 Waterloo 1815 Great War 1914–1918 2nd World War 1940–1945.

Carry on down the drove until it turns sharp left into Bussex Drove (it is no use taking a short cut to the farm unless you are carrying a ladder as the rhines are too wide to jump) and at Bussex Farm is a 1985 monument that tries to tell you a bit about the battle.

A bit more money and some help from the National Trust here might have produced something more elegant. Down Monmouth Road to the school (this looks like an ex-RAF building and so it was) where turn right into a cul-de-sac and take the narrow path to the church past the beehives. Westonzoyland Church has one of the finest towers and carved tie-beam roofs to be found in Somerset.

church. When the General Pardon was announced Scott came out of his hiding place and lived a normal life.

The other lucky rebel, Thomas Coad, was a militia man from Stoford. Put off by the lack of religious zeal in the Militia, he deserted at Axminster by walking down the bed of the river and then joined Monmouth's Red Regiment. He fought with a pike at Keynsham and again at Norton St Philip, where he was badly wounded in the lung and hand. He surrendered to Colonel Phelipps of Montacute, was treated for his wounds and imprisoned at Ilchester. Sentenced to be hanged at Wells, his sentence was not carried out and he was transported to Jamaica, where he was sold to Colonel Bach, a planter. Here he seems to have been well treated and became a lay preacher. In 1690 he was freed and managed to pay his own fare home. He wrote his *Memorandum*, which was eventually published in 1849 and is one of the most fascinating contemporary accounts of the rebellion.

THE AMAZING ESCAPE OF DR HENRY PITMAN

Henry Pitman and his younger brother, William, were Quakers from Sandford Orcas on the Dorset/Somerset border. Henry had trained as a doctor in Italy and had a deputy job in Yeovil. When they heard of the Monmouth rising the two brothers went to Bridgwater and Monmouth appointed Henry as his surgeon. He treated the wounded from both sides, but after Sedgemoor was captured and his horse stolen. He and his brother were imprisoned in Ilchester Jail (now no longer, but once the principal county jail) and tried at Dorchester. They were transported on the *Betty* from Weymouth to Barbados, then sold as slaves to Robert Bishop.

Badly treated, Henry decided to escape. His brother died, but with five other rebels he joined two debtors and made for the island of Tortuga off the coast of Venezuela in an open boat. They had an early escape when the boat was nearly discovered before they left, but they hid it under water so that they had to bail it out continuously when they were under way. At Tortuga, they had to live off fish and turtle eggs as there was no other food. They managed to survive and eventually an English privateer landed at the island and took off Pitman; the others did not want to leave so were left food and clothing. The ship took Henry to New York, which had recently been taken over from the Dutch, and then he took another ship back to Southampton. When he arrived he discovered that both he and his brother had been pardoned on 31 May 1687.

Henry settled in London, where he wrote and published his account *A Relation of the Great Sufferings of Henry Pitman*. Strangely the good doctor's adventures were not yet finished as he went back to Barbados as a free man and died there two years later in 1693. What became of the rebels left on Tortuga is unknown, but very few transportees returned and Pitman was one of the only men to write an account of their adventures. It must have been read by Daniel Defoe, who was also involved in the Monmouth Rising, but managed to avoid capture. Defoe used it, along with the account of William Dampier's rescue of Alexander Selkirk from Juan Fernandez Island, as a source for *Robinson Crusoe*.

Glencoe (National Trust for Scotland)

KILLIEKRANKIE
27 July 1689

Appearing like Montrose with a scratch army in support of the king, John Graham of Claverhouse, Viscount Dundee – a cavalryman by training – seems to have been a natural leader. One can imagine his army on the hill above Urrard House waiting for the word to charge on Mackay, who was carefully arranging his troops on the plateau below. Why didn't Dundee charge before Mackay was ready? Was there some instinct of chivalry that induced him to wait or was it really because he wanted the sun to shine in the face of his enemy? These points are not really answered, but the wait proved fatal. There is a quiet glade below the new main road where the Campbell of Urrard stone, visible from the edge of the road, now marks the spot. It is a very peaceful scene in spite of the traffic nearby and especially so as the National Trust centre is some distance away on the tourist road to Pitlochry. The dead of Killiekrankie rest in peace and the tourists walk elsewhere.

The battle of Killiekrankie was an isolated incident and does not really fit into the pattern of Jacobite risings. Viscount Dundee had assembled the loyal clans at Blair Atholl, including Irish troops under Colonel Cannon. He had very few horsemen but he knew that General Mackay with 5,000 regular government troops was out to capture Blair Atholl and he planned to ambush him in the Pass. The route winds along by the River Garry and Mackay's scouts spotted the Highlanders on the hill opposite, so Mackay drew up his force in a

Guided walk at Killiekrankie (National Trust for Scotland)

position roughly just above the old road with his right wing at Urrard House, in which he placed his sharpshooters. On his left wing was Brigadier Berthould Balfour's Dutch regiment and in the centre he had three small cannon. Dundee waited until the sun shone in his enemy's faces before charging down the slope to scatter the government troops. The Highland victory was conclusive, Balfour was killed but so too was Dundee, by one of the sharpshooters; Mackay escaped with some survivors. But the rebellion was soon over without a leader of the class of Dundee, for Cannon, next in command, could not control the Highlanders.

THE WALK (L)

Killiekrankie is an excellent place for a walk and, starting at the National Trust of Scotland centre on the old road, you take the footpath through the wood below. It starts off with a footbridge and in wet weather can be slippery. A stick is useful and good shoes or boots essential. The wood in August was alive with black Scotch Argus butterflies, not seen very often although a day later I saw some at Glen Shiel. There are some oak trees, newly planted; the Trust is planning to make this an oak wood and discourage beech as small plants do not grow under beech trees. The path drops to the River Garry where the diagonally shaped rock on the left of the railing is the Soldier's Leap. One of Mackay's men leapt 18ft (5m) to cross the Garry here and get away from his pursuers. The path then winds down to the left by the railway and the viaduct. High up on the last arch is the anonymous carved face of, perhaps, the stone mason or more probably the Victorian engineer who built the viaduct, still used by Inverness-bound trains today. The path winds through wild raspberry bushes, and the trees, mostly beech and oak but including a few elms – still alive in spite of the disease which has reached this area too – provide excellent shelter for the walker on a hot day.

After about ½ mile (.8km) the Balfour stone appears with a notice saying this is where he was cut down, apparently not understanding the Gaelic for surrender. The path now suddenly turns right over a metal bridge with the Garry far below. On the other side of the bridge is an aspen tree (Killikrankie in gaelic means the vale of aspen) easily recognised by its leaves, green on one side, silver on the other.

Climbing up the other side one comes to the modern Lynn of Tummel road bridge and car park. Across this take the turning right to Tenandry which goes up the steep hill to the hamlet of two houses, a farm and a church. The sign on the church said that the service was altered from 11.45am to 11am so that the parson could get back home in time to listen to the *Archers*.

At the top of the hill there is a nature reserve. This was a mass of wild flowers. Amongst others I saw the white grass-of-Parnassus flower, scarce now in Scotland and very scarce in England, scabious, ragged-robin, and lots of yellow lady's bedstraw, so-called for that is what it was used for in the crofts of olden times. Above, there were two buzzards with swept-back round wings like Hawker Hurricanes, and almost as deadly to smaller birds. They make a strange mew sound, sharp and easily heard by their prey.

Finally the walk goes back down to the river, over the road bridge by Old Killiekrankie station, over the railway bridge and turns right to the Trust centre. For those wanting tea there is an excellent restaurant about ½ mile (.8km) up the old road towards Blair Atholl and in the layby by the restaurant is a lane leading to the Campbell of Urrard monument on the actual battle site (now private land). The sheep field in front of this has a stone supposed to commemorate the death of Dundee.

This walk took an hour and ten minutes and covered 3½ miles (5.6km), but it can be extended to Loch Faskally and Pitlochry if wished.

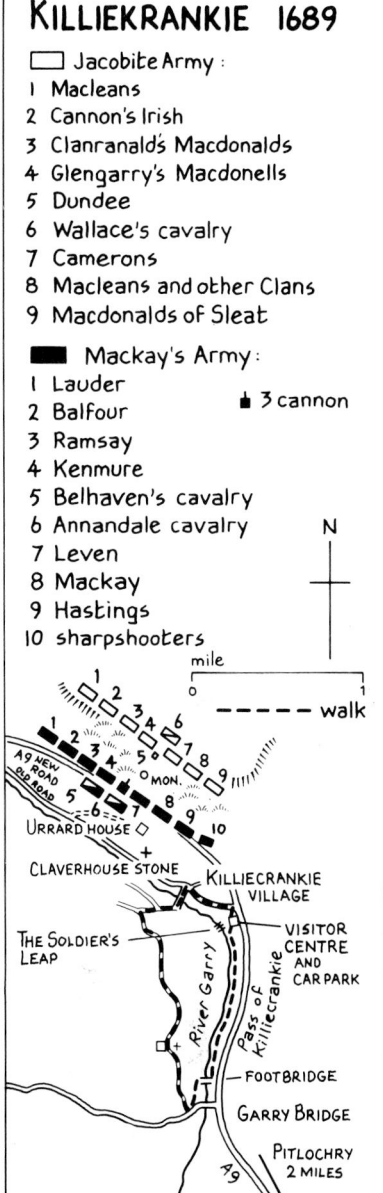

KILLIEKRANKIE 1689

☐ Jacobite Army :
1 Macleans
2 Cannon's Irish
3 Clanranald's Macdonalds
4 Glengarry's Macdonells
5 Dundee
6 Wallace's cavalry
7 Camerons
8 Macleans and other Clans
9 Macdonalds of Sleat

■ Mackay's Army :
1 Lauder
2 Balfour
3 Ramsay
4 Kenmure
5 Belhaven's cavalry
6 Annandale cavalry
7 Leven
8 Mackay
9 Hastings
10 sharpshooters

⚑ 3 cannon

---- walk

TO SEE NEARBY

Blair Atholl Castle Home of the Murrays, Dukes of Atholl. One room has Dundee's armour showing the bullet hole. In the ruined church is a very innocuous monument to him.

Clan Museum of the Robertsons The Robertson or Clan Donnachaidh has its museum at Bruar near Blair Atholl (see also page 11). It has several Jacobite relics.

PRESTON
13 November 1715

The failure of the 1715 rising was of advantage to the 1745 rising as there is a record at Avignon of no less than 500 men in attendance at the court of the Old Pretender. These are too numerous to list here but include:-

Duke of Ormond
Earl of Mar
Earl Marischal
Lord Southesk
Lord Panmure
Lord Lintithgow
Lord George Murray (Future commander in '45)
Lord Nithsdale (After his escape from London)
Lord Keith
Lord Ogilvy
Lord Erskine
General Cullen
General Hamilton
General Gordon
General Fraser
Brigadier Mackintosh of Borlum
Brigadier Hay
Brigadier Corbet

9 colonels, 5 Lieutenant Colonels, 9 Majors of Infantry, 24 Captains of infantry, 6 Lieutenants, 10 doctors and surgeons, 30 gentlemen, 35 Catholics, and two secretaries. With their retainers this list comes to 500.

It is not surprising that there were more plots and that the 1719 rising was soon to follow led by the Earl Marischal and his brother Lord Keith and that the younger ones like Tullibardine, Macdonald and Murray took a leading part in the '45 rising.

The first battle of Preston was a muddled three-day affair in August 1648. It led to the defeat of the Scots by Cromwell with no visible signs today of the battlefield other than a fine picture in the Harris Museum, Preston.

The battle of 13 November 1715 is of much more interest as it took place inside the town. At that time Preston was a small market town with an important bridge over the Ribble that took the traffic from the south to Carlisle and Scotland. The rising under Lords Kenmure, Wintoun, Carnwath and the Earl of Derwentwater took place in Kelso in early November, while Mar was marching out of Perth with the main body of the Jacobite army. Some 2,000 Mackintosh Highlanders under Brigadier Mackintosh crossed the Forth and, avoiding Argyll's government troops, marched to Kelso. There was an argument as to where to go next but Forster, appointed by Mar as 'General', suggested Preston where there was hope of support from the Lancashire Jacobites.

On 9 November Derwentwater's horse reached Preston and Lord Charles Murray led in the Atholl regiment the following day. On 11 November Mackintosh, Murray and others realised that General Wills was coming from Cheshire with dragoons and General Carpenter from Newcastle. Road blocks were set up. There was no attempt to block the bridge. Four barricades at each end of Fisher Street and on the Blackpool road were strengthened by naval cannon. The barricades held up Wills and the dismounted dragoons lost some men, but during the night many Scots deserted over Penwortham ford. When Carpenter arrived 'General' Forster sent out his friend Mr Oxburgh to make surrender terms and early on the 13th the Jacobites surrendered. The leaders were condemned to death and shut up in Newgate Prison, where three of them, Nithsdale, Forster and Mackintosh (see page 174), managed to escape,

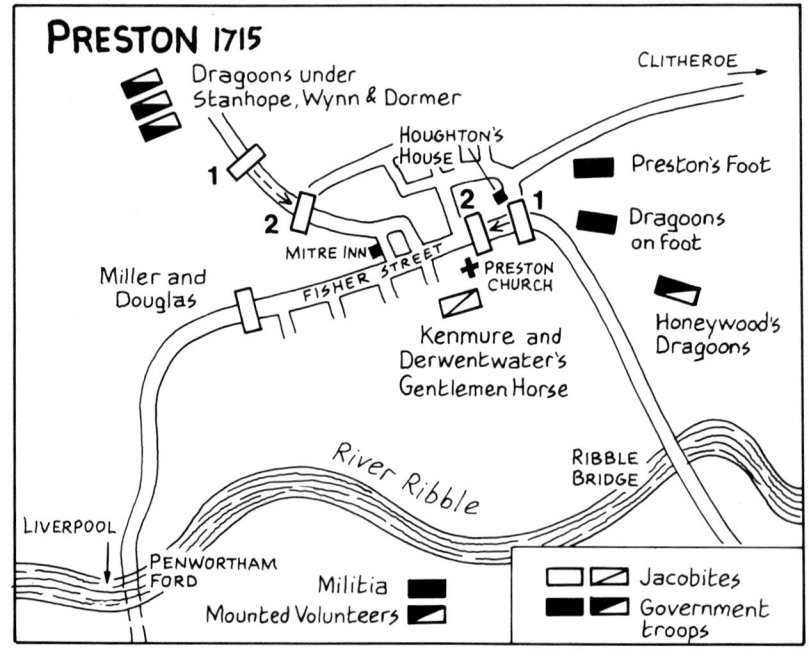

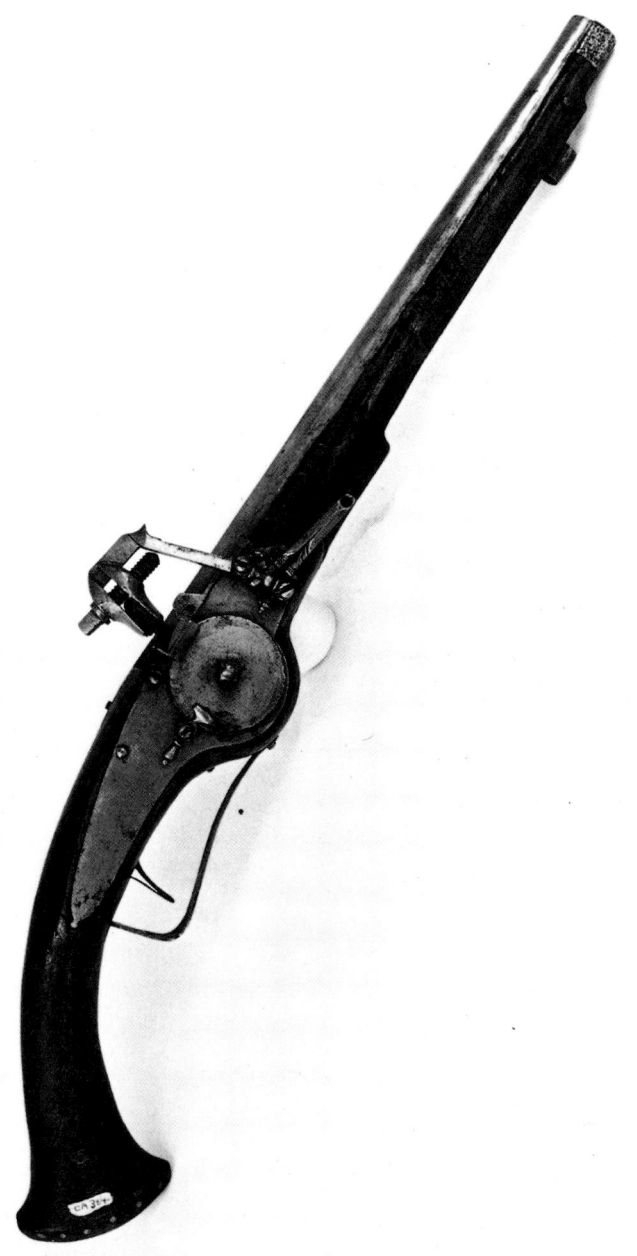

Eighteenth-century pistol of a type used at Preston (York Castle Museum)

Derwentwater and Kenmure were both executed. The rank and file were locked up in Preston Church for a month and many were transported. Some returned to Scotland and took part in the '45 rebellion.

OF INTEREST TODAY (S)

There is no monument to the Jacobite surrender and only a few relics in the Harris Museum.

The home of the Earl of Derwentwater, Langley Castle, is now a country house hotel near Haydon Bridge, Northumberland.

SHERIFFMUIR
13 November 1715

So close to Dunblane and Stirling the battlefield of Sheriffmuir is yet so wild and untouched even today. The armies faced each other across the road to Dunblane, the Jacobites at the Perth end and the government troops coming up from Dunblane. The farms on the moor are believed to be called after the stones erected for the fallen – hence Duthiestone, Cairnstone, Whitestone, Harperstone and Meiklestone. There are accounts of the remarkable bravery shown by men on both sides. The shepherd of Braco who joined Mar two days before the battle cut down seven dragoons in a ravine near the Loup of Pendreigh, where there is a large stone to record the deed. A dragoon stood in the Wharryburn and killed no less than ten Highlanders before he was slain.

Amongst items found on the battlefield are a rusty pistol, a 20in (50cm) dirk with an ivory handle and a leather covered glass bottle believed to have belonged to the Duke of Perth. No doubt there are other weapons still to be found.

The outcome of the battle, long a bone of contention between historians and supporters of both sides, is summed up in the old song:

> There's some say that we won
> And some say that they won,
> And some say that nane won at a' man;
> But one thing I'm sure,
> That at Shirramuir,
> A battle there was that I saw, man.
> And we ran and they ran,
> And they ran and we ran,
> And we ran and they ran awa' man.

Sheriffmuir in November is very bleak and is not a place to stay long. The two armies that assembled here in 1715 were fairly confident of victory. The

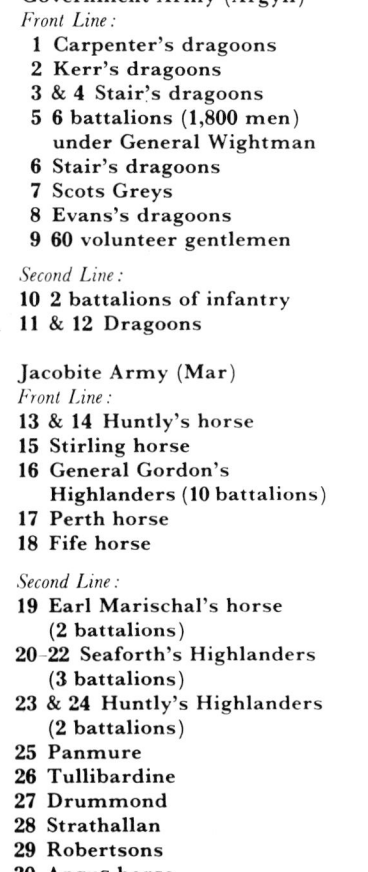

Government Army (Argyll)
Front Line:
 1 Carpenter's dragoons
 2 Kerr's dragoons
 3 & 4 Stair's dragoons
 5 6 battalions (1,800 men)
    under General Wightman
 6 Stair's dragoons
 7 Scots Greys
 8 Evans's dragoons
 9 60 volunteer gentlemen

Second Line:
10 2 battalions of infantry
11 & 12 Dragoons

Jacobite Army (Mar)
Front Line:
13 & 14 Huntly's horse
15 Stirling horse
16 General Gordon's
    Highlanders (10 battalions)
17 Perth horse
18 Fife horse

Second Line:
19 Earl Marischal's horse
    (2 battalions)
20-22 Seaforth's Highlanders
    (3 battalions)
23 & 24 Huntly's Highlanders
    (2 battalions)
25 Panmure
26 Tullibardine
27 Drummond
28 Strathallan
29 Robertsons
30 Angus horse
31 Reserve (800 men)

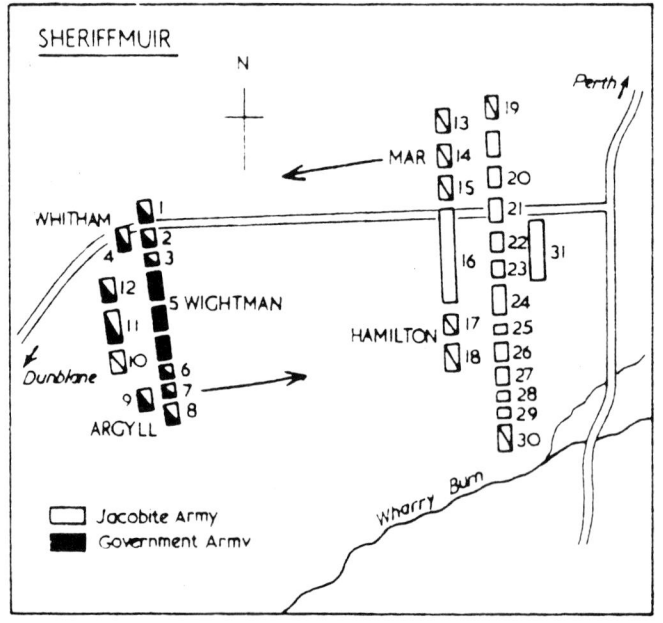

SGUR-URAN

FÒIR CÙ'MHME · NEC GAROTE CHROS

MACRAE
OF
CONCHRA

CLANN MHICRATH

MAR CHUIMHNEACHAN AIR CLANN MHICRATH A THUIT
AN CATH BLAR AN T SIORAMHAIR AIR AN TREAS LA DEUG
DE CHEUD MHIOS A GHEAMHRAIDH 1715 NUAIR BHA
IAD AG DION TIGHE RIOGHAIL NAN STIUBHARTACH
BHA BUIDHIONNAN NAN TAILEACH AGUS NAN AILSEACH
AN ORDUGH CATHA AIR SGIATH CHLI AN FHEACHD
GHAIDHEALACH AGUS DE NA SEOID SO BHA A MHOR-
CHUID LE AN CINN RI LAR AIG CRIOCH AN LATHA
THA AN CARN-CUIMHEACHAIN SO AIR A THOGAIL LE
COMUNN CLANN MHICRATH AIR AN TREAS LA DEUG
DE CHEUD MHIOS A GHEAMHRAIDH, 1915.

THE CLAN MACRAE

IN MEMORY OF THE MACRAES KILLED AT
SHERIFFMUIR 13TH NOV 1715, WHEN
DEFENDING THE ROYAL HOUSE OF STUART.
THE KINTAIL AND LOCHALSH COMPANIES
FORMED PART OF THE LEFT WING OF
THE HIGHLAND ARMY, AND FELL
ALMOST TO A MAN

ERECTED AT THE INSTANCE
OF THE CLAN MACRAE
SOCIETY.
13TH NOV. 1915.

THE ADVENTURES OF BRIGADIER MACKINTOSH OF BORLUM

The 1715 Rising was without doubt an inept affair. The Earl of Mar had no experience of commanding troops, and was a schemer rather than a leader. His choice of leaders, especially Thomas Forster who commanded at Preston, was most unfortunate; but he did find one loyal and devoted officer in Mackintosh of Borlum who was in his fifties and had military experience. His clan and the men under his command at the Braemar rising numbered 2,000 and Mar let him act independently, sending him to Fife and giving him vague instructions to cross the Forth, as far from Stirling as he could as Argyll controlled central Scotland for the Hanoverians. Collecting a number of small boats at Crail, Pittenweem and Elie in Fife they set out for the coast of East Lothian. Landing near Haddington they occupied Seton House. A party of them had to take shelter from Argyll's fleet on the island of May, but these men under Strathmore and Walkinshaw (father of Prince Charles's mistress) made their way back to Mar's army and fought at *Sheriffmuir*.

Mackintosh decided to attack Leith and his men captured the old fort there, setting free some prisoners and helping themselves to some much needed provisions in the Custom House, where they were approached by Argyll who withdrew as he had no artillery. The attack on Edinburgh never really started and Mackintosh withdrew to Seton before setting out to join Forster at Kelso. He was part of the Jacobite force that barricaded itself into *Preston* and was captured along with many others and taken to Newgate prison in London. He managed to slip off his irons at 11 o'clock at night, waited at the door of the prison until the servant opened it, knocked down this man and then the turnkey outside and, with the help of Charles Wogan and twelve others, broke out into the streets of London.

Earl of Mar, with a commission from James VIII in his hands, had about 10,000 men and, as many said, almost as many leaders. Against him was the Duke of Argyll with a smaller but much more professional army including artillery and better cavalry than the Jacobites. In his centre was General Wightman, one of the most competent of the government generals at that time. Argyll was determined to stop the Jacobites moving down to Stirling and threatening Edinburgh. As usual the Scots believed in a sudden charge and Mar's right wing of Macleans chased Whitham's men as far as Stirling. On the other wing Cathcart and his Scots Greys attacked Hamilton and only the bravery of the Fife horse stopped a rout. The Macraes were killed almost to a man and four cannon captured. Both Argyll and Mar were off the field at this stage and as the Master of Sinclair said later 'the spirits of the best men on earth must be broken by such leaders', so there was no further Jacobite advance and Wightman held his ground. Some say there was a traitor in Mar's camp, one Drummond, who took a message to Hamilton from Mar and, instead of telling him to attack, told him to retreat. The Jacobites lost some 800 men to Argyll's 300 and the field was left to Argyll. In spite of the landing of James later, the rising was soon over, for the defeat at Preston put an end to it more effectively than Argyll's half-victory at Sherriffmuir.

THE WALK (L)

To find the Macrae Monument take the little hill road just after Stirling University and carry on over the hill for about 6 miles (9.6km) until you come to the inn (closed) and turning left for Dunblane. About 1 mile (.8km) down by the forest there is a large monument on the right to the Macraes and next to it in August a mass of yellow loosestrife. The walk starts here and, to see the Gathering Stone, take a short path by the wall through the heather and turn left to a clump of fir trees. It can be seen beside a fallen fir. It has large iron hoops round it to stop anyone carrying it away.

Return to the road and take the path that runs downhill for about 2 miles (3km) through the Kippendavie estate to Dunblane. After Dykedale it becomes

In 1719 the commander of the Spanish force at *Glen Shiel* was none other than Mackintosh of Borlum newly arrived from France, and again he escaped. But he was recaptured in 1727 and confined to Edinburgh Castle, where he lived to the age of eighty-five. His wife, a former maid of honour to Queen Anne, was allowed to visit him in prison and they had a daughter, Winwood, a son Lachlan, who died before his father, and another son Shaw. Shaw's son became a highwayman, he was the last of the family.

a stone track and is used by citizens of Dunblane for exercising animals. The path ends in Leighton Avenue amongst suburban housing and then to St Mary's Drive and Glen Road. There is a bus back to Bridge of Allen and Stirling (about ten minutes).

We did this walk in October after visiting the Wallace Monument in the morning (it closes at the end of October) so that it was nearly dark by the time we got to Dunblane. But the route is downhill all the way and straight walking amongst heather and fir trees with the odd pheasant and partridge squawking by the side of the path. The shock of suddenly meeting suburbia is intense, and one hopes that the battlefield will still retain its unspoilt appearance.

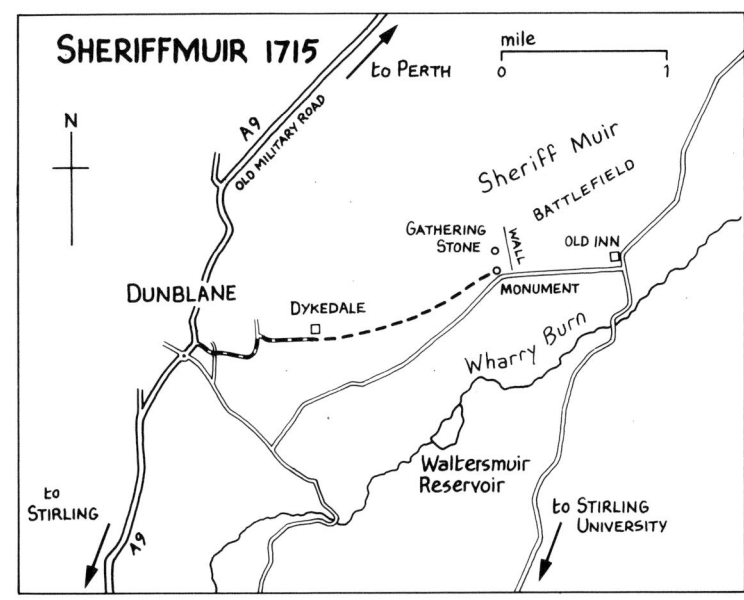

TO SEE NEARBY

Doune Castle, where English prisoners were put after Falkirk.

Battlefields Stirling Bridge, Bannockburn, Falkirk and Kilsyth.

Dunblane Cathedral.

175

GLEN SHIEL
10 June 1719

TO SEE NEARBY

Eilean Donan Castle is about 7 miles (11km) from the battleground and on the way you pass Loch Duich where the Spaniards are supposed to have flung their treasure. The little cairn by the road is in memory of a Campbell who was a shinty player. The castle is the home of the Macrae-Gilstrap family and two rooms are full of Jacobite relics. It was restored in the 1920s and has a causeway not there in 1719. If it had been properly defended by cannon, it would have been able to hold out longer against an attack by sea. The castle is open to the public in summer.

Five Sisters of Kintail For the mountaineer there is this fine ridge walk which can be done from nearby Ratigan Youth Hostel.

Skye Glen Shiel is en route for the island of Skye and some of the finest gabbro rock-climbing in Britain.

The Battle of Glen Shiel in the Western Highlands was a strange affair. On the Scottish side there were the Keiths – one of whom later became a Prussian field marshal – with 300 Spanish troops, arms and money. Arriving in Scotland at the same time were the Marquis of Tullibardine and the Earl of Seaforth, so there was an argument about leadership. Tullibardine seems to have won and set up an arsenal at Eilean Donan Castle. British ships *Worcester*, *Enterprize* and *Flamborough* appeared and bombarded the castle on 10 May. The forty-eight defenders surrendered and were transported to Leith. The castle was blown up and left as a ruin for two hundred years.

Meanwhile the main Spanish body and the few Highlanders – mostly Murrays and Macgregors – positioned themselves at the other end of Loch Duich where the pass is narrowest. It was a strange place to defend and not one a leader such as Dundee of Killiekrankie fame would have approved of. It is rocky, devoid of cover and General Wightman who set out from Fort Augustus to attack them with 1,100 men had the ideal weapon for the occasion – a cohorn mortar which created havoc amongst the Highlanders on the mountain. Lord Seaforth was badly wounded by a grenade and Montagu's men managed to get round the Highlanders on the mountain, routing them. The Murrays on the other wing had more success, killing the Dutch commander; but Wightman won the day and the Spaniards surrendered.

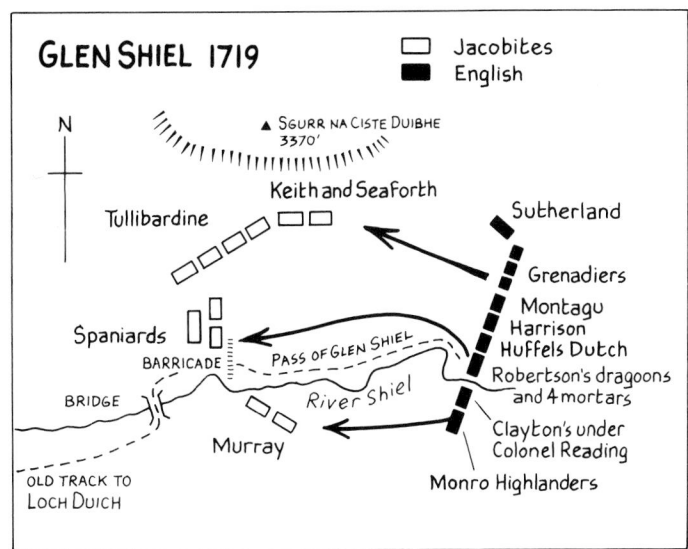

THE BATTLEFIELD TODAY (S)

This is easily found on the A87 as a small green boggy area with a cairn marking the spot where the leader of the Monro regiment fell attacking the Spaniards. The small bridge a few yards below was built in 1816, presumably on the site of an earlier bridge used by Wightman's advancing army. It is an ideal picnic spot and we found Scotch Argus butterflies in August by the waterfall. The banks of Sgurr na Ciste Duibhe are too steep to climb from here and the highlands on the other side of the river are also steep.

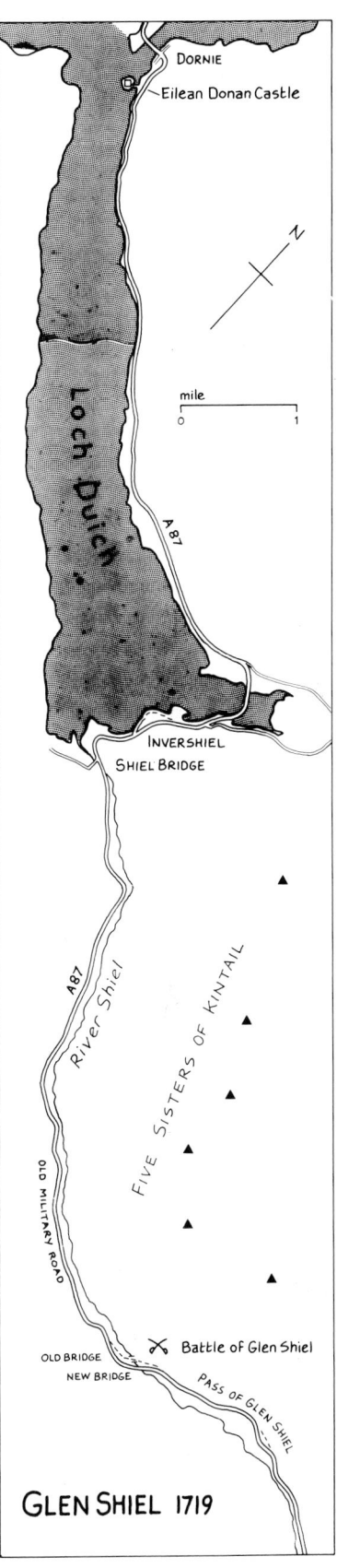

Eilean Donan Castle

177

The success of the 42nd Highlanders at Fontenoy made the Hanoverian government anxious to recruit more Highlanders to their ranks. The Earl of Loudoun was given the authority to raise the new regiment at Inverness in 1745. Before Prince Charles landed men were flocking to the colours. On 6 June the twelve companies were paraded with Colonel John Loudoun in command and John Campbell, later Duke of Argyll, as Lieutenant-Colonel. Eight companies were based at Inverness and the other four at Perth. Soon the two parts of the regiment were cut off by the Jacobite army. Some of Loudoun's men were present at *Prestonpans* where every officer and man of three companies was captured.

In February 1746, Lord Loudoun heard that Charles was at Moy Castle, seat of the Mackintosh chief, so he set out from Inverness to capture him. Lady Mackintosh discovered Loudoun's plans and sent young Lachlan Mackintosh to warn the prince. Arriving at five in the morning the lad gave the warning and Charles, with Lady Mackintosh's sons and her local blacksmith, a keen shot, hid beside the loch until the Macleods, in advance of the Highlanders, arrived. The blacksmith shot MacCrimmon, the piper of the Macleods, and the boys shouted so much that the rest of the Macleods rushed back to the main body where Lord Loudoun gave the order to retreat. This affair became known as the Rout of Moy.

The regiment was sent to Flanders and in 1748 it was disbanded in Perth.

(above right)
The £1 note of the Royal Bank of Scotland showing Edinburgh Castle. This remained in government hands throughout both the 1715 and the 1745 Risings (Royal Bank of Scotland)

(right)
French pistols (Wallace Collection)

PRESTONPANS
21 September 1745

When Prince Charles landed in Scotland in July 1745 and assembled the clans at Loch Shiel, he quickly raised a small army of about 1,000 men which, by the time he reached Edinburgh, grew to 2,500. There were notable absentees like the MacLeods and in Stirling the loyal troops, including Hamilton's and Gardiner's dragoons, were given a new general, Johnny Cope. Making for Inverness, Cope and his troops took ship for Dunbar where he landed on 17 September. Both Cromwell and Cope used Dunbar as a major troop supply port but other armies seem to have neglected it, so that today it has only a lifeboat station and a few fishing boats.

Lord George Murray, Charles's energetic general who had already fought for the Jacobites at Glen Shiel, left Edinburgh via the Salisbury crags, Duddingston and Falside Hill (see Pinkie, page 110). Cope took his army to Prestonpans where he lined a ditch between Bankton House and Riggonhead, keeping a close watch on the Scots who took up a temporary position near Tranent. The earlier Jacobites like Dundee might have attacked from the hill, but Murray, guided by a local laird's son, took his army in single file at 4am down a path over a bog through Riggonhead Farm to a new position facing back towards Edinburgh with his left on the edge of Seton Park (Camerons) and his right near Cockenzie (Macdonalds). In the second line were the Robertsons with their elderly chief, the men of Atholl and the Maclachlans. Waiting until the sun shone in the eyes of his enemies, Murray gave the order to charge and before they were properly organised Cope's army had the Highlanders on them. His artillery was all bunched up on the right wing and his infantry only had time to fire one round. Colonel Gardiner was killed and some 300 Hanoverians. About 1,600 prisoners were taken and only 30 Highlanders were killed, amongst them three young Cameron officers and David Thriepland of Fingask. Cope and some of his dragoons escaped to

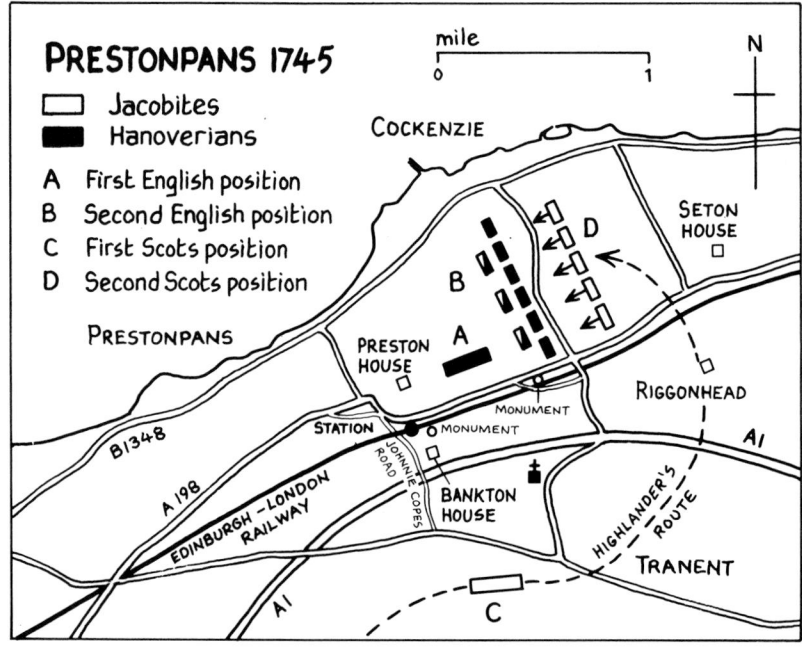

The Royal Bank of Scotland plc £1

£1

EDINBURGH CASTLE

TO SEE NEARBY

Prestonpans In the church is a monument to John Stuart of Phisgul 'barbarously murdered by four Highlanders near the end of the Battle fought at the field of Preston on the 21st September, 1745'. Presumably Stuart was either an innocent spectator or one of Johnnie Cope's local guides.

Seton Chapel Built for the Seton family on the site of an earlier church in 1513. The interior was damaged by troops in 1715. It is open to the public.

Dunbar, Pinkie (Falside Hill) and *Edinburgh* Edinburgh Castle has a museum of army relics and, although not specifically connected with the '45, is well worth a visit though alas Mons Meg, the cannon used in the Flodden campaign has retired from the battlements and is kept in the lower regions.

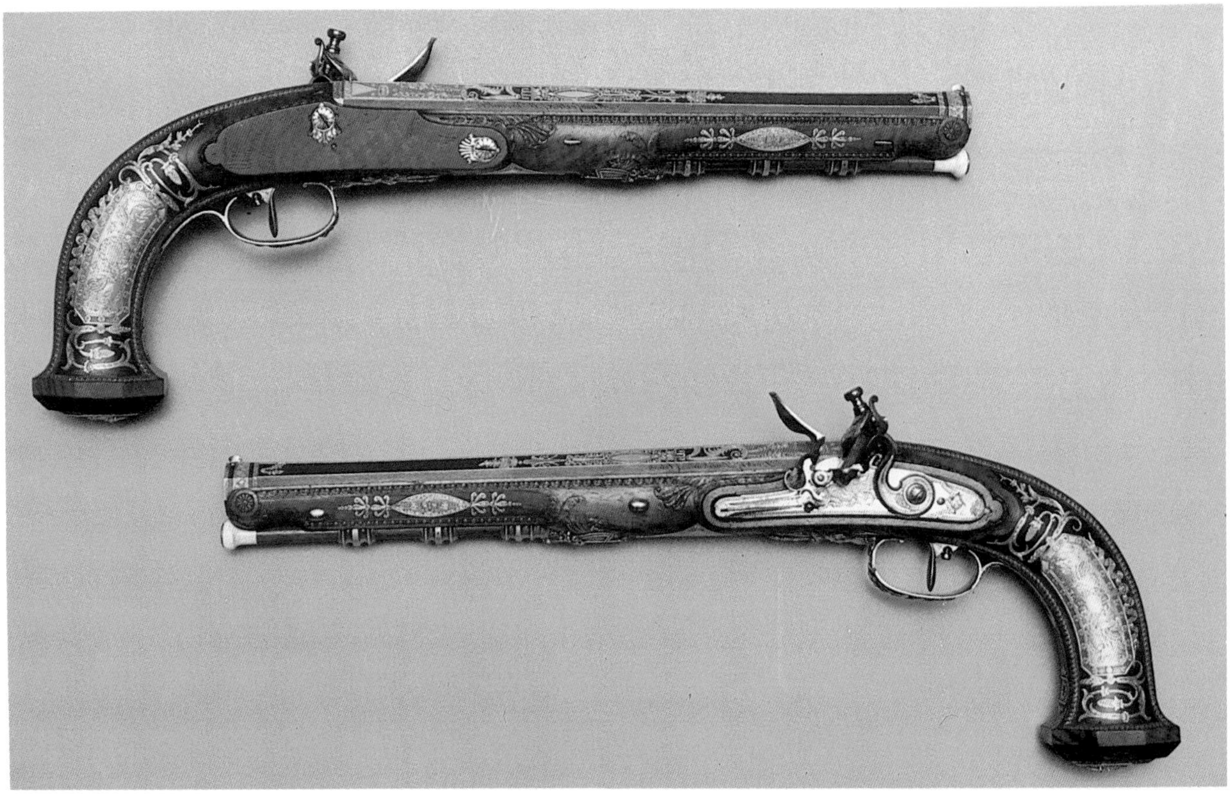

Berwick, but his carriage and papers were taken. The chief of the Robertsons was put in the carriage and his men took him in it back to Atholl as there were no horses to be found.

THE BATTLEFIELD TODAY (S)

There is a golden opportunity for the Scottish Tourist Board one day to open a path from Edinburgh to Tranent and Prestonpans following Murray's route. However the best way to see the battlefield is to take a train to Prestonpans station and lean out of the carriage to see the Gardiner Monument (on the Tranent side of the railway line) then carry on from the station down the road to the next bridge (Macmerry Road) where there is a simple monument to the '45 that stands on a neat piece of clipped grass by the side of the road. Preston House stands on the A198 still – this was where the wounded were taken, but there is no battle plan and the actual battlefield is very much an industrial area.

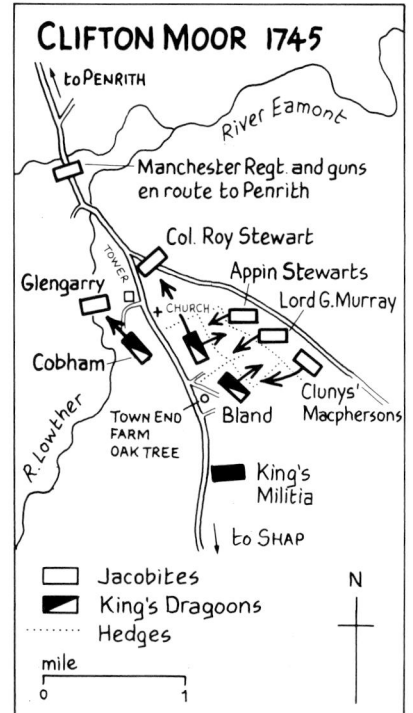

CLIFTON MOOR 1745

to PENRITH

River Eamont

Manchester Regt. and guns
en route to Penrith

Col. Roy Stewart

Appin Stewarts

Glengarry

TOWER

Lord G. Murray

CHURCH

Cobham

Clunys'
Macphersons

TOWN END
FARM
OAK TREE

Bland

R. Lowther

King's
Militia

to SHAP

☐ Jacobites   N
◣ King's Dragoons
.... Hedges

mile
0   1

CLIFTON MOOR
18 December 1745

After *Prestonpans* the Jacobites crossed into England but got no support, so turned for home at Derby. On retreating from Derby, Prince Charles's army was pursued by the Duke of Cumberland, and the Scots artillery in particular were a day behind the rest of the army at Penrith. Lord George Murray took command of the rearguard and sent for reinforcements from the prince who sent Colonel Roy Stewart and Cluny Macpherson's regiments to help, together with some of the Appin Stewarts. Murray placed them behind the many enclosure walls and hedges where they waited until dusk. When Cumberland's advance guard of Cobham's dragoons and Mark Kerr's dragoons with Bland's regiment advanced down the narrow lane the Highlanders charged with broad sword and targe and drove them back with about twelve killed on each side; but many of the Hanoverians were wounded including Bland's Colonel Honeywood. The pursuit was stopped and the prince's army marched into Glasgow on Christmas Day, leaving Cumberland behind at Carlisle.

THE WALK (M)

Clifton is a small village on the old A6 a few miles south of Penrith. Clifton Tower which belongs to English Heritage can be examined. Strangely the middle door is not locked and one can climb to the next floor but no further, so it is not a good place to see the battleground.

From the Tower proceed over the farm field to the stile over the wall that leads to Clifton Church, where some of the Hanoverian dead were buried. There is a monument to Bland's regiment just inside the gate which was erected by the King's Own Dragoon Guards when stationed in the area.

Inside, the church is mostly Victorian but has a very unusual carved wooden pulpit showing a nativity scene. In 1943 a gas pipe was eaten through by a rat and there was an explosion that blew out all the glass.

Carry on past the church and after a short time there is a footpath to Clifton Dykes that crosses the railway line. Here we found an attractive blue flower, about 2ft (60cm) high that could have been a cornflower; we saw it again later beside a footpath in Pitlochry. The path goes down to the field, which was full of standing corn so we retired to the road and past the Post Office to Town End Farm. Here on the left-hand side of the road is an oak tree where there is a small monument to two Scots killed in the battle.

TO SEE NEARBY

Carlisle Castle This has cells with some graffiti by Jacobite prisoners.

Brougham Castle at Eamont Bridge and *Penrith Castle* are ruins nearer Clifton that are worth a visit.

Bland's regimental monument in Clifton churchyard

FALKIRK
17 January 1746

After *Clifton*, Jacobites occupied Glasgow. After his retreat from Derby, Prince Charles found that Edinburgh was in government hands and so too was Stirling Castle. As most of his fresh recruits were in Perth, including some French arrivals, he decided to invest Stirling Castle. General Hawley, in command at Edinburgh with 8,000 men including dragoons, was a stern disciplinarian, but no match for Lord George Murray. The latter had positioned his army on Plean Hill, not far from Bannockburn and soon realised that the key to the position was to occupy Falkirk Moor, high above the little town. He marched his army there in two columns leaving the Duke of Perth with 1,000 men in the siege lines at Stirling.

Hawley was being entertained at Callander House by the Countess of Kilmarnock, rather like Lady Heron entertaining the Scots king before Flodden, and it was late in the afternoon before Hawley gave orders for Lord Ligonier, who led three dragoon regiments up Maggie Wood's Loan to attack the Highland left wing. One devastating close-range fire from the Macdonalds and the dragoons gave way hotly pursued by the Highland left wing.

Cobham's dragoons galloped down between the two armies and were fired at by all the Scots front line. The rain and cold prevented the Scots from being able to re-load, so they charged, as at Prestonpans, and four of the English regiments turned and fell back down the hill. Price's and Barrel's regiments stood firm and Lord Ligonier's right-wing troops too, so that a flanking fire checked the advancing Scots and Lord George had to advance his Atholl brigade in the second line to keep a check on the disordered front line. Lord Stapleton's picquets held the left of the second line and the Scots then entered Falkirk, Prince Charles finding General Hawley's missed supper much to his liking. Hawley lost some 280 men killed, wounded and missing. Lord Ligonier caught quinsy and died a few days later, and Sir Robert Munro's tomb can be seen in Falkirk Church. The Scots lost about 50 and the decision was made to retreat into the Highlands, although an advance to Edinburgh might have been successful.

THE BATTLEFIELD (S)

The battle site is found by taking the hill up past Falkirk railway station (B803) then turning right opposite the hospital then right again in a housing estate and, at the entrance to Bantaskin Park, is a monument, erected in 1927, to the battle. This is a small park with rowan trees and a delightful walk round it can be made by taking the bridge over the ravine (which formed part of the left wing of Lord George's position). Some sort of battle plan would be useful here and would make the site more interesting. Carry on down the hill past the end of the (disused) canal into Glenfuir Road and back to the main road. A short distance on the left is Rough Castle, one of the sites of the Antonine Wall.

The 1746 battle of *Falkirk* should not be confused with the action of 22 July, 1298, when William Wallace was defeated, when his horse deserted at a crucial moment, by King Edward I. The site of this battle was at Grahamston with the Scots occupying a position protected by a morass. Edward came from the Callendar Park direction and defeated his old enemy after a stiff fight, helped by his larger numbers and by the Scottish desertions. The area of this battle has now been built upon and it is difficult to work out where the action took place, and there is no monument.

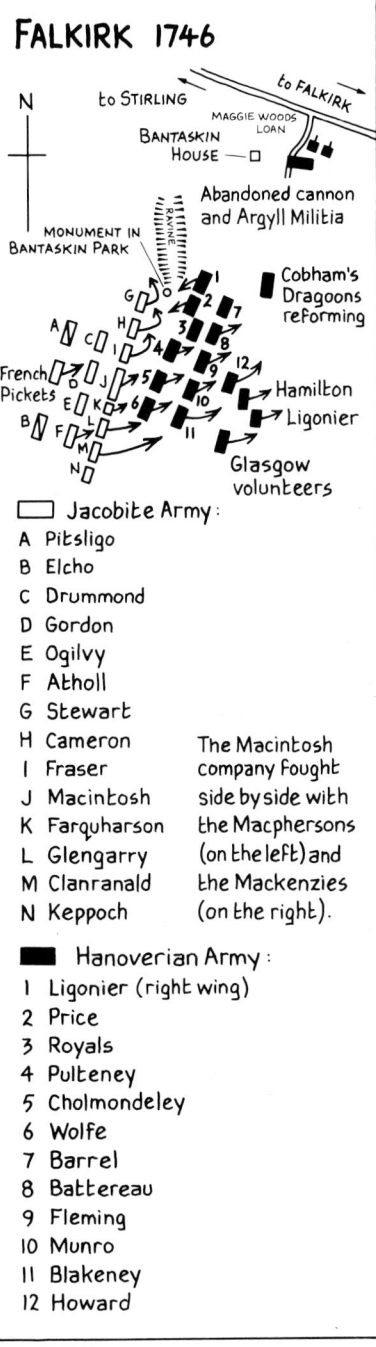

FALKIRK 1746

Jacobite Army:
A Pitsligo
B Elcho
C Drummond
D Gordon
E Ogilvy
F Atholl
G Stewart
H Cameron
I Fraser
J Macintosh
K Farquharson
L Glengarry
M Clanranald
N Keppoch

The Macintosh company fought side by side with the Macphersons (on the left) and the Mackenzies (on the right).

Hanoverian Army:
1 Ligonier (right wing)
2 Price
3 Royals
4 Pulteney
5 Cholmondeley
6 Wolfe
7 Barrel
8 Battereau
9 Fleming
10 Munro
11 Blakeney
12 Howard

TO SEE NEARBY

Linlithgow Palace ruins, where some of Hawley's men spent the night, stands impressively by a lake and are open at most times.

Battlefields Kilsyth, Bannockburn, Stirling Bridge, Sheriffmuir.

Falkirk Memorial in winter (R. Macowan)

(inset) *Silver mounted flint-lock pistol* (Wallace Collection)

CULLODEN MOOR
16 April 1746

Perhaps no battle arouses such feeling as Culloden. It was a disaster for Prince Charles's tired army which had failed a night attack on Cumberland at Nairn and returned exhausted and hungry to the field chosen by Sullivan as a suitable place to face the much larger Hanoverian army. Perhaps the battle is best described by the following extract from a letter home by Will Aiken, a young English officer on the right of the line:

Inverness Aprl 17th 1746

Dear Mother,

Yesterday we had a Battle with the Rebels and have obtained a complete victory the two armies met in Culloden Moore Between Nairn and this place we Drew up in two lines our Regt was in ye first we began the Action with Cannonading on Both Sides which lasted some time and then they came up to us in a very Bold arry But we gave them such a hot Reception with our Small Arms that they could not Bear it long But fairly fled we pursued them in good order over heaps of slain and it was a Gastly Sight to see some Dead some tumbling and wallowing in their Blood others not quite dead Crying for mercy we followed and slew them for three miles till the Dragoons were quite glutted with Gore we have taken a great number of prisoners and this day there are sholes of them Bringing in every hour so that this town will be full of them by tomorrow I Desire to thank Almighty God that I came off unhurt tho I was in the front of the battle where the Bullets flew like hail of our Regt poor Capt Grossett is killed and Captain Simpson had a ball throw his body but is yet alive one of our Regt killed the Lord Strathallan and took a purse of fifty guineas out of his pocket we took Lord Kilmarnock prisoner who had a wound in the Breast by a pistole shot he told me they were nine towsand threehundred that engaged us whom we Defeat only with our first

Flintlock musket of a type used at Culloden (National Army Museum)

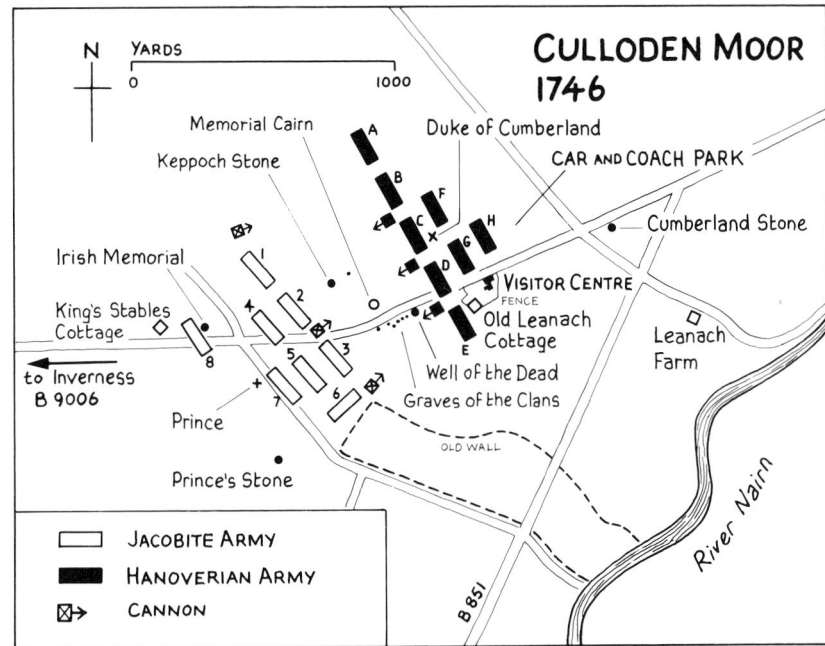

CULLODEN MOOR 1746

N YARDS
0   1000

Memorial Cairn
Keppoch Stone
Duke of Cumberland
CAR AND COACH PARK
Cumberland Stone
Irish Memorial
VISITOR CENTRE
FENCE
Old Leanach Cottage
King's Stables Cottage
Leanach Farm
to Inverness B 9006
Prince
Well of the Dead
Graves of the Clans
OLD WALL
Prince's Stone
River Nairn
B 851

☐ JACOBITE ARMY
■ HANOVERIAN ARMY
⊠→ CANNON

Jacobite Army
1 Macdonalds and Duke of Perth
2 Farquharsons, Macleans, Mackintoshes, Frasers, Stewarts of Appin, Camerons
3 Lord George Murray's Atholl Brigade
4 Irish under Brigadier Stapleton
5 Lord Drummond's Royal Scots, Lord Lewis Gordon
6 Ogilvy Regiment
7 Fitzjames Horse and Life Guards
8 Reserve under Lord Balmerino

Hanoverian Army
A Cobham's Dragoons, Kingston's Horse
B Pulteney, Royal Scots
C Cholmondeley, Price, Royal Scots Fusiliers
D Munro, Barrel
E Wolfe
F Battereau, Howard, Fleming
G Bligh, Sempill, Ligonier
H Blakeney

line of But Six Regts all the French have surrendered and I believe this unnatural Rebelion is put to an end . . .
Your Dutyfull Sun and humbl Sevt

Will Aiken

Charles was out-gunned, outnumbered and, for once, fighting on unsuitable ground. He escaped with the principal leaders but the Scots way of life was henceforth altered, tartan was banned and the Highlanders hunted down. It was the end of an era and never again was a pitched battle to be fought on British soil.

THE WALK (S)

The National Trust for Scotland looks after Culloden Moor and the new Visitor Centre, opened by Colonel Donald Cameron of Lochiel in 1984, has a restaurant, bookshop, study room and an excellent video cinema seating fifty where the visitor can see a twenty-minute film of the events leading up to the battle and its aftermath. To see Old Leanach Cottage you can leave at one end of the Centre; but you have to come back and pay to see the main battlefield, where there are wooden signs denoting where various regiments stood. The problem with this is that the whole battlefield is cramped as the Trust only own part of the site, as the rest is on the other side of the road. When you leave the centre you are on the Hanoverian side and the Cumberland post has a wild raspberry growing up it: some suitable comment by a Scottish gardener perhaps?

The trees have now been removed and the whole scene has a very sad atmosphere, which was heightened for me when I spent the night here in a tent in April 1975 and, finding the ground too hard, used a rope and a boulder to hold up the tent. It was a wild night and I dreamt of horses only to wake up suddenly to find the tent had collapsed on top of me and I was hearing horses disappearing into the distance. Were they ghost riders from Charles's army?

The Irish Memorial (1963), the Memorial Cairn, the Cumberland Stone, the Keppel stone and the Well of the Dead are all to be seen and for the archaeologist there are the Clavastone circles and cairns which have nothing to do with the battle.

TO SEE NEARBY

Cawdor Castle Open to the public and containing the muskets captured by the first Lord Cawdor at Fishguard (see page 186).

Auldearn Battlefield and the Boath Doocot (see page 143). One of Montrose's greatest victories.

FISHGUARD
21–23 February 1797

The events of February 1797 must have inspired Gilbert and Sullivan to write one of their comic operas. There are many anecdotes associated with the invasion that are beyond belief. When Tate's bedraggled army climbed the cliff and made their way to Tre Howel Farm, the farmer made a hasty escape. His servant, knowing how keen her employer was on his beer, walked a mile with a full pint so that he could have it when he reached his (rather mean) neighbour. The Fishguard Fencibles, who were assembling in Fishguard when notified of the invasion, decided to retreat to Haverfordwest. On the way they met Lord Cawdor's force coming in the opposite direction. Both sides stopped and a discussion took place to decide who was in command and where they should all go.

Finally the commander of the Fencibles, Wiliam Knox, was so incensed by Lord Cawdor's complaints that the fort at Fishguard had been abandoned, that he challenged him to a duel. No one seemed to want to get to grips with the French, who fortunately were mostly so demoralised or drunk with the large supply of port in the many farmhouses (a ship had been recently wrecked) that one Frenchman opened fire on a grandfather clock at Brestgarn Farm, scoring a hit and believing he had killed one of Cawdor's men.

To sum up, perhaps one can only say that, one of the least known British battles, Fishguard was in fact a surrender and only three people were killed. One regiment, the Pembroke Yeomanry, is entitled to wear the Fishguard battle honours so the battle has a place in this book. The pre-Napoleon war with France brought little rewards. The 'Glorious First of June' a few years before when Howe defeated the French fleet, and the blockade of French ports, were the only successes. General Hoche planned an invasion of Ireland with Wolfe Tone as his contact, but the Bantry Bay expedition was defeated by bad weather. A small force under Colonel Tate, an American from Charleston, was given 1,000 men, mostly gaol-birds, and three ships, the very latest muskets and ammunition, and instructions to burn Bristol. His ships however couldn't get past Lundy due to the wind, so they crossed to the Welsh bank and headed for Fishguard. One of the cannon in Fishguard fort fired at them, so Tate landed at Carregwastad Point, where his local guide showed him a path to Tre Howel farm, which became his headquarters. His men were soon looking for food and drink – finding the many bottles of port from the wreck – and although they fortified Llanwnda crags, they had no horses and not enough food to go further.

Meanwhile Lord Cawdor, who owned property in the area, took command of the assortment of militias, yeomanry and sailors numbering 575 men. He however decided to bluff Tate into thinking his army was enormous. The local Fishguard women in their red shawls and stove-pipe hats could look like guards in the distance and Tate, who never seemed keen to fight, agreed to a surrender in the local inn. The remarkable affair was over. Fishguard has never forgotten it, but the rest of the world soon did, little realising that neither Napoleon nor Hitler ever achieved the possession of such a large part of British soil for three days.

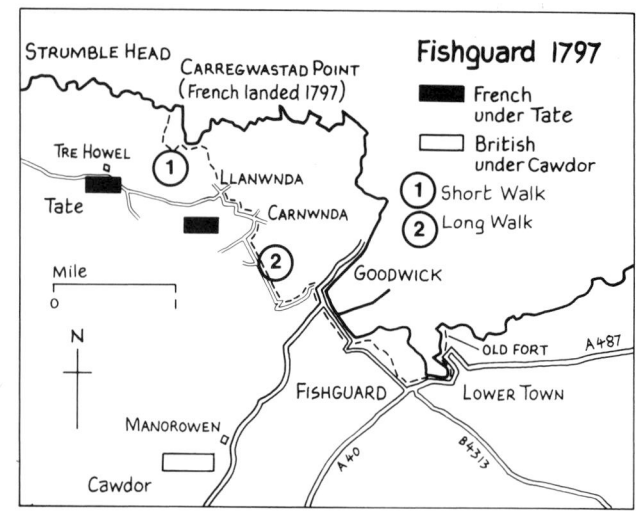

THE WALK (M and L)

Start at Llanwnda and take the new gated path towards Carregwastad Point. It is easy to follow on the map and goes down to a wooded gully full of small oaks and gorse then up to the large Victorian stone on the Point. There is another longer walk (2 hours) from Llanwnda down the hill to Goodwick sands past the monument to the surrender and up the other side to old Fishguard (see the Royal Oak and Jemima's monument in the church, she rounded up some French stragglers with a pitchfork) and then down the other side to the Old Fort, where there are some 1790 cannon in place. It is a delightful walk on a fine day. To see more of the coast, take the Pembrokeshire Coast Path walk, details of which can be obtained form the National Park Officer, Pembrokeshire Coastal National Park Department, County Offices, Haverfordwest, Dyfed, SA61 1QZ.

To see Tre Howel Farm, which is private, a public footpath from Carregwastad Point leads off the coastal path across two fields into Tre Howel lane. When taking this path we noticed a large peregrine falcon and, strangely, some feral pigeons that seemed quite unafraid of the large bird. A better way to see the cliff the French climbed would be by boat, which can be hired in Fishguard. Bicycles can also be hired at St Davids, and the area is well served by British Rail.

Royal Oak, Fishguard. Scene of the signing of the French surrender to Earl Cawdor in 1797.

SLAPTON SANDS
26–28 April 1944

The eternal problem of tanks in manoeuvres is that they are too large and heavy to cross rivers, often requiring existing bridges to be strengthened. It is sometimes too late to get special bridging equipment for them and it was not surprising that Nicholas Straussler, a Hungarian working in Britain, should come up with the idea of a floating self-propelled tank. The plans went before the Admiralty who said 'no' it was unseaworthy. Straussler, undaunted, turned to the War Office. They said 'yes' and numerous generals, including Eisenhower and Montgomery, were present at its demonstration.

Straussler fitted an inflatable canvas screen round the top of the tank just high enough for the gun to stick out over the top. The engine was given extra clutches, and two propellers were fitted aft. A special platform was erected for the commander and his crew of three were given submarine escape apparatus in case the tank sank. The driver had a special periscope, but otherwise the commander controlled the tank with a waterproof telephone.

Sherman tanks were adapted and became known as Duplex Drive Shermans or 'Donald Ducks' to the Americans. On Omaha beach no less than twenty-seven tanks sank, due partly to the rough sea, and only five actually made the beach.

The tank you can see at Slapton is an apt memorial to the men who died at Omaha (see page 189).

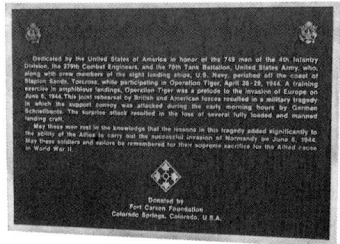

October 1987 monument to the American troops lost at sea in April 1944

The long sweeping beach lying between Dartmouth and Start Point in south Devon is known as Slapton Sands. In fact it is fine gravel and not sand, but the small village of Slapton is famous for Slapton Ley, an inland lake almost on the sea and a nature reserve for many varieties of waterfowl. There is a Field Studies Centre in the old village school.

There was a meeting in the Village Hall at Slapton on 13 November 1943 when all the inhabitants were given until 20 December to leave the area. Farmers had to move stock, pets had to be put down, valuables removed and the entire population of 7 parishes and 750 families, or 3,000 people, moved to other homes. The American forces moved into the area so soon afterwards that one lady, driving down a narrow road, had to have her car deposited by a crane in a field by the Americans as it was in their way. Pincher, a local dog, ran onto the sands and set off six land mines, so that every window in the village was shattered and the Royal Sands Hotel was in such a shaky state after the war that it was closed.

The village became infested with rats and even after D-Day the people couldn't come back until the Engineers had swept the beach and removed all mines and live shells. Water supplies, electricity and all damaged roads and houses had to be repaired. A shell had hit the church and fragments of shrapnel had to be removed from the pews.

The new monument on the beach next to the Sherman tank has the dedication:

> To 749 men of the 4th Infantry Division, the 279th Combat Engineers and the 70th Tank Battalion, United States Army, who with the crew members of the eight Landing Ships, United States Navy, perished off the coast of Slapton Sands, Torcross, while participating in Operation Tiger.

Operation Tiger was a full-scale exercise authorised by General Eisenhower that involved 30,000 troops landing at Slapton on a beach similar to that at Utah in Normandy. Unfortunately a flotilla of seven *Schnellboote*, a fast variety of E-Boat armed with torpedoes, attacked a convoy and sank eight Landing Ships before retiring at high speed. The landing craft were overloaded and many men were drowned in the dark. The affair was hushed up and today we still have little information about the tragedy. Where were the men buried? Why did the E-Boats not suspect that the invasion was coming to Normandy? Was there a spy who directed their approach? What was the Royal Navy doing? Sir Peter Scott in *The Battle of the Narrow Seas* mentions that the Germans has two E-Boat squadrons at Cherbourg, the 5th under Korvettenkapitan Bernard Klug and the 9th under Korvettenkapitan Gotz von Mirbach, that their fifteen boats were well led and in the Slapton Sands action that night were lucky because the American convoy's destroyer escort had been damaged in a collision and had withdrawn to Plymouth for repairs. When Klug and von Mirbach struck, they only had one small escort to deal with and they could easily avoid her. He also states that the flotilla was under direct control of the Führer der Schnellboote, Kapitan zur See Petersen, who was based at Scheveningen in Holland. It is likely that communications between Holland and Cherbourg would be very difficult at this stage of the war and the 5th and the 9th probably acted independently of Petersen's orders and maybe their report on the action never got through to Headquarters before D-Day.

Sherman floating tank at Slapton Sands, rescued by volunteers in 1984

The area today is a pleasant beach inhabited by fishermen and holiday makers. There is the Sherman tank rescued by a hotel owner in 1984 that has no connection with the tragedy (see also page 188). It was designed as a swimming tank with an aft propeller and canvas sides. One of the canvas strips was holed by another tank in an exercise and the tank slipped under water at high tide. The crew were all rescued and in 1984, with the help of the Royal Navy and many volunteers, the Sherman was dug up and hauled into its present position next to the monument which was unveiled on 15 November 1987 before a large crowd including many American servicemen.

In 1954, another monument was erected further along the beach which does not mention the tragedy at all. It is a 'thank you' to the villagers for leaving their land for so long as a training area for American troops.

THE WALK (L)

Slapton Sands are on the South West Coast path and a very easy stroll from here to Start Point and its lighthouse takes a couple of hours. The plain wooden signposts clearly show the route. In the other direction it is possible to walk into Dartmouth, but the coast path goes up the hill in places and it is not such an easy journey. Slapton can also be visited by boat from Dartmouth and on a fine day it would make a pleasant outing.

For those interested in walking the South West Way, it is advisable to contact the South West Way Association, I Orchard Drive, Kingskerswell, Newton Abbot, Devon TQ12 5DG. On payment of a small subscription a full list of accommodation and route maps can be obtained.

BIBLIOGRAPHY AND USEFUL ADDRESSES

Apart from the Aiken letters available at York Castle Museum, church pamphlets, battle leaflets (a particularly good one on *Flodden* for example) and the English Heritage magazine, the following works should be consulted.

Adair, J. *Cheriton, 1644* (Roundwood Press, 1973)

Barrett, C.R.B. *Battles and Battlefields in England* (Innes, 1896)

Bennett, M. *Lambert Simnel and the Battle of Stoke* (Sutton, 1987)

Binski, P. and Alexander, J. *Age of Chivalry – Art in Plantagenet England 1200–1400* (Royal Academy, 1987)

Brooke, H. *Visits to Fields of Battle in England* (Russell Smith, 1857: re-issued by Sutton, 1975)

Buist, F. and Tomasson, K. *Battles of the '45* (Batsford, 1962)

Burne, Colonel A.H. *Battlefields of England* (Methuen, 1952)

——. *More Battlefields of England* (Methuen, 1952)

Clarendon, Earl of. *The History of the Great Rebellion* (OUP edn, 1967)

Elcho, Lord. *The Affairs of Scotland 1744–6* (Mercat Press, 1973)

Firth, C. H. *Cromwell* (Putnam, 1901)

Gardiner, S.R. *History of the Great Civil War* (Longmans, 1901)

Grant, J. *British Battles at Land and Sea* (Cassell, 1890)

Hume-Brown, P. *History of Scotland*, vols 1–3 (Cambridge, 1901)

Kemp, H. *The Jacobite Rebellion* (Almark, 1975)

Kendall, P.M. *Richard III* (London, 1987)

Kinross, J.S. *Fishguard Fiasco* (Five Arches Press, 1974)

——. *Discovering Battlefields of England* (Shire, 1974)

——. *Discovering Battlefields of Scotland* (Shire, 1986)

——. *The Battlefields of Britain* (David & Charles, 1979)

Lander, J.R. *Government and Community – England 1450–1509* (Arnold, 1980)

Lang, A. *History of Scotland*, vols 1–4 (Blackwood, 1902)

Money, W. *The Battles of Newbury* (Simpkin Marshall, 1884)

Newman, P.R. *Atlas of the English Civil War* (Croom Helm, 1985)

Paston Letters (Everyman edn, 1906)

Robson, James. *Border Battles and Battlefields* (Rutherford, 1897)

Rogers, Colonel H.C.B. *Battles and Generals of the Civil War* (Seeley Service, 1968)

Ross, C. *The Wars of the Roses* (Thames & Hudson, 1976)

Seymour, W. *Battles in Britain*, vols 1 and 2 (Sidgwick & Jackson, 1975)

Shakespeare – Historical Plays, Poems and Sonnets (Everyman edn, 1906)

Taylor, A. *Minster Lovell Hall*, (HMSO, 1958)

Warner, P. *British Battlefields*, vols 1–4 (Osprey, 1973)

Wedgwood, C.V. *Battlefields in Britain* (Collins, 1944)

Woolrych, A. *Battles of the English Civil War* (Batsford, 1961)

Young, Brigadier P. *Edgehill* (Roundwood Press, 1968)

——. *Marston Moor* (Roundwood Press, 1970)

——. *Naseby 1645 – The Campaign and the Battle* (Century, 1985)

WALKING BOOKS

The following provide useful information on Fishguard, Lansdown Hill and The Standard respectively.

Barrett, J.H. *The Pembrokeshire Coast Path* (HMSO, 1974)

Richards, M. *The Cotswold Way* (Penguin, 1984)

Wainwright, A. *Coast to Coast Path* (Westmorland Gazette, 1978)

USEFUL ADDRESSES

The Ramblers' Association, 124 Finchley Road, London NW3.

Youth Hostels Association, Trevelyan House, 8 St Stephen's Hill, St Albans, Herts.

Camping Club of Great Britain, 11 Lower Grosvenor Place, London SW1.

Caravan Club Ltd, 46 Brook Street, London W1.

Automobile Association, Fanum House, Leicester Square, London WC2.

Royal Automobile Club, 85 Pall Mall, London SW1.

National Parks Commission, 1 Cambridge Gate, Regents Park, London NW1.

INDEX